ASIAN PHILOSOPHICAL STUDIES, NO. 2

KANSAS SCHOOL OF RELIGION
University of Kansas
1300 Oread Avenue
LAWRENCE, KANSAS 66044

Also in this Series:

No. 1 WANG YANG-MING: *The Idealist Philosopher of
16th Century China* by Carson Chang

CHINESE HUMANISM AND CHRISTIAN SPIRITUALITY

ESSAYS OF
JOHN C. H. WU

EDITED BY
PAUL K. T. SIH

St. John's University Press   Jamaica, N. Y. 11432

1965

This book is lovingly dedicated to
the memory of
Teresa Lee
beloved wife of the author and
god-mother of the editor

EDITORIAL INTRODUCTION

In the *Analects,* Confucius recorded his autobiography in these words:

At fifteen I set my heart upon learning.
By thirty I was on my feet.
By forty I was free from illusions.
By fifty I came to know the will of Heaven.
By sixty my ear was docile.
By seventy I could follow the dictates of my heart without overstepping
the boundaries of right.

This may be very well applied to the personal life of Dr. John C. H. Wu. At fifteen, he had already developed an extensive interest in learning. Together with his study in Chinese classics, he sought his higher education in Western thought. Thus he earned his Bachelor of Laws from the Comparative Law School of China, Soochow University, at the age of 22, and his doctorate of Jurisprudence from the University of Michigan the following year. Because of his intellectual maturity he was early drawn into an intimate friendship with Justice Oliver Wendell Holmes, who, then in his eighty's, was sitting on the bench of the United States Supreme Court.

At thirty, Dr. Wu had already begun his career in the legal profession. He was first the Dean of his alma mater, the Comparative Law School of China. Then, he became the President of the International Court of Shanghai. At the age of thirty-five, in 1934, he was entrusted by the National legislature with responsibility for drafting the "May 5th Constitution"—the foundation of the Constitution of the Republic of China which is still in force in Taiwan at the present time.

His professional success, however, did not satisfy him. His heart drew him on to higher achievements. Approaching his forty's, he had overcome all doubts, and, in 1938, he became a Catholic. The most significant contribution he made during this period was the completion of a Chinese translation of the New Testament and of the Psalms. These translations, in literary Chinese, provide a fruitful way of expounding the true meaning of the scriptures— an approach exemplified by Clement of Alexandria and deeply appreciated by St. Augustine.

At the age of fifty, when the Communists came to power on the continent, he knew the Divine will. Resigning from his diplomatic post as China's Minister Plenipotentiary to the Holy See, he came to the United States to enter the teaching profession. He taught first at the University of Hawaii and then at Seton Hall University where he is now a professor of Oriental Philosophy and Religion. He did this as a faithful follower of Confucius who was primarily a scholar and educator. In the words of Tsu Hsia, a disciple of Confucius, "When one has reached excellence as a public officer, he devotes himself to the study of culture . . ."

To say this is not to indicate that Dr. Wu is entirely a scholar who stresses primarily worldly achievements. Together with his Confucian discipline, he is also a true representative of Taoism. He is light-hearted, with a great love for simplicity and humility— the keynote of Taoist wisdom. It seems that he acts like a Confucian and feels like a Taoist. In fact, his Confucian training and Taoist insight both prepared him to embrace the Catholic faith.

Speaking of his spiritual odyssey, he once wrote:

I maintain that all spirituality must be founded on moral life; but on the other hand, moral life must, so to speak, bathe itself in the ocean of contemplation. Without contemplation, the moral life would tend to degenerate into a dry and narrow humanism. Without the moral life, contemplation would be empty and degenerate into quietism. Only Catholicism has perfectly harmonized the two opposite tendencies, as they are represented by Confucianism on the one hand, and Taoism on the other. For me, this harmony is well symbolized by a verse of Psalm 96:

"Clouds and darkness are round about him:
Justice and judgment are the foundation of his throne."

Confucianism had prepared me to appreciate the second line; Taoism had prepared me to appreciate the first line; but it is Catholicism which made me understand both of them in the unity of their whole.

To explain this spiritual unity, Dr. Wu has written many articles in addition to his books. Among his numerous writings, we select in this volume eleven papers, including the appendix. These, in our judgment, constitute an orderly presentation of his basic thought on the spiritual unification of Eastern and Western cultures within a Christian context.

The first and second articles deal with the Confucian tradition. Both the thought of Confucius and that of his principal follower, Mencius, are treated. The third essay on "The Spirit of Joy in Chinese Sages" combines the study of Chinese classical thought with a study of Chinese spiritual values.

The fourth and fifth articles discuss Taoist philosophy. Here Dr. Wu gives us new insights into both Lao Tzu and Chuang Tzu. This Taoist wisdom prepares us to appreciate the following sixth and seventh articles, "St. Thérèse and Lao Tzu" and "Thérèse and Céline." Here we find an extraordinary harmony between the way of Lao Tzu and the way of Saint Thérèse.

The eighth article poses the challenge of modernity and technology to the spiritual values of mankind. Dr. Wu's advice is to intensify our Christian way of life at this turning point in human history.

The central thought of Dr. Wu is found in the ninth and tenth studies. In these, he presents his conviction that there can be no real antipathy between the higher spiritual traditions of the East and West, but only a profound unity which we instinctively feel to be present but which we cannot yet bring to full expression. He realizes that a spiritual bridge between East and West is really possible if a sufficient number of dedicated people from the Oriental and Occidental cultures can see this need and work together for its realization.

The appendix contains Dr. Wu's "The Science of Love." It was written not long after his conversion in gratitude to his favorite Saint, the Little Flower. As it has been warmly received the world over, we include this at the end of the volume.

In making this book available to the public, I, as editor, feel most grateful to Dr. Wu. Both as his student and godson, I am indebted to him for his constant guidance in my intellectual and spiritual life. In editing his works, I drew once again the spiritual nourishment and inspiration he provides so abundantly.

Some of the works included in this volume have already appeared in printed form. We are grateful to the *Chinese Culture Quarterly* for allowing us to use "Mencius' Philosophy of Human Nature and Natural Law" and "The Spirit of Joy in Chinese Sages"; to the *International Philosophy Quarterly* for letting us reproduce "The Wisdom of Chuang Tzu: A New Appraisal." The article "Christianity, the Only Synthesis Really Possible Between East and West" was included in *Le Monde Attend L'Eglise*. We are thankful to Editions Fleurus for authorizing the inclusion of this in the present volume. Thanks are also given to Rev. Nicholas Maestrini, P.I.M.E., for permission to reproduce the article "The Science of Love."

Paul K. T. Sih
Director
Center of Asian Studies
St. John's University, New York

CONTENTS

Editorial Introduction   v

I   Confucius: The Man and His Ideas   1

II   Mencius' Philosophy of Human Nature and
Natural Law   15

III   The Spirit of Joy in Chinese Sages   39

IV   Taoism   53

V   The Wisdom of Chuang Tzu: A New Appraisal   61

VI   St. Thérèse and Lao Tzu: A Study in
Comparative Mysticism   95

VII   Thérèse and Céline   127

VIII   Technology and Christian Culture: An
Oriental View   145

IX   Christianity, the Only Synthesis Really Possible
Between East and West   157

X   Water and Wine: Chinese Ethics and The
Christian Faith   173

XI   The Science of Love   203

ix

CONFUCIUS:
THE MAN
AND HIS IDEAS

1. Historical Background

In order to understand the personality and the philosophy of Confucius, we must look at him against the historical background. The splendid Chou Dynasty was established by the end of the twelfth century B.C., and reached its zenith in the eleventh. By the tenth century it had begun to decline. In spite of a brief rally in the eighth century under the reign of King Hsuan, commonly called the era of Renaissance, the downward tendency was too strong to stem. The feudal system which had held the Kingdom together in its early stages was now gradually but steadily disintegrating. In fact, the seed of disintegration was sown in its very expansion, for in the process of expansion the centripetal forces were over-balanced by the growing centrifugal forces.

From the very beginning of the Chou Dynasty, lands were meted out to princes, mostly members of the collateral branches of the royal houses. For a period everything went well. The kings were good and able on the whole, and the local princes and other vassals remained faithful to the royal house. But as time went on, the principalities grew in population and strength, and when the reigning monarch happened to be weak, he could hardly control them. So an anomalous situation had arisen. In theory the local princes still owed allegiance to the king, but in practice most of them had their own axes to grind and paid no more than lip-service to the Throne.

Let me introduce a story which will serve to illustrate how hopelessly weak one of the kings was. Yu Wang, who reigned between 781 and 771 B.C., was enamoured of the beauty of one of the girls in his seraglio, by the name of Pao Ssu. He was so madly in love with her that in order to make her smile, he played a practical joke on his vassals. He ordered the kindling of the beacon fires, the signal for his vassals to rally against a raid of barbarians. When the vassals came in earnest, they found it was a joke; and their stupefaction made Pao Ssu burst into laughter. But woe to them that laugh at the expense of others, for they will weep. Not long afterwards, there was a real invasion on the capital and the beacon fires were lit in earnest, but no vassals came to the rescue, as they did not want to be fooled a second time. Yu Wang was killed and Pao Ssu taken captive. The situation was so bad that the next king, Ping Wang (771-720), had to move the capital eastward to Loyang. This marked the end of the Western Chou, and the beginning of the Eastern Chou. While the Dynasty was to last for over five centuries more, the center of interest had shifted from the royal house to the feudal states struggling for hegemony in the long period of chaotic disorder.

When Confucius was born, by the middle of the sixth century, things were going from bad to worse. Intrigues, murders, assassinations, rebellions, usurpations and notorious immoralities were the order of the day. He witnessed glaring discrepancies between name and reality. The unscrupulosity and hypocrisy of the local princes and their ministers, the corruption and inefficiency of the royal house, the ignoble lives of the nobility, the ungentle manners of the gentlemen, and finally the innocent sufferings of the poor and downtrodden conspired to goad him and other thinking minds to search for the causes of such strange phenomena and for the ways and means to remedy them.

In short, Confucius lived at a time when the king was not like a king, the princes not like princes, the ministers not like ministers, fathers not like fathers, sons not like sons, husbands not like husbands, wives not like wives, brothers not like brothers, friends not like friends—in a sense, men were not like men, for they seemed to have lost their humanity; and this was especially true of the ruling classes.

The ignobleness of the nobility and the fact that he himself was born poor and of "humble status"[1] made Confucius a sympathizer with the common people, opened his eyes to the most significant truth: that true nobility is not a matter of blood but of character and culture. A man is a true man insofar as he embodies humanity; and a gentleman is no gentleman if he is not gentle in fact. On the other hand, a commoner may rightly be called a gentleman if he had the qualities of one. As a matter of fact, Confucius and Mencius never tired of dwelling upon the intrinsic dignity of man. They anticipated Robert Burns bemoaning "man's inhumanity to man." This, as you will see, was a tremendous revolution, effected through the right definition of terms.

2. The Central Idea of Confucianism: Humanity

Confucius was the kind of man who could call a spade a spade. For example, on seeing a particular kind of bronze goblet popularly called "horn-gourd," he remarked in a spirit of irony, "A horn-gourd that is neither horn nor gourd. What a horn-gourd! What a horn-gourd!"[2]

Similarly, a man must be human; the whole duty of man is to cultivate his humanity. As Confucius said, "If a man is not human, what has he to do with rituals? If a man is not human, what has he to do with music?"[3] Humanity, however, has degrees; Confucius himself did not claim to have attained full humanity. All that he counseled his pupils to do was to desire it intensely and pursue it with all their might. Once a disciple of his said to him, "Not that I do not like your teaching, but my strength is not sufficient to follow it." Confucius answered, "He whose strength is not sufficient will only collapse in the middle of the journey. But now you deliberately draw the line before you start out."[4] He never ceased to encourage the timorous souls to start on the way of humanity. He said, for instance, "Is humanity far away? No, if only I desire humanity, lo! it comes."[5]

The *Analects* contains an extremely interesting comment on a stanza of a current love-song. The stanza runs as follows:

The flowery branch of the wild cherry,
How swiftly it flies back!
It is not that I do not love you;
But your house is far away.

Do you know what was the comment of Confucius? He said, "He really did not care for her. If he did, he would not have worried about the distance."[6]

It is in the nature of great hearts to love passionately. How passionately Confucius loved the virtue of humanity can be seen from some of his words. "If a gentleman abandons his humanity," he said, "how can he fulfill his name? A gentleman never quits humanity even for the space of a single meal. In moments of stress he cleaves to it; in seasons of peril he cleaves to it."[7] "To know it is good, to love it is better, but to rejoice in it is best."[8] "No man of true ambition and humanity will seek life at the expense of his humanity; on the contrary, he will, when necessary, give up his life in order to achieve his humanity."[9] Thus, to Confucius, humanity is dearer even than life.

But what exactly is the virtue of humanity? To answer this question, three angles will have to be envisaged, namely, Heaven, one's self, and one's neighbors. Vis-à-vis Heaven, Confucius said, "The man of true humanity serves God as his parent."[10] Vis-à-vis one's self, Confucius said, "To conquer one's self and return to what is right and proper, this is true humanity."[11] Besides, he advocates the cultivation and development of human nature, because human nature being God-given we owe it both to Heaven and to ourselves to cultivate it the best we can. As he said, "When nature prevails over culture, you get the boorishness of the rustic. When culture prevails over nature, you get the pedantry of the scribe. Only when culture and nature are duly blended do you get the true gentleman."[12] Vis-à-vis one's neighbors, Confucius said: "Who can realize humanity? Perhaps, it would take a sage to do it. Yet, even Yao and Shun felt their deficiency therein. For a man of true humanity is one who desiring to stand firm himself helps others to stand firm, and desiring to develop himself fully helps others to develop themselves fully. To be able from one's self to draw a parallel for the treatment of others, this may be called the art of humanity."[13]

From this it is evident that the realization of full humanity requires the most conscientious performance of one's duties toward Heaven, toward one's self, and toward others. Such is the ideal that Confucius set for himself and for all men. If his system is called humanism, it is a humanism in all its plenitude, in which no values of civilization are missing. In this system the virtue of humanity occupies the same position as charity does in the Christian religion. It is the queen of virtues, the bond of perfection. All other virtues are subordinated to it, and all talents and accomplishments minister unto it. As a matter of fact, Confucius himself expressed this idea in a magnificent passage found in *Li Ki*: "Gentleness and meekness constitute the essence of humanity: reverence and prudence, its foundation; broad-mindedness and generosity, its flowering; humility and courtesy, its function; ceremony and ritual, its manners; sharing and distribution, its expansion. A scholar combines all these qualities, but still he dares not claim full humanity."[14]

This is the central thread that runs through all the qualities and interests of this extremely many-sided and richly gifted man. His love of learning, his humility and self-knowledge, his keen responsiveness to all human values, his earnestness in improving himself, his readiness to admit mistakes, his patience and tact in teaching others, his indifference to honors and riches, his hero-worship, his willingness to learn even from his inferiors, his spirit of joy, his sense of humor, his deep understanding of the rhythm of tension and relaxation; all these seem to be inspired and enlivened by his one desire to be perfectly human, and at the same time, all of them contribute toward the realization of full humanity.

It is a common error to regard filial piety as the central theme of the philosophy of Confucius. The fact is that Confucius treated filial piety as the starting point of humanity, which, like charity, begins at home. For Confucius was not only an idealist, but also a very practical man, and as a practical man he believed in going step by step. With him, philosophy is no mere intellectual discipline, but constitutes the basis of social and individual behaviour. There is a beautiful passage in *The Golden Mean,* written by his grandson, Tse-Sze:

The moral life of man may be likened to traveling to a distant place: one must start from the nearest stage. It may also be likened to ascending a height: one must begin with the lowest step. The *Book of Songs* says:

"When wives and children and their sires are one,
'Tis like the harp and the lute in unison.
When brothers live in concord and peace,
The strain of harmony shall never cease.
The lamp of happy union lights the home,
And bright days follow when the children come."[15]

There is certainly a great charm in all this. But Confucius' vision is not bounded by the wall of the family. His point is simply this: If a man is not a good son at home, neither will he be a model citizen, or trust-worthy friend, or a true lover of mankind. To him, therefore, filial piety is just the first step in the way of universal love. It is unfortunate that later Confucians tend to treat the starting point as the central theme, thus narrowing the broad vision of Confucius and paving the way to a kind of detestable clannishness, from which China has suffered so much.

3. The Sincerity of Confucius

The ideal of full humanity, as you will see, is as high as it is broad. It is like a gigantic pyramid with Heaven for its apex and the earth for its base. As to its volume, it is composed of all the intricate relationships and activities of man, together with the infinitely variable circumstances of life. Evidently, such an ideal is not completely attainable in life, but it is just because of this that it furnishes perspective and opens glimpses of the infinite. If Confucius had not such a lofty ideal before him, he would not have been so utterly humble and matter of fact, nor so tolerant toward the failings of others. In this connection, let me quote one of his sayings which has impressed me most profoundly: "There are four things in the moral life of man, not one of which I have been able to carry out in my life. To serve my father as I would expect my son to serve me: that I have not been able to do. To serve my superior as I would expect my subordinate to serve me: that I have not been able to do. To act towards my elders as I

6

would expect my juniors to do to me: that I have not been able to do. To be the first to behave towards my friends as I would expect them to behave towards me: that I have not been able to do."[16]

Frankly, I have not come across a single Confucian scholar in the long history of China, who has made such a good confession of his failings as the master did. Confucius' greatness was built upon the solid foundation of deep humility, which is nothing else than self-knowledge. This is also the reason why he never ceased striving after perfection up to the end of his life. The *Analects* contains an interesting self portraiture on the part of Confucius. A certain Duke asked Tse Lu what he thought about Confucius, but Tse Lu did not make any answer, because he did not know what to say. Upon being told, the master said in good humor, "Why did you not say, he is simply so eager for improvements that he forgets his food, so happy therein that he forgets his sorrows, and does not even note that old age is at hand."[17]

The improvement of one's personality, for Confucius, does not depend upon the undertaking of big things: it depends upon how well you perform your ordinary duties. In his hands, the commonplace is transmuted into gold. To use his own words: "In the discharge of the ordinary duties of life and in the exercise of care in ordinary conversation, whenever there is shortcoming, never fail to strive for improvement, and when there is much to be said, say not more than necessary; words having respect to actions and actions having respect to words. Is it not just this thorough genuineness and absence of pretense which characterizes the moral man?"[18]

The thorough genuineness and absence of pretense on the part of Confucius can best be illustrated by an interesting episode in his life. Once he was gravely ill, and one of his disciples asked his fellows to serve as stewards for his funeral to emulate the style of official families. When Confucius got a little better, he remarked, "The scoundrel! He has gone on preparing these things behind my back. I have no stewards in my family and he wanted to pretend that I had. Whom do I deceive? Can I deceive Heaven?"[19]

4. Confucius' Faith in *T'ien* (Heaven)

Confucius had a lively faith in *T'ien* and that faith was the ultimate source of his greatness. For one thing, that faith convinced him that one's happiness depends upon the approval of *T'ien* rather than the praises of men, upon one's interior qualities rather than external things. Once he said, "I do not murmur against *T'ien,* nor grumble against men. My studies lie low, but my penetration rises high. *T'ien* alone knows me."[20]

For another thing, this living faith in *T'ien* explains why Confucius could be so composed and serene when faced with dangers of life. On one occasion, when one Huan T'ui wanted to kill him, he said, *"T'ien* having endowed me with virtue, what can Huan T'ui do to me?"[21] When he was trapped in a place called Ku'ang, he said, "Since the death of King Wen, has the mantle of culture not fallen on me? If *T'ien* had intended to destroy this culture, a latter-day mortal like me would not have been able to link himself to it. But if *T'ien* does not intend to destroy this culture, what can the men of Ku'ang do to me?"[22]

One of the most touching episodes of the life of Confucius happened on the borderland between the two states Chen and Ts'ai, where he and his disciples were surrounded by an army sent from his political enemies. Their food supplies were running out, and many of the followers were sick and depressed. But Confucius continued to lecture and read, play music and sing.[23] Knowing that his disciples were worried, he called Tse Lu in and put a question to him: *"The Book of Songs* says:

> Are we buffaloes, are we tigers
> That our home should be these desolate wilds?

Is it perhaps because our Way is wrong that we should have come to this pass?" Tse Lu answered, "Possibly we are not good enough to make people believe in us. Possibly, we are not wise enough to make others take our Way." "Is that so?" said Confucius. "If a good man is always believed in, then how would you account for the case of Po Yi and Shu Chi? If a man of wisdom can always have his way in the world, then how would you account for the case of Prince Pikan?" Tse Lu went out and Tse Kung came in.

Confucius put the same question to him: *"The Book of Songs* says:

> Are we buffaloes, are we tigers
> That our home should be these desolate wilds?

Is it perhaps because our Way is wrong that we should have come to this pass?" Tse Kung's answer was: "Master, your Way is extremely great. That is why the world cannot accept it. Why don't you, Master, compromise a little?" "Sze!" Confucius said. "A good farmer can sow and till the ground, but he cannot ensure the harvest. A good artisan can do his work skillfully, but he cannot ensure popularity. A good man can cultivate his Way so as to give system and order to it, but he cannot assure its acceptance by the world. Now, you don't cultivate the Way but only think of being accepted. Sze, I am afraid you do not set your aim high enough." Tse Kung went out and Yen Hui came in. Confucius repeated the question: *"The Book of Songs* says:

> Are we buffaloes, are we tigers
> That our home should be these desolate wilds?

Is it perhaps because our Way is wrong that we should have come to this pass?" Yen Hui answered: "Master, your Way is extremely great. That is why the world could not accept it. However, let the Master go on with it. What harm is there in not being accepted? Nay, the very fact that a man is not accepted by the world proves that he is a true gentleman. If we do not cultivate the Way, it is our shame. Now the Way has been thoroughly cultivated but is not resorted to, this is a shame to the rulers. What harm is there in not being accepted. The very fact that a man is not accepted would prove that he is a true gentleman." Confucius was so pleased with the answer that he smiled and said in a playful spirit, "Is that so? Oh son of Yen, if you were a rich man, I would like to be your butler!"[24]

5. The Harmony of Personality

But the wonderful thing about Confucius is that with all his child-like trust in Divine Providence, he believed in the necessity of human effort. He steered between the Scylla of quietism and the Charybdis of activism. He could be quiet without being a quietist, and active without being an activist. His personality represents a marvelous harmony of qualities which in a lesser man would jar one another. An inborn sense of balance served as the salt that kept all the qualities from degenerating into their opposites. He hitched his wagon to the stars, but he kept his feet on the ground. He was serious and yet he had a charming sense of humor. He was too moral to be moralistic, too pure to be puritanical, too broadly human to be all-too-human, too practical to be a mere utilitarian, and too consistently moderate to be immoderate even in the virtue of moderation. Confucius was not a man to go by half measures. His "golden mean" is not compromise, but harmony. His flexibility is not opportunism, but docility to the spirit. That he was not immoderately moderate can be seen from his whole-hearted love of music. When he heard the music of Hsiao in Ch'i, for three months he forgot the taste of meat, exclaiming, "I never thought that music could be so extremely fascinating."[25]

For Confucius music plays a crowning role in the formation of human character. He summed up his program of education neatly, thus: "Let a man be first incited by Poetry, then given a firm footing by the study of ritual and the laws of right behavior, and finally perfected by music."[26] Like all his pithy sayings, this is not to be taken too literally; but the idea it suggests is clear enough. The making of a perfect man follows three stages. First, the desire for goodness and wisdom must be aroused and nourished by means of Poetry or whatever corresponds to it. Then follows a second phase in which one is to be subjected to a thorough moral and mental discipline, in order to be confirmed in the right Way. Finally, one attains to the age of harmony when what was formerly done by effort becomes spontaneous, and all the virtues and talents that have so far been acquired are organically adjusted and harmonized, thus becoming, as it were, a second nature. In his own life, we can discern these three stages. He said, "At fifteen I set my heart upon learning. By thirty I was on my feet. By forty I was free from illusions. By fifty I came to know the will of *T'ien*. By sixty my ear was docile. By seventy I could follow the dictates of my heart without overstepping the boundaries of right."[27] It will be seen that he had completed the first phase around thirty. From that time up to around fifty he strictly disciplined himself in the exercise of moral virtues and in the purification of illusions and errors, which led him to the understanding of the will of *T'ien*. From fifty on, his ear was attuned to the still small voice of Wisdom, so that by the end of his life he could act with perfect freedom and peace of mind without fear of transgression. In other words, as he grew in ripeness, he was more and more assimilated to the spirit of music. He had waded through the realm of differentiations and entered the realm of Harmony. In that harmony, differentiations are not annihilated, but transcended and brought into a living unity.

I have always thought that there is something symphonic about the personality of Confucius. He combined in a most harmonious way the solidity of the northerner with the suppleness of the southerner. In this, he was characteristically Chinese. Recently, in reading the "Canon of Emperor Shun" in *The Book of History* I was thrilled to find a passage which confirms my surmise. The Emperor was appointing his Cabinet, which was composed of eight departments, among which was the Department of Music. He appointed Ku'ei to take charge of it, saying, "Ku'ei, I appoint you to be Director of Music, and to teach our sons, so that the straight-forward shall yet be mild; the gentle, dignified; the strong, not tyrannical; and the impetuous, not arrogant."[28] Now, this reminds me of what the disciples of Confucius said about him: "The Master was affable yet firm, commanding but not harsh, reverential but easy."[29]

In another part of *The Book of History,* nine virtues are mentioned, namely: Affability combined with dignity; mildness combined with firmness; bluntness combined with respectfulness; aptitude for government combined with reverent caution; docility combined with fortitude; straight-forwardness combined with gentleness; an easy negligence combined with discrimination; strength combined with restraint; courage combined with rectitude.[30] Does this not sound like a grand symphony composed of a magnificent series of counterpoints?

Prince Wu Chi-tseh, who was an elder contemporary of Confucius and for whom the latter had a profound admiration, was a great critic of music, beside being a great statesman. When he heard the singing of the Odes of Wei, he said, "Admirable! What harmony! There is grandeur and delicacy, like a dangerous defile yet easily traversed!" When he heard the singing of the Odes of Ta Ya, he said, "How wide! How harmonious and pleasant! Amid all the winding of the notes, the movement is straight onward." When he heard the singing of the Sacrificial Odes, he said, "This is perfect! Here is straight-forwardness without rudeness; winding without bending; nearness without pressure; distance without estrangement; changes without license; repetitions without satiety; deep sorrow without despair; immense joy without indulgence. . . . The five notes are harmonious; the airs of the eight winds are equally blended; the parts of the different instruments are well defined, but the whole is maintained in an orderly manner; the complete virtue of Chou, Shang and Lu appears united here."[31]

I cannot better conclude my essay than by borrowing these words of Prince Wu to give a hint of the "musical" personality of Confucius.

NOTES

[1] *Analects*, ch. 9.
[2] *Ibid.*, ch. 6.
[3] *Ibid.*, ch. 3.
[4] *Ibid.*, ch. 6.
[5] *Ibid.*, ch. 7.
[6] *Ibid.*, ch. 9.
[7] *Ibid.*, ch. 4.
[8] *Ibid.*, ch. 6.
[9] *Ibid.*, ch. 15.
[10] *Li Ki, Ai Kung Wen.* The whole sentence is: "The man of true humanity serves his parents as Heaven, and serves Heaven as he serves his parents." It is plain that Confucius' conception of *T'ien* is theistic rather than natural or pantheistic. For him, *T'ien* has will and intelligence, and *T'ien ming* is not fate but Divine Providence.
[11] *Analects*, ch. 12.
[12] *Ibid.*, ch. 6.

[13] *Ibid.*, ch. 6.
[14] *Li Ki, Ju Hsing.*
[15] *Chung Yung.*
[16] *Ibid.*
[17] *Analects,* ch. 7.
[18] *Chung Yung.*
[19] *Analects,* ch. 9.
[20] *Ibid.*, ch. 14.
[21] *Ibid.*, ch. 7.
[22] *Ibid.*, ch. 9.
[23] *Kung Tze Chia Yu,* 20.
[24] *Ibid.*, ch. 12.
[25] *Analects,* ch. 7.
[26] *Ibid.*, ch. 8.
[27] *Ibid.*, ch. 2.
[28] *Shang Shu, Shun Tien.*
[29] *Analects,* ch. 7.
[30] *Shang Shu, Kao yao Mu.*
[31] *Chun Ch'iu Tso Sze Chuan,* under the twenty-ninth year of Hsiang Kung, corresponding to 544 **B.C.**

MENCIUS'
PHILOSOPHY OF HUMAN NATURE
AND NATURAL LAW [1]

1. Human Nature as Essentially Good

Mencius was born in the tiny state of Tsou bordering the state of Lu, the native place of Confucius, both states being in the present Shantung. He was born in 371 B.C., a hundred and eight years after the death of Confucius, and died in his early eighties in 288 or 289 B.C. In this connection his English translator, James Legge, makes an interesting comment: "The first twenty-three years of his life thus synchronized with the last twenty-three years of Plato's. Aristotle, Zeno, Epicurus, Demosthenes, and other great men of the West were also his contemporaries. When we place Mencius among them, he can look them in the face. He does not need to hide a diminished head." [2]

He was linked up with Confucius by the fact that he received his education at the feet of the disciples of his grandson, Tsu Szu, reputed author of *The Golden Mean.*

A host of legends has grown up around his mother so that she became the ideal of motherhood in the Confucian tradition. [3] One legend has it that she changed her residence repeatedly until she found a proper environment for her son. At first they were living near a cemetery, and the boy amused himself with acting the various scenes which he witnessed at the tombs, perhaps, mimicking the lamentations of bereaved women. "This," said Mother Meng, "is no place for my son"; and she removed to a house in the market-place. The boy then took to playing the part of a salesman, vaunting his wares, and haggling with imaginary customers over the prices. Mother Meng sought for a new house, and found one at last in the neighborhood of a public school. There the versatile child's attention was taken by the various exercises of politeness which the pupils were taught, and he endeavored to imitate them. "This," said the mother, "is the proper environment for my son."

According to another legend, one time their house was near a butcher's. On a certain day the boy Meng asked his mother what they were killing the pigs for? "To feast you," she jested. Her conscience immediately reproved her for telling such an untruth. She said to herself, "When I was pregnant with this child, I would not sit down if the mat was not placed in the correct manner, nor did I eat any meat unless it was cut in the right way, for education should begin in the womb. Now that his intelligence is opening, to deceive him would be to teach him untruthfulness!" With this she went and bought a piece of pork in order to make good her words.

The external events of Mencius' life are easily told. He never held any public office. Although he had interviews with many rulers, none of them was seriously interested in his political ideas and his program of benevolent government. Like Confucius he was primarily a teacher, and he had numerous students. His conversations with his students and friends, and his interviews with the kings and other ruling powers constitute the contents of the book known as *Meng Tzu*. No book exercised a greater influence upon the minds of Chinese scholars. It was a required reading for all students throughout the ages. But unlike other required readings, the book of *Mencius* was simply fascinating even to the teenagers.

Even in the early days of this century, when the modern school had begun to be introduced in China, *Mencius* was still used as a text on ethics and Chinese literature. You can hardly imagine how electrified we boys were when the instructor, an old Confucian scholar, read aloud, or rather chanted, the sonorous sentences of Mencius. There was a frankness, even brusqueness about him that appealed to us boys. The very style was full of vital spirit.

The book begins with an account of the first encounter between Mencius and a monarch. It reads as follows:

Mencius saw King Hui of Liang. The king said, "Sir, since you have not minded the distance of a thousand li in coming here, may I not presume that you must have something whereby to profit my kingdom?"

Mencius replied: "Why must Your Majesty speak of 'profit'? Humanity and justice are all that is necessary. When the king thinks of the ways and means of profiting his kingdom, every great officer will be thinking of the ways and means of profiting his family, and every common man will be thinking of the ways and means of profiting himself. When the high and the low are scrambling for profit, the kingdom itself would be in grave danger. . . . For if profit is preferred to justice, the whole country will end by being a scene of mutual snatchings. On the other hand, no *humane* man would ever abandon his parents, nor would a *just* man ever prefer his own interests to those of the sovereign. I wish Your Majesty would also speak in terms of humanity and justice, rather than in terms of profit."[4]

But while Mencius was always talking of humanity and justice, he was no mere social idealist. It is because of his philosophical realism that he could set such great store by these virtues. His claim to lasting fame in the history of Chinese thought lies in his well-thought-out philosophy of human nature and the natural law. His starting point is that human nature is something ordained by Heaven, and therefore it cannot be otherwise than good in its original essence. The whole line of his thinking is in agreement with the opening passage of *The Golden Mean,* which was authored, if not by Tsu Szu himself, at least by his disciples who were teachers of Mencius. It reads: "What is ordained by Heaven is called 'Nature.' Following out this Nature is called the *'Tao'* (or the *natural law*). The refinement of the natural law is called 'culture.' "[5] Putting this ontological insight in a teleological form, Mencius said, "He who has exhaustively studied all his mental constitution knows his nature. Knowing his nature, he knows Heaven. To preserve one's mental constitution and nourish one's nature, is the way to serve Heaven."[6]

Thus, the mandate of Heaven, human nature, and culture form a continuous series. The natural law is to be found by the mind in human nature itself, and to be further developed and applied by the mind to the ever-widening human relations under infinitely variable circumstances.

Now, how does Mencius conceive of human nature? He starts from the fundamental insight that human nature is essentially good. But can such a thesis be maintained in the face of so much wickedness in the human world? Some preliminary explanation is necessary.

What Mencius meant by human nature is the essential nature of man as distinguished from that of birds and beasts. He did not deny there are elements or natural tendencies, which man shares with other animals. He said, for instance, that sex and nourishment are the two great desires of man, but these desires belong to the lower nature and do not constitute his distinctive mark as a human being. It is man's moral and intellectual nature that constitutes his very essence, without which he would be no better than a tiger or a wolf.

"In a human being," Mencius said, "some elements are noble, while other elements are small. The great must not be injured for the sake of the small, nor the noble for the sake of the element of inferior value. He who nourishes the small elements in him is a small man; he who nourishes the great elements is a great man."[7] He illustrates this by saying, "A man who is specially devoted to eating and drinking is counted a base character. Why? Because he nourishes the little at the expense of the great."[8] In other words, we do not live to eat, but eat to live, and, for Mencius, to live is to live like a man.

In another passage, Mencius explains his doctrine of the essential goodness of human nature by pointing out that he was speaking of the basic orientation of human nature to goodness, although the fulfillment or frustration of it depends upon external causes. The passage is worth quoting in its entirety:

> The disciple Kung Tu said, "Kao Tzu holds that human nature is neither good nor evil. Some others maintain that human nature may be made to do good, and may be made to do evil. This is why under the regime of Wen and Wu, the people became fond of goodness, while under the regime of Yu and Li the people became fond of violence. There are also others who say that some men are by nature good, while others are by nature evil. This is why even under such a sage ruler as Yao there was still a wicked man like Hsiang, with such a father as Ku Sou there yet appeared a son like Shun, and with the tyrant Ch'ow for their ruler (and their nephew, too) there yet appeared Viscount Ch'i of Wei and Prince Pi Kan. Now you maintain that human nature is good. Can it be that all the others are wrong?"

Mencius replied, "It is by looking at its original condition and tendency that we can see that human nature is constituted for the realization of goodness. This is what I mean in saying that it is good. If men do what is not good, the guilt cannot be imputed to their natural powers."[9]

Mencius further clarified his doctrine by introducing the idea of normality. He was speaking of the normal nature, which is derived from the norms or patterns set up by Heaven and affixed to different species of things. He quoted a significant stanza from *The Book of Songs*:

Heaven gives birth to the teeming people,
Fixing a norm upon the nature of everything.
All men being endowed with this normal nature,
They have a natural love for the beauty of virtue.[10]

Confucius had uttered a eulogy upon this by saying, "I should think that the maker of this ode knew well the Law of Nature!" To this Mencius added a thoughtful comment: "We may thus see that to every faculty and relationship there must belong its law, and that since the people possess this normal nature, they therefore love its normal virtue."[11]

Between one man and another there may be accidental differences but there can be no essential differences. There may be a difference in degree, but never a difference in kind. Otherwise they could not both belong to the same mankind.

Mencius further developed the idea of normality by showing that most differences are due to environmental influences, and that even deviations from the normal are restricted in their natural limits. The following passage will be found to be particularly interesting for the analogical reasoning of which Mencius was such a master:

In good years the young people often acquire a habit of dependence. In bad years the young people often take to violence. This is not due to the differences in their natural endowments as conferred by Heaven. It is owing to the different things by which they allow their minds to be ensnared and engulfed.

Take for instance the barley. Let the seed be sown and covered up. The ground being the same, and the time of planting again the same, it will grow luxuriantly and ripen in the fullness of time. If there be inequalities of produce, it must be due to the thickness and thinness of the soil, to the sufficiency and insufficiency of rain and dew, and to the different ways of farming.

In fact, all things which belong to the same kind or species are similar to each other. Why should we doubt in regard to man, as if he were a solitary exception to the rule? The sages and we are the same in kind.

As Lung Tsu aptly put it, "When a cobbler undertakes to make a pair of sandals without knowing the measure of the feet, he does not end by producing a bushel basket." Sandals must be like sandals, because all men's feet are similar in form.

So with the mouth and flavors. All mouths have the same relishes. The great cook, Yih Ya, only discovered before me what my mouth relishes. If his mouth, in its relish for flavors, were of a different nature from the mouths of other men, in the same way as dogs and horses are not of same kind with us, how can you explain that all men seem to appreciate Yih Ya's culinary art? . . . .

So it is with the ear. In the matter of music, all the world agree in their appreciation of the art of Master Kwang. This is because the ears of all men are like one another.

And so it is with the eye. In the case of Tzu Tu, all people recognized her beauty. Any one who did not would have been as good as eyeless.

Now, since men's mouths agree in having the same relishes, their ears agree in enjoying the same sounds, and their eyes agree in recognizing the same beauty, can their minds alone be without anything which they would agree in approving. What, then, are the things universally approved by the minds of men? I should say, Reason and Justice! In regard to these, the sages merely discovered before us what our minds all agree in approving. Therefore, Reason and Justice delight our minds, just as tender meat delights our mouths.[12]

2.   The Four Incipient Tendencies in Human Nature

Mencius further developed his theory of human nature by pointing out certain tendencies springing spontaneously from the mental constitution or structure of man.

Let me reproduce here a dialogue between Mencius and the philosopher, Kao Tse:

Kao Tse: Nature is like a bubbling fountain. If you direct it to the east, it flows eastward; and if you direct it to the west, it flows westward. Human nature is no more inclined to good or evil than water is inclined toward east or west.

Mencius: True, water is indifferent to east and west. But is it indifferent to high and low? Human nature tends to goodness just as water tends to the low places. There is no man who does not tend to goodness, just as there is no water that does not tend to the low places. Of course, if you splash the water, it can be forced to leap higher than your forehead. If you dam it and drive it, you can even make it go up a hill. But is this water's nature? It is the external pressure that causes it to act that way. In the case of man's being made to do evil, his nature is dealt with in this way.[13]

Another dialogue between the two philosophers:

Kao Tse: The nature (of man) is like a willow tree, and moral rectitude is like a cup or a bowl. To make goodness and justice out of human nature is like making cups and bowls from the willow tree.
Mencius: But can you make cups and bowls by following the nature of the willow? Or do you have to do violence and harm to the tree before you can make cups and bowls from it? If you have to do violence and harm to the tree in order to make cups and bowls, do you also have to do violence and harm to human nature in order to be good and just? Your doctrine will lead the world to treat goodness and justice as a great calamity.[14]

Mencius does not maintain that man is born perfect; but he does maintain that the perfect development of man's moral personality is rooted in his nature. For him, a man's perfection consists in the full development of the four cardinal virtues: Humanity, Justice, Propriety, and Prudence. But these four virtues have their seeds or "beginnings" in nature.[15] Concerning Humanity, he says: "All men have a mind that cannot bear to see the sufferings of others. The ancient kings had this commiserating mind, hence they had a commiserating government. When a commiserating government is run with a commiserating mind, to bring the world to peace and order is as easy as turning one's palm."[16] Then he gives a very interesting instance to illustrate the fact that all men have a mind that commiserates. "Now, when men suddenly observe a child about to tumble into a well, everyone of them will experience a sense of alarm and sympathy."[17] They will instinctively stretch out their hands to protect the child from falling. They do it "not to make friendship with the child's parents; not to seek reputation from their neighbors and friends, nor to avoid the cries of the child. From this instance, it is plain that anyone who has no senti-

21

ment of sympathy would not be a man."[18] In this connection, I have come across a strikingly similar idea in a modern book. "A single situation often involves both perceptual and moral intuition. For example, if a blind man started to walk directly in the path of an on-coming automobile, every normal person who could lay a restraining hand on him would certainly do so."[19] There lie between Mencius and us twenty-four centuries. But human nature has remained essentially the same.

> The mind that commiserates or sympathizes is the beginning of Humanity. The mind that detests evil as something shameful is the beginning of Justice. The mind that defers to others is the beginning of Propriety. The mind that distinguishes right and wrong, and true and the false, is the beginning of Prudence. These four beginnings are to the mind what the four limbs are to the body. Having these four beginnings and yet saying that one is not capable of goodness is to play the thief with oneself; to say that his ruler is not capable of good government is to play the thief with the ruler. Since we all have the four beginnings within us, if we know how to develop and fulfill them, they will be like a fire beginning to burn or a spring beginning to flow. If we develop them to the full, they will suffice to embrace the four seas. If we do not develop them, they will not be sufficient even to serve one's parents.[20]

The four beginnings or incipient tendencies of human nature are capable of infinite development. Thus, with Mencius, nature does not exclude culture. On the contrary, if nature remains uncultivated, it will run to ruin, and this explains the existence of evil. In a magnificent passage, which Chinese scholars love to recite, Mencius lays stress on the cultivation of nature:

> The trees on the Ox Mountain were once beautiful. Being situated, however, in the suburbs of a large city, they were hewn down with axes and hatchets; how could they retain their beauty? Still through the growth from their vegetative life day and night, and the nourishing influence of the rain and dew, they were not without buds and sprouts sprang out. But then came the cattle and goats, and browsed upon them. This is why it appears so bare and stripped. When people see its bare appearance, they tend to think that there was no wood from the beginning. But is it due to the original nature of the mountain? Similarly, it cannot be said that there is no love and justice in the inherent nature of man. But the way in which a man loses the proper goodness of his mind is just like the way in which those trees were

denuded by axes and hatchets. Hacked at day after day, how can it retain its excellence? Still there is some growth between day and night, and in the peaceful air of the morning, the mind feels in a degree those inclinations and aversions which are proper to humanity; but the feeling is very feeble. And then it is fettered and destroyed by what the man does during the day. This fettering takes place again and again; the restorative influence of the night is not sufficient to preserve the original goodness of his nature; and when the still small voice of the conscience is smothered, his nature is scarcely distinguishable from that of the irrational animals. When people see that man is like an irrational animal, they tend to think that from the beginning he had no capacities for good; but is this due to his nature?[21]

3. The Realization of Our Essential Nature

While Mencius saw the essence of man in his rational and moral nature, he was not a rationalist. In the first place, his theory of human nature is built upon an ontological basis. In the second place, he was realistic enough to see the necessity of *gradualness* in the development and fulfillment of the incipient tendencies of human nature.

Whether in cultivating the natural law in our inner life, or in applying it to human relations in the political community, we must do it with patience and prudence. The four "beginnings" or incipient tendencies of our nature are like the seeds which require time to sprout, to grow and to ripen. Mencius stresses the importance of the full development of the virtues by a homely analogy. "Of all seeds the best are the five kinds of grain, but if they do not come to ripeness, they are not as good even as the tares. So it is with the virtue of humanity: all depends upon its maturation."[22]

The whole duty of a man is to actualize fully his essential nature; and this is to be accomplished by cultivating and nourishing the rational and moral virtues until their influence comes to dominate and permeate his whole being. As Mencius puts it in an illuminating passage: "What the superior man considers his true nature cannot be increased by the largeness of his sphere of action, nor diminished by his dwelling in poverty and adversity: for his heart is fixed on his own portion. The superior man realizes that his true nature consists in the virtues of humanity, justice, propriety, and wisdom. These are rooted in the mind; they manifest themselves as a mild harmony appearing in the countenance, a rich fullness in the back. They spread even to the four limbs; and the four limbs seem to understand their biddings without being told."[23]

An interesting phase in the realization of a man's essential nature is the gradual permeation and assimilation by it of what Mencius calls "the vital spirit,"[24] which corresponds to what Plato speaks of as "the passionate or spirited principle."[25] With Mencius, as with Plato, this passionate principle, or vital spirit, is a necessary ally of the rational principle if the unruly desires of man are to be kept in order. Without the help of the vital spirit, the essential nature of man would be like a powerless monarch.

For Mencius, "The will is the leader of the vital spirit; and the vital spirit pervades and animates the body. The will is the ruler, and the vital spirit is subordinate to it."[26] His advice therefore is "Maintain firm the will, and do not let the vital spirit grow beyond its control."[27] For, as he further explains, "When the will is concentrated, it moves the vital spirit. But when the vital spirit is concentrated, it would move the will."[28] The important thing is to inform the vital spirit with the spirit of justice, thus keeping it in the service of the will. Mencius shows us clearly that when the vital spirit is nourished by the spirit of justice, it is lifted up to a higher plane, and, instead of weakening, it will grow immensely. In this light we can understand more clearly the following words:

> I know how to nourish my vast vital spirit. . . . It is not easy to describe it in words. For it is a spirit extremely great and extremely strong. When nourished by rectitude and kept integral, it fills up all between heaven and earth. It is a spirit that must be mated to justice and natural law. Without these it would be starved. In fact, it is born of an accumulation of justice, not something which justice invades from outside and takes to itself. Its very life depends upon justice. For whenever your conduct does not satisfy your conscience, the vital spirit suffers starvation.[29]

The nourishing of this spirit is the work of a life-time. The mind must be always watchful, but must never be over-solicitous so as to become a meddlesome "improver." Mencius warned against impatience by introducing a beautiful parable. "Let us not be like the man of Sung. Once upon a time there was a farmer in the state of Sung who, being grieved that his corn did not grow faster, went to pull it up that it might look taller. He then returned home with a look of stupid complacency, and said to his folks, 'O I am really tired out today. I have been helping the corn to grow by leaps and bounds.' His son ran to look at it, and lo and behold! The corn was all withered."[30] "There are few people in the world," Mencius commented, "who are not dealing with their own nature as this man did with his corn—forcing it mechanically to grow taller in stature."[31] "Some consider all labor a futility and therefore abandon all effort; they are those who do not even weed their corn. The hasty 'improvers,' on the other hand, are those who up-root it: they not only waste their labor, but do great harm."[32]

4.   Some Practical Applications

So far I have been dealing with Mencius' teachings relating mainly to self-cultivation. To sum up, Mencius teaches that the supreme task of a man is to be a man. We owe our nature to Heaven, and we are accountable to Heaven for what we have done with it. The essential nature with which Heaven has endowed all men is the same, and it is good. This essential nature of man reveals itself in its dynamic aspect in the four incipient tendencies which are the seeds of the four virtues of humanity, justice, propriety and prudence. The incipient tendencies spring spontaneously from human nature as it is originally constituted by the ordinance of Heaven. Being spontaneous, they are not the results of conscious reflection. But as they grow, they become conscious orientations, transplanted, as it were, upon the mind. This, I think, is what Mencius meant when he said that the virtues are rooted in the mind. According to him, we can still recapture the passage of the incipient tendencies from the subterranean ground of our nature to the light of our rational mind, especially in the small hours of the morning when the conscience is more active than during the rest of the day when we are distracted by many things.

Constant returns to our original orientation are necessary, not because we need not grow to our full stature, but because we want to be sure that we are growing in the right direction as determined in our original orientation.

Now, what exactly is growth? It means the increasing fulfillment of our essential nature. Essence alone does not constitute the whole man as an existential being. To realize our essence, therefore, can only mean to fill our existential being with our essential nature. From the essential goodness to the existential goodness is a long process and to Mencius the main task of all philosophy and learning is to discover the proper ways of conducting ourselves during this long process of realization. To be true to our nature, we must, of course, pursue the good and avoid the evil. To pursue the good means, for Mencius, to practice the virtues of humanity, justice, propriety and prudence and to avoid the evil means to refrain from things contrary to these. This is the law or way of nature, which seems to be clear in its general outline. But difficulties arise when we are confronted with concrete situations in life and pressed for an answer as to what under the particular circumstances is the humane, just, fitting, and prudent thing to do. Often what seems humane may not be just, and what seems prudent may not be appropriate. The determination of the right solution of a concrete problem does not grow directly and spontaneously from the mind, but requires much reflection and arguments pro and con, as the works of Mencius so amply show. In fact, in his discussions with kings, friends, and disciples, Mencius employed all his wits and knowledge, natural as well as acquired, and often resorted to analogies drawn from his immense stock of learning and experience.

Mencius was a man of genius. My only reservation about him is that at times he seems to be too sure of the rightness of his views. He never admitted his own errors and defects as Confucius occasionally did. There must be something wrong with a man who is always in the right and never in the wrong.[33]

But the great charm of Mencius lies in the fact that whether he was right or wrong, he never failed to give the reasons why he thought the way he did. What is more, in most cases you feel that the position he took has an inevitability about it, or at least possesses a sound kernel of truth in it.

The freedom and frankness with which he presented his views to human dignitaries is mainly due to his conviction about the nature of real nobility. To his mind, there are two different kinds of nobility, the nobility of man and the nobility of Heaven. The former, to which kingship and the governmental ranks belong, is transitory and extrinsic; while the nobility of Heaven, which consists in the actualization of our essential nature, is in the form of virtues, and which therefore is open to all men as men, is permanent and intrinsic.[34] Furthermore, kingship and offices are instituted not as ends in themselves, but as means to an end; the happiness of the people. "In a country," he said, "the noblest element is the people; next come the Protecting Spirits of the land and grain; the lightest on the scale of values is the ruler. Therefore to win the hearts of the people is to become an emperor, to win the heart of the emperor is to become the ruler of a state; and to win the heart of the ruler of a state is to become a great officer. When the ruler of a state endangers the altars of the Protecting Spirits of the land and grain, he is to be removed and another put in his place. Likewise, when the sacrificial victims are flawless, the millet in its vessels all pure, and the sacrifices offered at their proper seasons, if yet there should ensue drought or flood, then the Protecting Spirits of the land and grain are to be removed and others consecrated in their place."[35]

Thus, on the human plane, the people are the ultimate sovereign from whom all political authorities are derived, and the people's well-being is the paramount consideration.

In one memorable interview with King Hsuan of Ch'i, Mencius expounded his philosophy of the government as a trust which may be withdrawn when the trustee has proved himself unfaithful or unequal to the charge. "Suppose," he said "that one of your Majesty's servants were to entrust his wife and children to the care of his friend, while he went himself to the state of Ts'u for a trip, and that, on his return, he should find that the friend had caused his wife and children to suffer from cold and hunger—how shall such a one be dealt with?" "He shall be cast off as a friend," replied the King. Mencius proceeded, "Suppose that the chief criminal judge could not regulate and control the officers under him, how should he be dealt with?" "Dismiss him," was the answer. Mencius proceeded further, "If within the four borders of your kingdom there is no order and peace, what is to be done?" The King looked to the right and to the left, and spoke of other matters.[36]

The same king once asked Mencius "Is it true that T'ang banished Chieh, and King Wu overthrew Ch'ow?" Mencius answered, "It is so in the historical records." "May a subject put his sovereign to death?" asked the King. Mencius' answer was: "He who outrages humanity is called a robber; and he who outrages justice is called a ruffian. The robber and ruffian we call a mere fellow. I have only heard of executing the fellow Ch'ow for his monstrous crimes, but I have not heard of murdering a monarch, in his case."[37]

King Huei of Liang fared no better with Mencius than King Hsuan. Blaming the king for his lack of provident measures for the people's livelihood, Mencius put a question to him: "Is there any difference between killing men with the sword and doing it with governmental measures?" There is none," answered the king. "Now," rejoined Mencius, "in your stalls there are fat beasts; in your stables there are fat horses. But your people have the look of hunger, and in the fields lie the bodies of men famished to death. This is feeding beasts with human beings. When beasts devour one another, men detest them for doing so. A king is supposed to be the parent of the people, but when his governmental measures lead to the fattening of the beasts at the expense of human lives, what kind of a parent is such a king? Confucius once said, 'The man who first introduced the practice of having wooden images of living persons buried with the dead, must have died without issue.' He made this remark because that man had made the semblances of living men to accompany the dead. How much worse is the case of one who causes his people to die of hunger?"[38]

Mencius did not expect the king to feed the people; but he did expect him not to interfere with farming by sending people to the wars of aggrandisement, and to lay down certain beneficent laws— what we would call social legislation—for preserving the natural resources of the country. That he was not a mere star-gazer can be seen from some of the practical measures which he considered the minimum of what a true government should do: If the seasons of husbandry be not interfered with, the grain will be more than can be eaten. If close nets are not allowed to enter the pools and ponds, the fish and turtles will be more than can be consumed. If axes and hatchets are not allowed to enter the hill-forests except at the proper times, the wood will be more than can be used. Then the people will be able to nourish their living ones and bury their dead ones properly, and they will entertain no resentment against the government. This is the first step in the kingly way."[39]

Only when a minimum of livelihood is secured can the government go on with plans of education by which manners may be beautified and moral duties inculcated. The one function of the government is to bring about and secure those conditions under which every man may have time and freedom to cultivate his own person and to realize his full humanity. "The root of the empire is in the state; the root of the state is in the family; the root of the family is in the person."[40]

The philosophy of Mencius may be called an "ontological humanism." All laws and policies are to be ordained to the end of the fullest realization of the God-conferred nature of man. For Mencius, to be faithful to this God-conferred nature and realize it fully is the only way of serving God. It is also the only way of attaining happiness. He quoted two lines from an ancient Ode, which may well be taken to be a summing up of his own philosophy:

> Strive always to accord with the law of Heaven:
> This is the proper way of seeking for much happiness.[41]

With regard to the expression "the law of Heaven," or "the mandate of Heaven," which is a translation of the Chinese *"T'ien Ming,"* I must bring out two points in clarification of the sense in which Mencius understood it. First, "Heaven," as used by Mencius, is just another name for "God." This will be clear from the following remark:

> When Heaven is about to bestow a great mission or charge upon some one, It invariably begins by exercising his mind with suffering, toughening his sinews and bones with toil, exposing his body to hunger, subjecting him to extreme poverty, and frustrating all his plans. All these methods are meant to stimulate his mind, strengthen his nature, and increase his abilities.[42]

Thus, Heaven possesses supreme wisdom and long-range purpose, in other words, Intellect and Will, which are the two components of Personality.

My second point is that the term *"Ming"* has various meanings, as understood by Mencius and other Confucianists of the same School. The first meaning is that of a particular "appointment" or "design" relating to an individual person or group of persons. This meaning finds an illustration in the above passage. A second meaning is that of a general "Providence," as when we say that Heaven provides for all, even including the whole creation. In the case of man, Heaven gives him life and equips him with a body-soul together with all the physical and psychical capabilities. A third meaning is that of a specific "ordination" or "constitution" or "norm" which Heaven attaches to every class or species of beings as its proper essence. When we speak of *"Tien Ming"* in connection with the nature of man, the third sense alone is appropriate. This is illustrated by the proposition: "What is *ordained* by Heaven is called 'nature.'"

In other words, it is not the creative or providential will of God, but His prescriptive and normative will as fixed upon the human species, which constitutes our essential nature as man: and it is from this essential nature that flow the principles of the natural law.

The following passage is of capital importance in Mencius' philosophy of human nature and the mandate of Heaven, but in order to grasp the true meaning of the passage we must keep in mind the different senses in which both of the terms "nature" and "mandate" are used:

> For the mouth to desire sweet tastes, the eye to desire beautiful colors, the ear to desire pleasant sounds, the nose to desire fragrant odors, and the four limbs to desire ease and rest—these things, indeed, belong to man's nature (*Hsin*). But seeing that they are governed by the mandate of Heaven (*Ming*) the superior man does not say of the pursuit of them, "It constitutes my nature (*Hsin*)." On the other hand, love between father and son, justice between sovereign and minister, propriety between guest and host, the aspiration of the intelligent man to virtue, and the sage's fulfillment of the Natural Law—these belong to the mandate of Heaven (*Ming*). But seeing that our nature (*Hsin*) participates in them, the superior man does not refer to them as the "Mandate of Heaven (*Ming*)."[43]

It is to be noted that in the first part of this passage, *"Hsin"* indicates the *existential,* not the essential, nature of man, and *"Ming"* indicates the general Providence of Heaven. In the second part, on the other hand, *"Hsin"* indicates the *essential* nature, and *"Ming"* indicates the normative will of Heaven affixing a law peculiar to human nature as such. Only the latter constitutes the proper nature of man, because it is something that Heaven confers on man as man. But seeing that the word *"Ming"* has other meanings, Mencius prefers to call it *"Hsin"* rather than *"Ming."* This does not mean that Mencius isolated nature from Heaven, but only that so far as man is concerned, to develop his Heaven-endowed nature is the proper way of obeying the will of Heaven. To be more specific, the four seeds of virtue which Heaven has planted in man must be cultivated and developed to the full. If we are bent upon this task, we are sure to succeed, because Heaven would never have charged us with anything without giving us the power to accomplish it. Virtue, therefore, is something which can always be obtained by seeking, while external things, such as riches, and honors, are not within our control. The whole lesson boils down to this: Seek the nobility of Heaven, and you are sure to find it. Do not seek the nobility of man, because in the first place you are not sure to find it by seeking, and in the second place it is of no intrinsic value, even if we should obtain it. In the third place, even the external things like riches and honors, in fact, all the vicissitudes of life, are within the control of Heaven, but they are not something upon which we are to concentrate our attention. Mencius has summed it up in a pregnant sentence: "There is nothing which is beyond the pale of *Ming,* but it is for us to receive as our own that *Ming* which is proper to us."[44]

5. Mencius on Law and Morals

Mencius was not a jurist. He was primarily a moral philosopher. But he saw the importance of laws in the government of a country. He said, "When the ruler has no principles to guide his administration, and his ministers have no laws to observe in the discharge of their duties, then in the court obedience is not paid to principle, and in the office obedience is not paid to rule. Superiors violate the principles of justice, and inferiors transgress the penal laws. It is only by a fortunate chance that a state under such conditions can still be preserved."[45] On another occasion he said, "If a ruler has not about his Court those devoted to the laws and scholars who dare to maintain what is right against his caprices, and abroad there are no hostile states to worry about, his kingdom will generally come to ruin."[46]

What he advocated was a combination of moral virtues and laws. For, as he said, "Goodness alone is not sufficient for the exercise of government; laws alone cannot carry themselves into practice."[47]

It must be admitted, however, that Mencius, like most Confucianists, had a tendency to idealize the ancient rulers and therefore preferred the old laws to the new. Commenting on two lines which he quoted from an ancient Ode—

Erring in nothing, forgetful of nothing,
Observing and following the old statutes—

he remarks, "Never has any one fallen into error who followed the laws of the ancient kings."[48]

The extreme emphasis that Mencius laid on the solidarity of the family and on the duty of filial piety sometimes raised difficult questions which even he could not easily solve. For, as one can well imagine, there are situations in which the interests of one's family may clash with the interests of the state. One such question was brought up by a disciple of Mencius, T'ao Yin. "Suppose that at the time when Shun was Emperor and Kao Yao was the Chief Justice, Ku Sou should murder a man, what would have been done in the case?" Mencius said, "Kao Yao would simply have arrested him." "But would Shun not have forbidden the arrest?" "Oh no," was the reply. "How could Shun have forbidden it? The Chief Justice had received the law from a proper source." "What then would Shun have done?" The answer of Mencius is characteristic. "Shun was a man who regarded the abandoning of everything under heaven as throwing away a worn-out sandal. He would have stolen away the prisoner and, carrying him on his back, escaped together into concealment, living somewhere on the sea-side. There he would have remained all the rest of his life, cheerful and happy, forgetting the empire."[49]

I am sure that this is what Mencius himself would have done, but I am not so sure whether the Emperor should have abandoned his public duties without even a resignation. After all, the empire is not a piece of private property which one could throw away like a pair of old shoes.

Confucianism, by over-emphasizing family relations, created many troubles for the public peace and order. For one thing, it considered it a sacred duty for a son to avenge the blood of his father killed by another. It continued to be so considered long after private revenge was expressly forbidden by the laws. This conflict between law and moral ideas was one of the burning questions throughout the history of China, until about a century ago, when people began gradually to realize that private revenge was wrong even from the moral point of view.

Although Mencius did not encourage private revenge, he seems to have taken it for granted. He said, for instance, that if you kill your neighbor's father, then your neighbor would kill your father.

Mencius was insistent upon the traditional three-year mourning for the death of one's parent. This was also one of the instances where he seems to have mistaken a mere determination of the natural law to be one of its essential principles. An overassertion of natural law often leads to unnatural results. For instance, in the codes of many dynasties, there was a provision that it was a crime to beget a child during the period of mourning for one's deceased parents. It was not until the fourteenth century that this was abolished at the insistence of an emperor who found that provision to be against human nature.

In conclusion let me say that Mencius' philosophy of the natural law is in substantial agreement with the classic natural-law tradition of the West, as represented by Plato, Aristotle, the Stoics, St. Thomas Aquinas, Richard Hooker, Hugo Grotius, and Edmund Burke. In his recent book, *Plato's Modern Enemies and The Theory of Natural Law,* Professor John Wild of Harvard addresses himself to the question: "What is precisely meant by the doctrine of natural law, and who are its authentic representatives in the history of Western thought?"[50] After a comprehensive survey, he has brought out five basic points which its authentic representatives share in common, in spite of their differences in minor details. I shall present the five criteria of the authentic philosophy of natural law in my words. (1) Norms are not man-made; they are derived from the objective order of the universe which pre-supposes God as the Supreme Ordinator. (2) Each being is endowed with a nature, an essential structure which it shares with other members of the same species. The being we are concerned with in ethics and jurisprudence is man. The natural law is founded on the specific nature of man and the essential tendencies determined by this nature. (3) Those essential tendencies are expansive and dynamic and demanding further development and fulfilment. In Mencius' philosophy, we have seen the four incipient tendencies which, if not impeded, would grow by their intrinsic orientation to fulfilment in ripe virtue. (4) In view of distracting forces, there is need of a rational direction of these tendencies toward their natural end. Mencius has explained the need of such direction by the mind and the need of enlisting the help of the passion-nature in the task. (5) The attainment of the end is recognized as the one thing necessary for man, that is, the realization of his humanity to the fullest extent, which is at the same time the way to do the will of Heaven. In the words of Mencius, "all things of the universe are found complete within me. To return to oneself and find oneself true to one's nature—herein lies the summit of happiness."[51]

I know of no philosophy, whether in the East or in the West, that fulfills the above criteria more perfectly than that of Mencius.

Finally let us consider whether Mencius' doctrine of the essential goodness of human nature is compatible with the Christian conception of the fallen nature. On this point I want to quote illuminating words of Pius XII:

> Without taking into account the fleeting opinions which have appeared at various periods, the Church has affirmed the value of what is human and what is in conformity with nature. Without any hesitation she has sought to develop it and place it in evidence. She does not admit that in the sight of God man is mere corruption and sin. On the contrary, in the eyes of the Church Original Sin did not intimately affect man's aptitudes and strength, and has left essentially intact the natural light of his intelligence and his freedom.

Man endowed with this nature is undoubtedly injured and weakened by the heavy inheritance of a fallen nature deprived of supernatural and preternatural gifts. He must make an effort to observe the natural law—this with the powerful assistance of the Grace of Christ—so that he can live as the honor of God and his dignity require.[52]

Of course, Mencius had no idea of Original Sin. But when we remember that he was speaking only of the essential goodness of human nature rather than the natural goodness of man as an existential being, and when we recall how earnestly he harped upon the necessity of human effort and patience in bringing about the actualization of the essential tendencies or potentialities of human nature, we would marvel how close his conception is to that of Christian philosophers. On the other hand, the difficulties involved in his philosophy of the essential goodness of human nature and the diversity of views among outstanding Chinese philosophers about the nature of man, show how impossible it is to have a perfectly satisfactory answer to this thorny question without the light of the Revelation. For, as the Psalmist says:

In Thy light shall we see light.[53]

NOTES

[1] This article is based upon a public lecture delivered at Pittsburgh's first Natural Law Institute sponsored by The St. Thomas More Society, Duquesne University and the University Catholic Club, on October 18, 1956. This explains the popular nature of some of the passages. Some parts have been expanded considerably.

[2] James Legge, *The Life and Works of Mencius* (London, 1875), p. 16.

[3] Some of the legends are to be found in *Lieh Nu Ch'uan* (Biographies of Virtuous Women).

[4] Book I, ch. 1. This and other quotations in this article are my own translations. I dare not claim that they are free from errors. I hope the reader will point them out to me, when he finds them inaccurate.

[5] The opening sentence of *Chung Yung*.

[6] Book 7, Part 1, ch. 1, art. 1.

[7] Book 6, Part 1, ch. 14, art. 2.

[8] Book 6, Part 1, ch. 14, art. 6.
[9] Book 6, Part 1, ch. 6, arts. 1-6.
[10] Book 6, Part 1, ch. 6, art. 8.
[11] *Ibid.*
[12] Book 6, Part 1, ch. 7, arts. 1-7.
[13] Book 6, Part 1, ch. 2, arts. 1-3.
[14] Book 6, Part 1, ch. 1, arts. 1-2.
[15] Book 2, Part 1, ch. 4, art. 6. The original is the "four incipient beginnings or tendencies." The cardinal virtues enumerated by Mencius are different from those of Aristotle, which are Justice, Temperance, Fortitude and Prudence, I rather think that Mencius' list is more complete, because Humanity, or fellow-feeling, or sympathy, seems to me fundamental.
[16] Book 2, Part 1, ch. 4, arts. 1-2.
[17] Book 2, Part 1, ch. 4, art. 3.
[18] Book 2, Part 1, ch. 4, arts. 3-4.
[19] Hall, *Living Law of Democratic Society.* (Bobbs-Merrill, 1949), p. 75.
[20] Book 2, Part 1, ch. 4, arts. 5-7.
[21] Book 6, Part 1, ch. 8, arts. 1-2.
[22] Book 6, Part 1, ch. 19.
[23] Book 7, Part 1, ch. 21, arts. 3-4.
[24] Book 2, Part 1, ch. 2, art. 11.
[25] According to Plato, the Soul of man has three parts: the rational principle, the passionate or spirited principle, and desire. In the conflict between reason and desire, the passionate principle should be "arrayed on the side of the rational principle." The whole description is to be found in *The Republic,* Book VI. The similarity between Plato and Mencius is truly remarkable. With Mencius, in human nature there are also three parts: (1) the rational principle; (2) the vital spirit; (3) desire. In self-culture, everything depends upon the alliance of the vital spirit to the rational principle. This is brought about through the will which is rooted in reason but at the same time is more directly related to the vital spirit than reason is.

In another respect Plato is similar to Mencius. As Dr. Paul K. T. Sih has pointed out in his article "The Natural Law Philosophy of Mencius" (*New Scholasticism,* XXXI, No. 3 1957, pp. 317-337. Mencius was to Confucius what Plato was to Socrates.
[26] Book 2, Part 1, ch. 2, art. 9.
[27] *Ibid.*
[28] Book 2, Part 1, ch. 2, art. 10.
[29] Book 2, Part 1, ch. 2, arts. 12-14.
[30] Book 2, Part 1, ch. 2, art. 16.
[31] *Ibid.*
[32] *Ibid.*
[33] For example, Mencius' criticisms against Motze are very superficial. He was swayed by passions. Motze's *chien ai* was not equal love, but universal love, which admits of degrees. But Mencius does not seem to have

given Motze a fair hearing.

[34] Book 6, Part 1, ch. 16, art. 1.
[35] Book 7, Part 2, ch. 14, arts. 1-4.
[36] Book 1, Part 2, ch. 6, arts. 1-3.
[37] Book 1, Part 2, ch. 8, arts. 1-3.
[38] Book 1, Part 1, ch. 4, arts. 3-6.
[39] Book 1, Part 1, ch. 3, art. 3.
[40] Book 4, Part 1, ch. 5.
[41] Book 4, Part 1, ch. 4, art. 3.
[42] Book 6, Part 2, ch. 15, art. 2.
[43] Book 7, Part 2, ch. 24, arts. 1-2.
[44] Book 7, Part 1, ch. 2, art. 1.
[45] Book 4, Part 1, ch. 1, art. 8.
[46] Book 4, Part 1, ch. 1, art. 9.
[47] Book 4, Part 1, ch. 1, art. 3.
[48] Book 4, Part 1, ch. 1, art. 4.
[49] Book 7, Part 1, ch. 35, arts. 1-6.
[50] P. 103.
[51] Book 7, Part 1, ch. 4, arts. 1-2.
[52] Address to Philosophers participating in the International Congress of Humanistic Studies, on September 25, 1949.
[53] Psalms 35:10.

THE SPIRIT OF JOY
IN CHINESE SAGES

1. Joy and Music

"Where there is music there is joy," says one of the ancient Chinese classics, *Li Ki,* as rendered by James Legge. A literal translation of the same sentence would be "Music is joy." In fact, joy and music are represented by one and the same character. When it is intended to denote music, it is pronounced "yueh"; when it is intended to denote joy, it is pronounced "lo." But the same word is used in both cases. From this you can easily realize how inseparable the spirit of joy is from the spirit of music.

According to the Chinese way of thinking, music is joy, and joy is music, because both of them are essentially bound up with the idea of Harmony.

In *The Treatise on Music,*[1] the origin of music is traced to the harmony of the cosmos. It says: "The breath of earth ascends on high, and the breath of heaven descends below. These in their repressive and expansive powers come into mutual contact, and heaven and earth act on each other. (The susceptibilities of nature) are roused by the thunder, excited by the wind and rain, moved by the four seasons, and warmed by the sun and the moon; and all the processes of change and growth vigorously proceed. Thus it was that music was framed to indicate the harmony between heaven and earth."[2] In another place, it says, "Great music expresses the harmony of heaven and earth."

Now, heaven and earth constitute the Macrocosm, while man is Microcosm. If a man achieves a harmony within himself corresponding to the harmony of the Big Cosmos, then the spirit of joy will swell up spontaneously from the depths of his being, indicating that he is one with the Cosmos.

In other words, joy comes from the perfect realization of one's personality, which in turn depends upon the achievement of interior harmony. As music is the art of harmony *par excellence,* it is little wonder that the ancient Chinese sages laid such emphasis on the cultivation of music as a means of developing the human personality. Let one example illustrate the point. It is recorded in *The Book of History* how Emperor Shun appointed his Cabinet, including the Prime Minister and Ministers of Agriculture, Education, Justice, Public Works, and so forth. What interests me particularly is the appointment of the Minister of Music. The Emperor said, "Ku'ei, I appoint you to take charge of music, to teach our sons to be straightforward and yet mild, to be generous and yet firm, to be strong without being rude, and to be simple without being arrogant."[3]

Confucius was in the grand tradition when he announced his program for the education of his pupils: "First arouse their interest in learning by means of poetry; then establish their character by making them practice the rules of propriety; finally, harmonize their personality by means of music."[4] It is only in the last stage that one attains the spirit of joy. As Confucius put it, "To know it is not so good as to like it; and to like it is not so good as to rejoice in it."[5]

But, just as there are different styles of music, even though all of them are good, so there are different levels or modes of joy. Joy, as understood by the Confucianist sage, was not exactly the same as the joy of the Taoist, and both in turn differed from that of the Buddhist. The only thing in common to the three schools is that their joy is sharply distinct from, and superior to, the sensual pleasures of the world.

2. The Joy of Confucius

The atmosphere of joy in which Confucius lived begins to radiate in the very first pages of his book of *Analects*. In fact, it sets the tone of the whole book. These are the opening words:

> The Master said, "Is it not a true delight to learn and to practice constantly what one has learned? Is it not a real joy to see men of kindred spirit gathered from distant places? Is it not characteristic of the gentleman not to be saddened even when his qualities are not known by others?"[6]

Here we find the joy of learning, the joy of fellowship, and the joy of the perfect development of one's personality without regard to recognition by the world. Confucius described himself as "a man who is so eagerly absorbed in learning and teaching as to forget his meals, and who finds such joy in it as to forget all his worries, being quite oblivious of the coming on of old age."[7]

Among his pupils, the one for whom Confucius had the greatest love was Yen Huei. Indeed the Master never tired of praising him. He said: "How good is Huei! With a single bamboo bowl of rice, and a single ladle of cabbage soup, living in a miserable alley! Others could not have borne such distress, but Huei has never lost his spirit of joy. How good is Huei!"[8] In this bit of praise for his disciple, Confucius showed his admiration for people whose joy comes from within and is not dependent upon the external circumstances of life.

In terms of practical life, it may be said the Confucian joy comes from the awareness that one has well acquitted oneself of one's duties. Tseng-shen, another of the great pupils of Confucius, once said, "Every day I examine myself on three points: In planning for others, have I failed in conscientiousness? In dealing with my friends, have I been wanting in sincerity? In learning, have I neglected to practice what my Master has taught me?"[9]

Yet, great as he was, Tseng-shen was considered much less gifted than Yen Huei. In fact, Confucius referred to Tseng-shen as "stupid," presumably because the latter had to interpret joy for himself in terms of particular individual actions, whereas Yen Huei seemed to rise above these small details.

Stupid or not as he might have been in the mind of the Master, Tseng-shen has been the model whom most later Confucian scholars have patterned their lives upon; the simple reason for this is that Yen Huei was *inimitable*. Only the more gifted ones have dared to aspire to Yen Huei's level of joy, and, to my knowledge, none has ever quite reached it. His was indeed a true greatness, described by Tseng-shen in these words: "Clever, yet not ashamed to consult those less clever than himself; widely gifted, yet not ashamed to consult those with few gifts; having, yet seeming not to have; full, yet seeming empty; offended against, yet never reckoning."[10]

Yet, in spite of the intellectual quality of his notion of joy, Confucius did not believe it necessary to reject the small good things and the comforts of life. He only counseled moderation in our enjoyment of them. His teaching on moderation is well illustrated in "The Song of the Cricket." This composition was written in a sort of antiphonal style, the alternate verses to be sung by a group of feasters and a "moderator." It goes like this:

The Song of the Cricket

The Feasters:

The cricket sings in the hall,
The year is late in the fall.
Let's dance and sing today;
The sun and the moon wouldn't stay.

The Moderator:

Do not go to extremes,
Forget not your noble dreams.
See how the prudent boys
Restrain themselves in joys.

The Feasters:

The cricket sings in the hall,
The year'll take leave of all.
Let's dance and sing tonight
To catch time in its flight.

The Moderator:

Enjoy you surely may,
But heed what the elders say.
If you have no control,
You may soon lose your soul.

The Feasters:

The cricket sings in the hall,
The year is beyond recall.
Let's make the best of life:
Time's like a butcher's knife.

The Moderator:

I know that life is brief;
But too much joy brings grief.
Beware of the charms of beauty:
True peace is found in duty.

Nor does Confucian joy disregard human love. In the *Book of Songs,* which is said to have been compiled by Confucius himself, and which he never tired of recommending to his pupils, and even to his own son, there are love poems of the best sort.

Confucianism seeks harmony in human relations, and when it expresses itself in poetry, it radiates a certain fragrance of sympathy that warms the heart. Nothing that is of interest to man as man is alien to it. It does not despise any human feelings, affections, desires, and appetites; it only insists that they should conform to the ideal of harmony.

3. The Joy of the Taoists

While the Confucianists sought for joy in the harmony of the *human* world, the Taoists found their joy in the harmony of existence between the *individual* and the *universe.* They aspired to transcend the human hive, and to live in the bosom of Nature. A typical expression of the Taoist ideal is the poem by Lu Yun, who lived in the 4th century:

Beyond the dusty world,
I enjoy solitude and peace.
I shut my door,
I close my windows.
Harmony is my spring,
Purity my autumn.
Attuned to the seasons,
My cottage becomes a universe.

Lu Yun's ideal man, although he lived in isolation, was really no isolationist, because he was one with the universe, his spirit being tuned to the rhythm of Nature. Unlike the Confucianist, who found happiness chiefly in the fellowship of like-minded people, the Taoist felt at home when he was alone in communion with Nature.

It is not surprising then, to find that, while Confucianism set great store by scholarship, Taoism accounted scholarly learning of little worth and even advocated its abandonment.

You have heard Confucius say that riches and honors improperly obtained were so many fleeting clouds to him. The Taoist seems to go a step further. To him all riches and honors, whether properly or improperly obtained, are nothing. As the great Taoist, Chuang Tsu, put it, the man of the Tao "lets the gold lie hidden in the hill, and the pearls in the deep; he considers not poverty or money to be any gain, he keeps aloof from riches and honors, he rejoices not in long life, and grieves not for early death; he does not consider prosperity a glory, nor is he ashamed of indigence; he would not grasp at the gain of the whole world to be held as his own private portion; he would not desire to rule over the whole world as his own private distinction. His distinction is in understanding that *all things belong to the one treasury,* and that death and life should be viewed in the same way."[11]

The joy of the Taoist is the joy of non-attachment, of interior freedom. It lacks the warmth of the Confucian joy, but there is a breeziness about it which gives refreshment to the spirit. A good illustration will be found in "The Fisherman's Songs," written by Prince Li Yu. Note that these songs were written by a prince, who, despite his life in a palace, was miserable and envied the freedom of the fishermen. Here are the words of Prince Li Yu:

The Fisherman's Songs

The foam of the waves stimulates endless drifts of snow.
The peach-trees and the pear-trees silently form a
    battalion of spring.
A bottle of wine,
An angling line,
How many men share the happiness that's mine?

An oar of spring breeze playing about a leaf of a boat.
A tiny hook at the end of the silken cord.
An islet of flowers,
A jugful of wine,
Over the boundless waves liberty is mine.

Many a Chinese scholar began as a Confucianist, but as he grew older, he became more and more Taoistic in his ways of thinking and feeling.

In the teachings of Taoism can be found the beginning of that spiritual detachment which was arrived at by the Christian saints and which is so wonderfully summed up in these paradoxical lines written by St. John of the Cross: "To possess everything, desire to possess nothing. To be everything, desire to be nothing."

4. The Joy of the Buddhists

We come, now, to Zen Buddhism, which, to my mind, is a typically Chinese product. The German philosopher, Hermann Keyserling, in his book, *The Travel Diary of a Philosopher,* speaking of Confucianism and Taoism in China, says: "Kung Fu Tse (Confucius) and Lao Tse represent the opposite poles of possible perfection; the one represents the perfection of appearance, the other the perfection of significance; the former, the perfection within the sphere of the materialized, the latter, within the non-materialized; therefore, they cannot be measured with the same gauge."

On the whole, I think that Keyserling's appraisal is right, if we confine our study to the natural wisdom of man. But if Confucianism and Taoism represent the opposite poles of possible perfection, one may wonder: Where does Buddhism come in? I think it represents an attempt to harmonize the two poles by transcending them both. The Zen Buddhist aspires to reach the Other Shore by standing right where he is. He sees all things in the light of eternity. For him every experience in life, however ordinary it may be, is charged with wonderful significance, because it is a springboard from which to jump into the ocean of mystery. Apparently he is living in the same world as others, but subjectively he is living in a new heaven and a new earth. His joy is the joy of sudden awakening, upon which one gets a glimpse of the very nature of things. In his momentary raptures, all fears and sorrows are forgotten, and life is no more than a play on motion picture film. In such a state, one acquires a sense of universal compassion for all sentient beings.

The Zen Buddhist, viewing the universe in the light of eternity, is unmindful of all the billions of years of its existence and sees it as a magical flower blooming only for a single instant and then disappearing forever. Or, to change the figure of speech, all the pageants of life seem to him like the speeding of a racehorse watched through a crevice in a wall. Yet, with the Zen masters, while all apparently permanent things become transient, the most transient things acquire an eternal significance. The notes of a singing bird, the fragrance of a flower, the rippling of a brook, the casual reunion of old friends, the whisper of a lover, the echoes of a church bell—all these things have an eternal quality, bathed as they are in the ocean of mystery. The spring flowers look prettier, and the mountain stream runs cooler and more transparent. This may be called aesthetical contemplation. This is why the greatest Chinese artists have drawn their inspiration from Zen Buddhism.

Let me relate to you a charming anecdote about the great Zen Master, Hsuan Sha. One day, Hsuan Sha had ascended to his speaker's platform and was ready to deliver a discourse, when he heard the twitter of a swallow outside the hall. Abruptly, he remarked to his audience, "What a wonderful sermon on reality!" Thereupon, he came down from the platform and retired to his room.

Many of the poems of the T'ang Dynasty are saturated with the spirit of Zen. I will quote one which I like very much, and which seems to me to express a sudden invasion of eternity into the realm of time:

> *A Night-Mooring Outside the City of Soochow*
> *By Chang Chi*
>
> The moon has gone down;
> The crows are cawing;
> The sky is filled with frost.

The maple-trees and the fisherman's lanterns
Accompany my fitful slumbers.
Suddenly, from the Cold Hill Temple beyond the city
of Soochow,
Come echoes of the midnight-bell to a passing boat!

C. G. Jung calls Zen Buddhism "one of the most wonderful blossoms of the Chinese spirit." Now, what is the most fundamental characteristic of the Chinese spirit? To my mind, it is the union of the abstract with the concrete; of the universal with the particular; of utmost unearthliness with complete earthliness; of transcendental idealism with a commonplace practicality. This union is not a matter of theoretical synthesis, but a matter of *personal experience*.

The idea that the ordinary duties of one's daily life are charged with spiritual significance, is typically Chinese. Dr. Suzuki finds in this an expression of the Chinese people's characteristic industry and practicality. Hence he finds it quite logical for the Zen teachers to insist on service to others—doing for others—as the expression of an understanding of spiritual values. For, says Dr. Suzuki, mystics are always practical men—not too absorbed in things unearthly or of the other world to be concerned with the needs of this life.

Once again, we find in the thinking of the Chinese sages the beginning of an approach to the perfection of the Christian saints. I know one person who attained a sudden awakening such as I have just described—an awakening of the transitory and fluid nature of the cosmos, which ordinarily appears so solid and so permanent—by the reading of the four-line poem expressing the philosophy of Zen Buddhism. It was written by Sui Yang-ti:

Flowers and Moonlight on the Spring River

The evening river is level and motionless—
The spring colors just open to their full.
Suddenly a wave carries the moon away
And the tidal water comes with its freight of stars.

This poem is innocent enough, but it opened the interior eye of that reader to the transitory nature of the Cosmos, which ordinarily appears so permanent. Thus, Zen makes you see into the work of creation, although it does not claim to interview the Creator Himself.[12]

Shakespeare was steeped in the spirit of Zen. Shakespeare who made Prospero declare near the end of The Tempest:

> Our revels now are ended. These our actors,
> As I foretold you, were all spirits and
> Are melted into the air, into thin air;
> And, like the baseless fabric of this vision,
> The cloud-capp'd towers, the gorgeous palaces,
> The solemn temples, the great globe itself,
> Yea, all which it inherit, shall dissolve
> And, like this in substantial pageant faded,
> Leave not a rack behind. We are such stuff
> As dreams are made on, and our little life
> Is rounded with a sleep.

It would seem that the spirit of Zen leads only to a negative result, and has nothing to contribute toward joy. Yet, the realization that we are all passing shadows does a great deal by way of lifting the burden of sorrows from the heart of a sufferer. It also prepares the way for a true religious life, for by showing that there is no abiding city in this world, it gives a salutary warning to the spirit of man against seeking rest where it cannot be found.

5. Conclusions

In this paper I have tried to depict three types of joy corresponding to the three schools of philosophy that have permeated the spirit of the Chinese people throughout the ages. Confucianism is humanistic, and its joy is the joy of a virtuous life. Taoism is pantheistic, and its joy is the joy of feeling at one with the cosmos. Zen Buddhism is otherworldly, and its joy comes from the sudden illumination concerning the nothingness of the visible world. I have only touched upon the joy of Christian saints, because this belongs to a higher order than that of the sages.

The Christian joy contains all the three forms of joy that were known to the Chinese sages. It knows the Confucian joy, which springs from fraternal love and filial piety; but it transcends it, just as the theological virtues transcend the moral virtues. The Christian saint knows also the joy of the Taoistic sage, but he does not content himself with a promiscuous union with the creation; he rests in the Creator and enjoys his union with the whole creation in Him; through Him, and for Him. The Taoistic union with Nature is somewhat like free love, which may give momentary joys; but the Christian union with Nature is like the Sacrament of Marriage, which is a source of deeper and more stable joy, foreshadowing eternal bliss and borrowing therefrom a heavenly luster. The Christian saint, above all, knows the ecstatic and rapturous joys of the mystics, but, unlike the Buddhists, his transports are not self-induced—he simply rides on the tides of the Holy Spirit.

The Christian joy springs from three levels: Nature, man and God, with God as the Ultimate Source. This is why the Christian saints could sincerely fraternize with Nature without being drowned in the ocean of the cosmos. St. Francis loved and enjoyed Nature with the liberty of spirit characteristic of the children of God. He had all the joys known to the pantheists and more, and at the same time he did not have to regard himself as a cosmic ganglion. Similarly, St. Vincent de Paul and Father Damien loved their neighbors so generously as to be glad to suffer with them and for them. How many missionaries have laid down their lives for their fellow-beings in the far-distant countries! But nobody would accuse them of being all-too-human and sentimental. St. Paul was made joyful in his contemplation of God, but he was at the same time as sober as any Confucian gentleman in his dealings with men, and as unattached as any Taoist hermit or Buddhist bonze to human riches and glories. Only grace can fulfill the aspirations of nature.

From these examples it should be clear that the Christian saints possess a higher and richer joy than the pagan sages ever did. Compared with the Christian joy, the joys of the philosophers are but crumbs from the real Feast of Life. In truth, there is something pathetic about them; they are, at best, groanings and yearnings for the Joyful News of the Incarnation, for the restoration of the Garden of Delight. But what about those Christians who pass through their lives so joylessly that they have to seek external pleasures and excitements to kill time? They do not even seem to know what the Oriental sages knew so well: unless one finds happiness in the interior life, one will not be happy anywhere else. For, as Christ has told us, "The Kingdom of Heaven is within you."

Now it is the aim of the Christian apostolate to preserve and to perfect—not to destroy—whatever of truth it finds in the traditions of a people, and there are many such elements in the teachings of the Chinese sages—Confucius, Lao Tse, and the teachers of Zen Buddhism. These teachings have left their influence upon the people in many parts of the world. Hence, it is good for all who would promote the Christian apostolate in our times, and especially for those who would be prepared for a "philosopher's apostolate," to know where the seeds of truth are to be found in the Oriental fields of thought. Upon the trees of culture which spring from these seeds, we may hope to engraft the life-giving Gospel revealed by the Author of all grace and truth and the Source of all our hope for happiness.

It is here that the oriental ideas of harmony and joy have value, for "Gospel" means "Joyful News." It is only when we appreciate and radiate from ourselves the joy embodied in the Christian Gospel that we can effectively work as missionaries. Too many Christians fail to reflect this Divine joy. They live as though Christ had never been born, crucified, and risen from the dead, and yet they talk about "Christianizing" others! In their endless searching for happiness in the transient and meaningless pleasures of the world, they are indeed seeking after husks fit only for the swine. The Oriental sages at least appreciated the little crumbs of the Bread of Truth which they found in their lifelong searchings. Were they far wrong in identifying joy with music? I think not, because music is the art of harmony *par excellence*. The sages knew that joy follows from interior harmony. They knew, also, that interior harmony means development of the human personality.

NOTES

[1] *Li Ki,* Book 17.

[2] Legge, *Li Ki,* Book 17, par. 31.

[3] *The Canon of Shun.*

[4] *Analects,* 8:8.

[5] *Ibid.,* 6:18.

[6] *Ibid.,* 1:1.

[7] *Ibid.,* 7:18.

[8] *Ibid.,* 6:9.

[9] *Ibid.,* 1:4.

[10] *Ibid.,* 8:5.

[11] *Chuang Tzu Chi Chieh* (cf. "The Wisdom of Chuang Tzu: A New Appraisal" of this book, No. 1) ch. 12, pp. 64-65.

[12] Suzuki, *Essays,* p. 261.

TAOISM

Taoism can be studied under two different aspects: as *philosophy* and as *religion*. This article is not concerned with Taoism as a religion, which was a later invention hardly connected with the original philosophy of the Tao as propounded by Lao Tzu and Chuang Tzu. Taoism as philosophy or wisdom of life had its beginnings in the earliest times known to us, long before the sixth century B.C., the Age of Lao Tzu and Confucius. Although Lao Tzu, the author of the famous *Tao Teh Ching,* is generally recognized as the founder of Taoism, many of its basic ideas are to be found scattered in earlier writings, especially the *Shu* or *The Book of Documents,* upon which Confucius drew heavily and which could not have been unfamiliar to Lao Tzu, although he did not quote explicitly from this or any other books.

The central insight of Taoism is that humility or lowliness is the foundation of all greatness. For this is the Tao or Way of Heaven. As the *Tao Teh Ching* puts it: Therefore, the Sage embraces the One, and becomes a pattern to the world. He does not make a show of himself, hence he shines; does not justify himself, hence he becomes known; does not boast of his ability, hence he has true merit; does not brandish his success, hence he endures long; does not compete with anyone, hence no one can compete with him. Indeed, the ancient saying: 'Bend and you will remain whole' is no idle word. Nay, if you have really attained wholeness, all things will flock to you as to their home.[1]

In the *Book of Documents,* we find that when Shun wanted to transmit the throne to Yu who had successfully "pacified" the Flood, he paid him a compliment in these terms: You have worked diligently in the service of the country; you have been sparing in your expenditure on your family. Yet you are not elated and self-complacent. I am deeply impressed by your virtue. It is precisely because you do not brandish your achievements that no one in the world can contest your ability. It is precisely because you do not boast that no one in the world can deny your merit.[2]

Again, in the *Book of Documents* we find: "August Heaven has no special favorites; it gives its help only to the virtuous. The hearts of the people are not fixed upon (a particular leader), they cherish only the beneficent."[3] So, Lao Tzu: "The Way of Heaven has no special favorites; it always goes along with the good ones."[4] "The Sage has no fixed preconceptions; he makes the people's wishes his own."[5]

Again, the idea of bearing the guilt of the people on one's own shoulder finds expression several times in the *Book of Documents*. For example, T'ang, the Founder of the Yin Dynasty, at his inaugural sacrifice to God, made a solemn announcement to the people: "Let everyone of you keep the laws, so that he may receive blessings from Heaven. The good in you I will not dare to conceal; nor will I dare to forgive myself for the evil in me. All things are clearly recorded in the mind of God. May the sins of my people in all parts of the country fall upon my person! May my own sins never be visited upon my people anywhere!"[6]

This "scapegoat" idea finds a philosophic expression in the *Tao Teh Ching*: "Therefore, the Sage says, 'To receive the dirt of a country is to be the Lord of its soil-shrines; to bear the calamities of the country is to be the King of the world.' True words sound paradoxical."[7]

A very distinctive feature of Taoistic philosophy is the doctrine of *wu-wei*. *Wu-wei,* which has been variously rendered as "non-action," "non-assertiveness," "passivity," "spontaneity," "non-activeness," "non-attachment," etc. I have rendered it as "non-ado." The idea of *wu-wei* comprises two aspects, physical and mental. Physically, it implies that our actions should not exceed what is essential to the accomplishment of a given aim. We must not engage in activity for activity's sake. This doctrine inclines toward leading a quiet life and warns against being busy about many things. Mentally, *wu-wei* implies that even if we are called upon to perform a necessary function for the welfare of the people, and even if we have accomplished our work, we must never be attached to what we have done, knowing that our true happiness does not lie in what we do, but in what we are. *"When you have done work, retire!* This is the Way of Heaven."[8]

That this idea of *wu-wei* was well-known to Confucius is evident in some of his sayings, e.g.: "Speaking of 'ruling by *wu-wei,'* there can be no better exemplification of it than Shun! For what did he do? He did nothing but reign courteously and serenely with his face due south."[9] "How sublime were Shun and Yu! They possessed the whole world, but they were not attached to it!"[10]

The great contribution of Lao Tzu toward the formation of Taoism as a school of thought was twofold. In the first place, he gathered together many grains of wisdom scattered through ancient documents and put them into a little volume. Being the curator of the royal archives at the court of Chou, he must have read much and pondered on the ups and downs of the dynasties. Taking a long-range view of history, he must have won certain profound insights into the "timeless Tao" which, unchangeable in itself, is at the back of the variable fortunes of the human world. Only an extremely well-fed mind, with a natural gift of keen observation, could have discovered so many paradoxes of life. Let a few samples suffice: "Fill your house with gold and jade, and it can no longer be guarded. Set store by your riches and honors, and you will reap a crop of calamities."[11] The covetous and aggressive ones may succeed for a moment, but they are never rich and powerful enough and the very causes of their temporary success lead inevitably to their downfall. "For a whirlwind does not last a whole morning, nor does a sudden shower last a whole day."[12] On the other hand, he must have observed that the truly great men in history have been those who thought least of their own glory or interests but were minded only on giving peace and rest to the people. "Therefore, the Sage wants to remain behind, but finds himself in front; reckons himself out, but finds himself in. Is it not because he is selfless that his self is fully realized?"[13] Again: "The Sage does not take to hoarding. The more he lives for others, the fuller is his life. The more he gives, the more he abounds."[14]

To Lao Tzu, even the moral virtues must not be cultivated deliberately and with a *possessive spirit*. As he says, "High virtue is not self-virtuous; therefore it has virtue. Low virtue never frees itself from the sense of virtuousness; therefore it has no virtue."[15] For true virtue springs naturally and spontaneously from our union with the Tao or the Way of Heaven. Now, the Tao is the Origin of the universe and the "Mother" of all things.[16] It is the mystery of mysteries. It is essentially indefinable in human language and inexplicable by human reasoning. In order, therefore, to be united with the Tao, one must withdraw from all the mundane lights into the depths of his own soul. "Where the Darkness is at the darkest, there is the door to all subtleties."[17] To attain inner illumination, one has to follow the way of *unknowing*. "Block all the passages! Shut all the doors! And to the end of your days you will not be worn out. Open the passages! Multiply your activities! And to the end of your days you will remain helpless."[18] "Without peeping through your window, you can see the Way of Heaven. The farther you go, the less you know."[19] Where Confucius advocates learning, Lao Tzu stresses the necessity of *unlearning*. "Learning consists in daily gaining; but the practice of the Tao consists in daily losing. Keep on losing and losing, until you reach the state of Non-Ado. Non-Ado, and yet nothing is left undone!"[20]

Lao Tzu's symbol for the Tao is the Hsuan P'ing, the Mysterious Feminine. "The Spirit of the Valley dies not. It is called the Mysterious Feminine. The doorway of the Mysterious Feminine is the Root of the universe."[21] In an interesting chapter of autobiographical nature, he describes how foolish and dull and useless he is by the worldly standards, but concludes with a child-like candor that in one thing alone he excels others, that is, he *"knows the value of feeding upon the Mother."*[22]

His symbol for *Teh* or Virtue—which is the effect crystallized in the person united with the Tao—is the *new-born Child*. "One who is deeply steeped in Virtue is akin to the new-born Child."[23]

His symbol for the functioning of the Tao is the *water*. "The highest form of goodness is like water. Water knows how to benefit all things without striving with them. It stays in places loathed by all men. Therefore it comes near to the Tao."[24] Again: "Nothing is softer and weaker than water; yet in attacking the hard and strong it is irresistible."[25] The glory of the sea is derived from the tendency of water to seek out the low places. "How does the sea become the king of all streams? Because it lies lower than they!"[26]

As a practical counsel on personal cultivation, Lao Tzu recommends what he calls his "Three Treasures." The first is *mercy*. The second is *frugality*. The third is *not daring to be the first in the world*. Only the merciful is capable of the heroic. Only the frugal will be able to be truly generous. Only the retiring is capable of true leadership. On the other hand, to try to be heroic without being merciful, to be generous without being frugal, and to be a leader without forgetting oneself, is the surest way to court death. He further says that "Heaven will come to the rescue of the merciful, and protect him with Mercy."[27]

Practically all the essential doctrines of Taoism are covered by this little book of Lao Tzu, which contains only about five thousand words. But it is so sententious and pregnant with meaning that the average reader would easily miss many of its subtle points. The far-reaching influence of the Taoistic way of thinking and feeling about life is largely due to Chuang Chou (or Chuang Tzu, who lived around 369-286), who was not only a man of profound insights but also a man of literary genius. He had the gift of illustrating profound truths with intriguing stories and tantalizing paradoxes. The *Book of Chuang Tzu,* over ten times larger than the *Tao Teh Ching,* has been a source of inspiration to Chinese scholars and poets through the centuries. It contains many discourses on the nature of the Tao. The following specimen is typical: "The Tao carries within itself reality and unfailing truth, but it is beyond action and without form. It may be transmitted, but cannot be received as one's own. It may be attained, but cannot be shown. It is its own origin, its own root. Before heaven and earth came to exist, it Eternally *is*. It divinizes the spirits and gods, and gives birth to heaven and earth. It is above the zenith, but it is not high. It is beneath the nadir, but it is not low. Prior to the universe, yet it is not ancient. Prior to human history, yet it is not old."[28]

To be united with the Tao is to transcend, in spirit, time and space; to be indifferent to the vicissitudes of life, in a word, to be a *free man*. Having attained the transcendency of the Tao, one acquires also its immanency and becomes "united with the great community of existence." One feels one with Nature.

To attain this state, one has to pass through certain disciplines, similar to the *yoga* of the Hindus and Buddhists. Chuang Tzu brings out a number of such practices, among which are "the fast of the Mind" and "sitting and forgetting." It is significant that Chuang Tzu, in expounding these practices, should have put his words into the mouths of Confucius and his beloved disciple Yen Hui.

The Fast of the Mind. Yen Hui was going to the State of Wei, to see the Prince of Wei in order to offer his advice so as to reform his character. On taking leave of Confucius, he told him what he intended to do. He said that he would keep himself inwardly straight, but outwardly yielding. He continued: To be inwardly straight is to be a fellow of Heaven; and a fellow of Heaven knows that the "Son of Heaven" (the King) and himself are both children of Heaven, and does not care a whit whether his words are approved or disapproved by men. Such a one is called a guileless Child. This is what I mean by being a fellow of Heaven. To be outwardly yielding and adaptable is to be a fellow of men. . . . What others do I will also do. In this way, I shall be free of blame. This is what I mean by being a fellow of men. . . .In my remonstrances, I will cite the words of the ancients, so that even though they are actually condemnatory of his conduct, they do not come from me but from the ancients. In this way, my straightforwardness would give no offense. This is what I would call "being a fellow of the ancients." Will this do?" Confucius replied, "Oh no, it will not do! You have too many designs and methods but too little flexibility. You may, indeed, avoid blame; but that is all. How can you expect to transform him, seeing that you are still taking guidance from your own mind?" Yen Hui said, "Well, this is as far as I have arrived, and I can advance no farther. Can you show me the way?" Confucius said, "You must first *fast,* then I will tell you." Yen Hui said, "My family is poor. For several months I have tasted neither wine nor flesh. Is this not fast enough?" "No," said Confucius. "This is a ritual fast, not the fast of the mind." "What is the fast of the mind?" asked Yen Hui. Confucius replied: "Concentrate your will upon the One. Do not listen with the ear, but with the mind. Do not listen with the mind, but with the spirit. The function of the ear is limited to hearing;

that of the mind is limited to forming concepts and symbols. But the spirit is an emptiness ready to receive all things, for where there is emptiness the Tao itself will fill it. Emptiness is what I mean by fast of the mind,"[29]

Settled in Forgetting. Chuang Tzu puts this doctrine into the mouth of Yen Hui, making him teach Confucius. Yen Hui once said to Confucius, "I am making progress." Confucius said, "What do you mean?" "I have forgotten love and justice," said Yen Hui. "Very well," said Confucius, "but that is not enough." Another day, Yen Hui reported that he had forgotten the rites and music. This again failed to impress Confucius. A third day, Yen Hui reported that he had been inured to forgetting. Confucius became excited and asked what he meant. Yen Hui replied, "I have dropped the body and limbs and discarded intelligence and consciousness. Having been freed from the body and knowledge, I have become one with the Infinite. This is what I mean by being 'inured to forgetting.' " Confucius said, "To be one with the Infinite is to have no more preferences. To be thoroughly transformed is to have no more fixations. In this you have gone ahead of me. Let me follow in your steps."[30]

With Chuang Tzu the philosophy of Taoism reached its summit. Later works have not contributed anything new to the teachings of Lao Tzu and Chuang Tzu. Their ideas and their mode of thinking have become a ~~haven~~ leaven of Chinese thought, without which neither Zen Buddhism nor Neo-Confucianism would have been possible.

NOTES

[1] Ch. 22.
[2] *Ta Yu Mu.*
[3] *Ts'ai Chung Tzu Ming.*
[4] *Tao Teh Ching,* ch. 79.
[5] *Ibid.,* ch. 49.
[6] *T'ang Kao.*
[7] Ch. 78.

[8] *Tao Teh Ching,* ch. 9.
[9] *Analects,* 15:4.
[10] *Ibid.,* 8:18.
[11] *Tao Teh Ching,* ch. 9.
[12] *Ibid.,* ch. 23.
[13] *Ibid.,* ch. 7.
[14] *Ibid.,* ch. 81.
[15] *Ibid.,* ch. 38.
[16] *Ibid.,* ch. 1.
[17] *Ibid.*
[18] *Ibid.,* ch. 52.
[19] *Ibid.,* ch. 47.
[20] *Ibid.,* ch. 48.
[21] *Ibid.,* ch. 6.
[22] *Ibid.,* ch. 20.
[23] *Ibid.,* ch. 55.
[24] *Ibid.,* ch. 8.
[25] *Ibid.,* ch. 78.
[26] *Ibid.,* ch. 66.
[27] *Ibid.,* ch. 67.
[28] *Ta Chung Shih.*
[29] *The Book of Chuang Tzu,* ch. 4: "The Human World."
[30] *Ta Chung Shih.*

THE WISDOM
OF CHUANG TZU:
A NEW APPRAISAL[1]

1. Life[2]

Very little is known of the life of Chuang Chou, whom we usually call Chuang Tzu or Master Chuang. Even the year of his birth remains uncertain in spite of innumerable attempts by later scholars to determine it. All that we can say is that he was a younger contemporary of Mencius (371-289 B.C.), although the two seem never to have met and exchanged views, since there is no mention of each other in their works. This should not surprise us, if we remember that the books that we call *Meng Tsu* and *Chuang Tzu* did not exist during the lifetime of their respective authors; they were compiled by their disciples. Even if they had heard of each other, neither of them would have felt warranted in criticizing the other's views on mere hearsay. From all available evidence, Chuang Chou was born in the city of Meng in the state of Sung (in the present Honan province) in the decade between 370 and 360 B.C., and died probably in his early eighties.

In his younger days he served as a clerk for a few years in a local government, but later lived in complete retirement, making his livelihood as a sandal-maker,[3] with fishing for his hobby or as a by-profession. He was married, outliving his wife by a few years. *The Book of Chuang Tzu* contains an interesting account of his behavior on the occasion of his wife's death:

> When Chuang Tzu's wife died, Hui Tzu came to condole with him,

but found him squatted on the ground singing a song while beating time on a bowl. Hui Tzu said, "Your wife has lived with you for life, brought up children, aged, and died. It is bad enough if you don't wail over her. But now you are even singing and beating time on the bowl. Is this not going too far?" "Not so!" replied Chuang Tzu. "Her death at first afflicted me as it would anyone in the same situation. But upon reflection I came to see that in the beginning she had no life, nor even bodily form, not even breath, forming an indistinguishable part of a chaotic mass. A change occurred and there was breath; another change occurred, and there was bodily form; still another change, and there was life; now she has just undergone one more change and arrived at death. All these are only the phases of a process, like the procession of the four seasons: Spring, Summer, Autumn, and Winter. There now she sleeps peacefully in the Boundless Mansion. If I were to go about crying and wailing for her, I should be acting like one who has no understanding of the principle of predestination. That's why I have refrained."[4]

The "Hui Tzu" mentioned in the above passage was none other than the Hui Shih who was the leading dialectician of the age. He was noted both for his logical acumen and his immense learning. At the same time, he must have been a man of practical ability; for he was for some time the prime minister of the state of Liang. He had an analytical mind without any profound convictions. With all his versatility and remarkable talents, he fell short of true genius. On the whole, he was antipodal to Chuang Tzu. Yet the two men seem to have had an irresistible attraction for each other. Whenever they met, they engaged in a battle of wits, with Chuang Tzu always coming out the victor. This is no surprise, seeing that those encounters were recorded by Chuang Tzu's disciples. Let me give a sample here. One day, Chuang Tzu and Hui Tzu were promenading together on a bridge over the Hao river. "How freely the minnows are darting about!" observed Chuang Tzu, "such is the happiness of fish!" "Since you are not a fish," said Hui Tzu, "how do you know the happiness of fish?" "And since you are not I," came the quick retort, "how do you know that I don't know the happiness of fish?" To which the logician answered "Just as I, not being you, do not know you, so you, not being a fish, do not know the happiness of fish. My point is conclusively proved!" But Chuang Tzu, refusing to be confined by this conceptual straightjacket, remarked, "Let us go back to your original question. You asked me how I knew the happiness of fish; this very question implied that you already knew that I knew. Well, I knew it then and there on the bridge."[5] In other words, what Chuang Tzu relied upon for knowledge was intuition and direct perception, and he refused to be hoodwinked by the logician's trick.

While Chuang Tzu was by far the greater philosopher of the two, yet it cannot be denied that Hui Tzu's arguments sharpened his wits and brought his genius to full flowering. We do not know exactly how Hui Tzu felt about Chuang Tzu; on Chuang Tzu's part at any rate, there was a real affection for Hui Tzu. In fact, after Hui Tzu's death, Chuang Tzu missed him intensely, as perhaps one master chess-player would miss his erstwhile rival. One day, passing by the grave of Hui Tzu, he looked round and said to his companions:

> Once a painter got a spot of paint on the tip of his nose, no thicker than a fly's wing. He sent for the great carpenter Shih to chip it off. Shih plied his adze breezily and chipped off the paint neatly, leaving the nose uninjured and the painter standing undisturbed. When Prince Yuan of Sung heard about it, he summoned Shih to try it on him. Shih declined, saying, Your servant used to be able to do it; but not now, because the one who used to serve as my foil has long since died. Likewise, in my case, since the death of this master, I have lost my foil, and have found no one else with whom I can speak as I did with him.[6]

Chuang Tzu was a recluse, but after all no man is an island, and even a recluse has need of the stimulus of human companionship and friendship to bring out the best in him. He was a recluse only in the sense that he desired to remain out of government. Once the King Wei of Ch'u sent two emissaries to Chuang Tzu with the offer of premiership and found him fishing with an angling line. When they broached the subject to him, he kept on holding his rod without turning his head, saying, "I hear that in Ch'u there is a sacred tortoise which has been dead now some three thousand years, and that the prince keeps its shell carefully enclosed in a hamper on the altar of his ancestral temple. Would this tortoise rather be dead and have its shell thus venerated, or would it rather be alive, wagging its tail in the mud?" The two officers said, "Of course, it would rather be alive wagging its tail in the mud!" "Then leave me in peace," said Chuang Tzu, "for I, too, want to wag my tail in the mud!"[7]

Chuang Tzu was living in an age—the era of Warring States—in which there was a remarkable development of technology and military science. Clever politicians were trying to outwit each other. The States were engaged in a deadly struggle for existence and supremacy. All branches of knowledge useful in this struggle were highly prized by the ruling powers. Moral philosophers like Mencius traveled from one State to another with the hope of influencing the rulers to base their government upon benevolence and justice rather than upon material interests. The rulers were not so much impressed by the philosophers' grandiose talk as amused by their impracticality.

To Chuang Tzu the world scene must have looked like a terrible tragedy written by a great comedian. He saw scheming politicians falling into pits they had dug for others. He saw predatory States swallowing weaker States, only to be swallowed in their turn by stronger ones. Thus the much vaunted utility of the useful talents proved not only useless but self-destructive. On the other hand, he saw the supreme utility of the useless. He illustrated these truths in a conversation with Hui Tzu, of which Father Thomas Merton has produced a version as accurate as it is beautiful:

Hui Tzu spoke to Chuang Tzu and said:

> I have a large tree.
> People call it "stinktree."
> The trunk is so swollen,
> So knotted,
> No one can get a straight plank
> Out of it.
> The branches are so crooked
> You can't cut them up
> In any way that makes sense.
> There it stands, beside the road.
> No carpenter will look at it.

Chuang Tzu replied:

> Have you ever watched the wildcat
> Crouching, spotting its prey,

This way it leaps, and that way,
High and low,
And lands at last in the trap.
But have you seen the Yak?
Great as a thundercloud
He stands in his might.
Big? Sure,
He can't catch mice.
So, for your big tree. No use?
Then plant it in the wasteland
In emptiness
Walk idly around,
Sleep under its branches;
No axe or bill prepares its early end.
No one will ever cut it down.
Useless? You should worry![8]

In an age when there was so much ado about nothing, Chuang Tzu's gospel of uselessness and non-ado should be as refreshing as the breeze and shower on a hot summer day. And with what humor he propagated his gospel!

Chuang Tzu used to say, "Everybody knows the use of usefulness, but nobody seems to know the use of uselessness."[9] However, even uselessness is not without its drawbacks. It may sometimes lead one into dire penury, and so it did with Chuang Tzu. Once he was so poor that he had to go to a certain Marquis for a loan of some rice. "Yes," said the Marquis, "I am just about collecting the revenue of my fief, and I will then lend you three hundred ounces of silver. Will that do?" At this Chuang Tzu flushed with anger and said:

> Yesterday, on my way coming here, I heard a voice calling me. On looking round, I saw a goby in the cart-rut. "Come, goby fish," I said, "what are you doing here?" "I am Minister of Waves in the Eastern Sea," said the goby, "I wonder if you can get me a pint of water to save my life." I replied, "Yes, I am going south to see the kings of Wu and Yueh, and I will request them to lead a stream from the Western River to flow toward you. Will that do?" At this the goby flushed with anger and said, "Just now I am out of my element, and in a helpless situation. A pint of water is all I need to keep alive. But to talk to me like this—you might as well put me in a stall of dry fish at once."[10]

We are not told whether Chuang Tzu succeeded in getting the

needed rice from the Marquis. I presume he did, there being no news about his being starved to death. But did he get the loan by uselessness? Or was it not rather thanks to his wit and humor? However, if he were not so steeped in uselessness, he might not have been so witty and humorous. Being something of a fisherman, he seems to have had a deep empathy with the fishes, so that their images frequently swam across his mind. If he knew their happiness, he also felt their sorrows. For instance, he said, "When the springs are dried up, the fishes huddle together on the dry land, moistening one another by their gasping and wetting one another by their milt. How much happier they would be if they were swimming in the rivers and lakes, quite unconscious of themselves and their neighbors!"[11]

This is his allegorical way of castigating the practice of moral virtues in separation from their spring, the Tao. However, Chuang Tzu should have known that even in our interior life there are days when the inner fountain is running dry and we find ourselves stranded in the cart-rut, and the only way to keep ourselves alive is to borrow a little water near at hand.

In order to understand and enjoy Chuang Tzu, we must take him with a grain of humor. For Chuang Tzu was not merely a profound thinker, but also a humorous man. He remained humorous even on his deathbed. Upon learning that his disciples were planning to give him a grand burial, he said to them, "I have heaven and earth for my coffin and shell, the sun and the moon for my twin-jades, the stars for my pearls and jewels, and all our fellow-beings for my mourners. Are not my funeral paraphernalia amply provided for? What could you add to them?" The disciples said, "We are afraid that the crows and kites would eat our Master." "Well," replied the dying man, "Above ground, I shall be food for the crows and kites: below, I shall be food for the mole-crickets and ants. Now you want to rob the one to fatten the other. What partiality!"[12]

As he had lived, so he died, a free spirit. His death probably occurred some time between 290 and 280 B.C. We do not know exactly the year of his death any more than we know about the year of his birth. But to Chuang Tzu, as to all men of wisdom,

"Any day is a good day to be born, and any day is a good day to die."[13]

2.   His Notion of the Tao

The last chapter of the Book of Chuang Tzu contains a critical survey of the major philosophers of all schools, including the "scholars of the States Tsou and Lu," Mo Ti, Sung Hsin, Yin Wen, Shen Tao, Kuan Yin, Lao Tan, Chuang Chow, and Hui Shih. This chapter has been considered by all historians of Chinese philosophy as the most important source material for the period covered, although it is generally agreed that it was not written by Chuang Tzu himself but by one of his disciples. For the purposes of the present article, two points are of especial interest. In the first place, before it enters into a treatment of the different schools, it highlights the six disciplines, namely, *The Odes, History, The Rites, Music, The Book of Change,* and *The Spring and Autumn Annals,* as the common cultural heritage, and pays an unstinted compliment to the "scholars of Tsou and Lu," in that they had mastered and elucidated the principles of the six branches of learning. Then it sums up the ideal of the whole tradition as "the way of sageliness within and kingliness without."[14] Here Confucianism and Taoism are completely united.

The second point that strikes me is the masterful summing up of the spirit of Chuang Chow and his philosophy in a few bold strokes. Let me translate the passage as accurately as I can:

> Among the ancients there were those whose approach to the Tao took the line of musing on the Formless Void, on the transformation and ceaseless change of things, on death and life, on the union of heaven and earth, and on the movements of the Spirit that comes and goes mysteriously and suddenly, no one knows whence or whither. They enjoyed the pageant of all things, but knew that there is no abiding home among them. With oblique and roundabout arguments, hyperbolic language, and unbridled fancies, he often gave free play to his mind, not, however, to the extent of losing his spirit of impartiality. For it was not in him to look at anything from just one angle. Seeing that the contemporary world had become earthbound and muddled in spirit, so that serious talks on the Tao would hardly find an entrance, he drew concrete instances from everyday life to illustrate the principles, introduced quotations from recognized sages to buttress

Truth, and made use of parables and allegories to reach the multitude. He had a personal communion with the spirit of heaven and earth, yet he did not look down upon his fellow beings. Nor did he make himself a judge of other people's rights and wrongs; in this way he lived peacefully in the midst of conventional society. Although his writings are far from the beaten track, his criticisms of the world are presented in such a way that nobody could take offense. The style is uneven, but it is humorous and charming. It seems as though he spoke out of the fullness of his heart, so that the words flowed with an irresistible spontaneity. Above, he made friends with the Creator; below, he associated himself with those who had transcended life and death and risen in spirit above the realm of time. In dealing with Ultimate Reality he was comprehensive and broad, opening up new vistas, and at the same time he was profound and free. In dealing with the Supreme Principle it can be said that in his vision all things with their luxuriant diversity and mutual contrariety constitute a harmony oriented upwards to the One. However, in his response to the process of transformation and his interpretation of things, his reasons are infinitely variable and adaptable, although never divorced from their starting point. Mystical and dark, no one has touched the bottom of his depths.[15]

Perhaps, the best way to plumb Chuang Tzu to the bottom is not to try to do it, but let the bottom fall off of itself. However, this does not mean that we cannot make a study of his thoughts which he has articulated in his writings. What does he say about the Tao? What are his ideas about life and death? How does he conceive of the distinctions and relations between the virtue of the Tao and moral virtues? What is his ideal and his way of perfection? What is his genuine attitude towards government, technology, and civilization? All these questions will be briefly dealt with in this article. First, as to his notion of the Tao.

The Tao as the Absolute

To Chuang Tzu the Tao alone is absolute. It is not only the way, but the Origin and the End of the universe and all things in it. It is at once creative, normative, and directive. It is present in all things, yet it cannot be identified with anything in particular. Immanent in the universe, it nonetheless transcends it. It is not merely the Supreme Ultimate, but the Infinite. It is the Unique, yet it is the cause of all changes. It is the mystery of mysteries, which evokes in the minds of thinking people a perennial sense of wonder. The wiser the man, the more amazed he is by this Mystery. Only the ignorant fools think that they know.

Since the Tao alone is the Absolute, it follows that everything else is relative, including all human opinions and traditions. It is only with regard to these that Chuang Tzu may be said to be a "relativist" precisely because he was a pilgrim of the Absolute; and that he was sceptical of the views of the various schools precisely because he had a childlike faith and confidence in the Tao. If he resorted to subtle and paradoxical reasonings, it was because he wanted to beat the sophisticated dialecticians in their own game. At the source of his humor and apparent frivolities there lies a high seriousness.

The Tao as it is in itself defies all human understanding and human language. What Lao Tzu and Chuang Tzu have attempted to do is to describe, obliquely and in a negative way, some of its *effects* in relation to the existent universe and human world. Chuang Tzu's notion of the Tao appears essentially the same as that of Lao Tzu. But Lao Tzu was a Sage, scanty of words and pregnant in his utterances; while Chuang Tzu was a man of genius who articulated, by graphic descriptions and intriguing stories, what was implicit in the epigrams of his Master. Chuang Tzu was to Lao Tzu what Mencius was to Confucius. As a prose-writer, he was peerless in ancient China; such as Tao Yuan-ming and Li Po, *(and even outstanding poets)* have drawn their inspiration from the writings of Chuang Tzu. But his influence has not been confined to the field of literature. It has permeated Chinese thought. There has not been a single first-rate thinker, whether among the Chinese Buddhists or among the Neo-Confucians, who did not have his mind liberated and fructified by some of the insights of Chuang Tzu. Even Ch'eng Hao (1011-1085), one of the great pillars of Neo-Confucianism, while taking Chuang Tzu to task for his ignoring of the Rites, was open-minded enough to assert that "there are good things in his presentation of the principles of Tao."[16]

Here we must be content with a few samples of what he thought about the Tao. First as to the transcendent aspect of the Tao, he says:

The Tao carries within itself reality and unfailing truth, but it does not need to resort to action and is without form. It can be transmitted, but not received as one's own. It can be attained but cannot be seen. It exists in and through itself. Before heaven and earth came to exist, it eternally is. It spiritualizes the spirits and deities; it gives birth to heaven and earth. It is above the zenith without being high. It is beneath the nadir without being low. Prior to the universe, yet it is not ancient. Anterior to all antiquity, yet it is not old.[17]

Again:

The Tao causes fullness and emptiness, yet it is neither fullness nor emptiness. It brings about growth and decay, but It is neither growth nor decay. It makes the beginning and the end, but It itself does not begin or end. It gathers and scatters things, but is itself neither gathered nor scattered.[18]

So long as he was dealing with the Tao's transcendence, he spoke, as he had to, in terms of "neither this nor that," reminding us of the "neti, neti" of the *Brihad-Aranyaka Upanishad,* as well as the *via negativa* of Christian mystics. But when he was dealing with the immanent aspects of the Tao, he did not hesitate to make affirmative statements, as, for instance, in the following passage:

Tung Kuo Tzu asked Chuang Tzu, "That which you call the Tao— where is it?" Chuang Tzu replied, "It is present everywhere." "Can you tell me more definitely?" "It is in the ant," said Chuang Tzu. "As low as that?" "It is in the panic grass." "Ah, even lower than the ant!" "It is in the potsherd." "Oh, can it really be so low!" "It is in ordure!" Tung Kuo Tzu made no comment.[19]

Tao as the Creator

Tao is beyond the distinction of personal and impersonal. It is neither and both. In speaking of the Tao, St. Paul's adage that "the letter kills, but the spirit gives life" has an unintended pertinency. Any word we use about it—be it a noun, a pronoun, a verb, an adjective, or even a preposition—would kill if it is taken literally. It does not kill the Tao, but it kills the one who sticks to it, or rather gets stuck on it like a fly on flypaper. For instance, if we use "He," we are liable to think of the Tao as a being with characteristics more human than divine. If we use "It," we are liable to think of the Tao as a thing as lifeless as a stone, or as ghostly as an abstraction. All words we employ in speaking about the Tao must be taken analogically and evocatively. To Chuang Tzu, the whole universe is but a finger pointing to the Tao.[20]

In several passages, Chuang Tzu spoke of the Tao as the Creator, or "He-Who-Creates-Things." At moments he entered into an I-Thou relation with the Tao:

> O my Master! O my Master! You mingle and blend all things without being harsh; You bestow blessings upon endless generations without being charitable; You are older than the highest antiquity without being aged; You brood over and sustain the whole universe, and carve all things into an infinite variety of forms without resorting to artificial skill. This is what I would call the Joy of Heaven.[21]

Chuang Tzu used the terms "Heaven" and "Tao" interchangeably. Both terms designate the One *ne plus ultra*. But when viewing It as the Creator, he usually called It "Heaven," which is equivalent to "God."

To Chuang Tzu, Heaven is not completely unknowable. It is knowable remotely through our concepts of its attributes. We know It, for instance, as—

> The Great Unity, The Great Mystery, The Great Eye (that is, The Omniscient), The Great Maker, The Great Boundlessness (The Omnipresent), The Great Truth, The Great Ordinator.[22]
>
> As Great Unity, It unifies all things; as Great Mystery, It explains all things; as Great Eye, It watches all things; as Great Maker, It sustains all things; as Great Boundlessness, It is present in all things; as Great Truth, It sets an infallible pattern to all things; as Great Ordinator, It maintains all things in order.[23]

These concepts constitute, for Chuang Tzu, the sum total of our knowledge of Heaven. They only serve as so many pointers to Heaven itself. Although Heaven is, in some sense, manifested in these concepts as well as in the laws of nature and in the cosmic process, yet Its inner essence remains as hidden as ever. Besides, before the universe came to be, Heaven eternally *is*. On the other hand, all the names we could think of come from the finite world. How could we hope to fathom the Infinite with a finite measure?

"This being the case," Chuang Tzu declared, "our understanding of It is as if there were no understanding; our knowledge of It is as if there were no knowledge. Only by unknowing can we hope to know it."[24]

It is truly remarkable that all the great mystics of the world talk the same language. To take just one instance out of a legion, St. John of the Cross has likewise said that neither the intellect, nor the will, nor the memory of man can ever lead to a direct understanding of God, and that "in order to reach Him, a soul must rather proceed by not understanding than desiring to understand; and by binding itself and setting itself in darkness rather than by opening its eyes in order the more nearly to approach the ray Divine."[25]

The most characteristic feature of Taoism lies in its emphasis on the unconscious and spontaneous, in opposition to the Confucian emphasis on conscious effort and rational thinking. They are antipodal to each other, but together they form a living polarity of tension and relaxation, the articulate and the inarticulate, waking and sleeping, reason and intuition, remembering and forgetting, increasing and decreasing, acquiring and letting go. But just as Confucian scholars cannot all be equally tense and articulate, so the Taoistic mystics differ among themselves in the degrees of relaxation and silence. The following story of two men of the Tao is one of the most tantalizing inventions of Chuang Tzu:

> Nieh Ch'üeh the Toothless enquired of P'i I about the Tao. P'i I said, "If you keep your body under proper control, and your gaze fixed upon a single point, the harmony of Heaven will eventually descend upon you. Fold up your knowledge, and concentrate your mind upon One, and the Divine Spirit will come to dwell in you, Virtue will adorn you with its own beauty; and Tao itself will be your house. You will be as innocent and simple as a new-born calf which reckons not how it came to be."
>
> While P'i I was still speaking, he found that Nieh Ch'üeh had dozed off into a sleep. He was greatly delighted, and walked away, singing as he went:

> > Body like dry bone,
> > Mind like dead ashes!
> > True and solid is his knowledge,
> > No longer seeking for how and why.

O happy darkness that frees the mind
Of all purpose and design!
What manner of man is he?[26]

Tao as Indwelling in Us

It is in his treatment of the Tao as indwelling in us that Chuang Tzu shows his most profound spiritual insights, which put him in the company of the great mystics of the world. Gifted as he was as a speculative philosopher, he was even more remarkable in his single-hearted love of the Tao and his intense desire to be united with it.

Lao Tzu had said, "Where the Dark is at its darkest, there is the gateway to all spiritual insights."[27] Chuang Tzu developed this profound truth in a masterful way. In describing the man of supreme Virtue (that is, the man who is united with the Tao), he wrote:

> He contemplates Darkness and listens to Silence. In Darkness he alone sees the Dawn; in Silence he alone hears Harmony. As he enters deeper and deeper into his contemplation, he touches the Real. As he grows in spirituality, he grows also in all his vital powers. In this way he places himself in intimate relation with all things. Having absolutely nothing, yet he replenishes all things. Always on the move, yet he gives rest to all.[28]

No one could have written like this if he had not in some way experienced it in himself.

To lose one's self in the Tao is to transcend time and space; to accept the vicissitudes of life with equal peace; in a word, to become a free man. And, what is more wonderful, when one is intensely and vibrantly aware of the transcendence of the Tao, one will participate in some degree also in its immanence and become united with the great community of existence. But it should be noted that with all his feeling of oneness with the universe, he cannot be dubbed a "pantheist." He never identified himself with the universe. Nor did he identify the universe with the Tao. Even when he spoke of losing one's ego in the Tao, he thought of it only as the necessary way to self-realization. If I am forced to give him a label, I would call him a "panentheist,"[29] or at least the prototype of one.

It is through the indwelling of the Tao in us and our union with it that we become "children of Heaven." The following passage deserves our close attention:

> One whose interior house is filled with great peace radiates the light of Heaven. When one radiates the light of Heaven, the man sees his true self. When a man's spiritual life reaches this state, he is confirmed in the Tao. Being confirmed in the Tao, the merely human in him leaves him, and Heaven takes care of him. Being rid of the merely human, he becomes a subject of Heaven. Being in Heaven's care, he can be called a son of Heaven. This is something which cannot be acquired by learning, nor attained by effort, nor understood by understanding. To know how to rest in the unknowable is the summit of knowledge.[30]

This is a state in which "There is no doing and yet nothing is left undone."[31] It does not mean that the man will become idle like a pig and quiet like a doll. His life may be filled with activities and accomplishments, but he realizes at heart that it is not he but the Tao in him who does it all. He sees so clearly his dependence upon Heaven and Its Tao that to claim any credit for what is accomplished through him would be to pick Heaven's pocket. This is why Chuang Tzu went to the extent of saying, "The Creator, in rewarding a man, does not really reward the merely human in him, but rewards the Divine in him."[32]

3. Life, Death, and Dreams

Chuang Tzu did not believe, as later degenerate Taoists came to believe, in the cult of physical immortality. He never searched for the elixir of life, nor did he ever practice alchemy. When he spoke of the "True Man" whom water could not drown, nor fire burn, nor death kill, he was really speaking of the spirit or soul of man, which is not something physical and is therefore beyond the realm of time and space. The spirit is called the "True Man" in the sense that it is a man's true self or higher self. This true self existed before his birth as a human being, and when he dies the true self returns home, as it were, to its original state. It continues to exist, although its existence is beyond time and space. His conception of the state of the soul after death corresponds closely to what Christians call eternal life. In fact, to his mind this eternal life is so *real* that, compared with it, our life on earth is like a dream as compared with our waking life. Human beings are the passing shadows of their spirits or true selves.

But whatever our faith may be concerning our state after death, still death is a grave event. Even though it cannot kill the soul, the dissolution of the body is, to put it moderately, not a very pleasant thing, nor is the parting, however temporary, from our dear ones. I suspect that Chuang Tzu, being endowed with a most sensitive soul and exceptionally imaginative mind, was somewhat obsessed with the idea of death. The very fact that he so often spoke of it shows that he must have had an intense fear of death coupled with an intense curiosity about the afterlife. Hamlet's question, "To be or not to be," must have been lurking in some unsuspected corner of his mind. The haunting specter of death helped to call out some of his profoundest insights in his attempt to exorcise it. For instance, he speculated that death may be an unexpected boon:

> How do I know that our love of life is not a delusion? How do I know that he who loathes to die is not like the man who, being a lost child from his earliest days, does not even know that he has a home to return to. The Lady Li Chi was the daughter of a humble warden of Ai. When the State of Tsin first got hold of her, she wept till the front part of her dress was drenched with her tears. But when she came into the Prince's mansion, sharing with him his comfortable bed and feasting daily on delicate meat, she began to repent of having wept in the beginning. How do I know that the dead are not wondering why they should have clung so desperately to life?[33]

In another passage he calls death "The Great Return." The following words are presented as coming from the mouth of Lao Tzu in an imaginary dialogue with Confucius:

> Man's life in this world is like the flitting shadow of a white pony on its run as seen through a crack in the wall. A momentary flash, and it disappears! Like jets of water from the bubbling fountain, men spring out and return to their source. By one transformation they are

born, by another transformation they die. At the point of dying, all living beings become miserable and men feel sad. But it is only the removal of the bow from its sheath, or the shedding off of a shell. There may be some confusion amidst the yielding to the change, but the spiritual soul and animal soul are taking their leave, and the body will follow them. This is the Great Return![34]

He often spoke of life as a dream and death as "the Great Awakening," as in the following passage:

When a man is dreaming, he does not realize that he is dreaming. Sometimes he even dreams that he is awake and goes on to interpret the dream he has just had. Only when he awakes does he realize that it was all a dream. So, when the Great Awakening comes, one will realize, that this life is a Big Dream. Yet fools consider themselves as awake, knowing for sure that "*this* is the prince and *that* is the shepherd." Oh, what cocksureness! Confucius and yourself are both dreams; and I who say that you are dreams am likewise a dream.[35]

Chuang Tzu was not a dreamy man. It was rather because he was more awake than most others that he perceived a higher Reality than the reality of this life. To say that life is a dream is a very different thing from saying that life is an illusion. To Chuang Tzu, even dreams have a certain degree of reality, only not quite as real as waking life. But compared with the "Great Awakening," our waking life becomes a Big Dream, which, while belonging to a higher level of reality than our dreams, is infinitely lower than Reality itself. Chuang Tzu's is a thorough-going realism, with Heaven and Its Tao as Supreme Reality, the Cosmos as the most real of existing things, and all other things as more or less real. His belief that even our dreams have a certain degree of reality finds a good illustration in the following account of a dream:

Some time ago, Chuang Chou dreamed that he was a butterfly, fluttering freely hither and thither, to all intents and purposes a butterfly! The butterfly was conscious only of its happiness in its untrammeled freedom with no thought whatever of Chuang Chou. A little while later he awoke and found the same old Chuang Chou lying quietly in bed!

But there is no knowing whether it was then Chuang Chou dreaming that he was a butterfly or whether it is now the butterfly dreaming that it is Chuang Chou. But since it is certain that Chuang Chou and butterfly are two different beings this is a good instance of Metempsychosis.[36]

Sometimes Chuang Tzu put his own philosophy of life and death into the lips of a dying man. The following discourse is supposed to have come from the mouth of one Tzu Lai on his death-bed:

> If parents should order their son to go east, west, south, or north, the son would promptly follow their bidding. Now, *Yin* and *Yang* are more to a man than his parents. Since they have brought me to the brink of death, I should be a very stiff-necked fellow indeed, if I should demur to their will, which, besides, cannot be wrong in any case. The Great Cosmos, having in the past clothed me with a body, charged me with the strenuous task of living, and blessed me with a peaceful old age, is now resting me with death. That which has taken such good care of my life will certainly take good care of my death.
>
> Suppose that as a great founder is casting his metal the metal should jump up saying, "You must cast me into a mo-yeh sword!" What would the founder think but that there is something uncanny about that metal? So, if any man should think that having once been a human being, he must always be cast in the form of a human being, the Creator could not but consider him an uncanny man. As for me, I have always thought of the Cosmos as an immense smelting-pot, with the Creator as the Supreme Founder. Therefore, whatever He wills, I will. Soundly I have slept; calmly I shall awake![37]

Here some explanation seems to be called for. In introducing *Yin* and *Yang* and the Cosmos, Chuang Tzu may possibly be taken for a pantheist. But it must be noted that at the end he spoke of the Cosmos as a smelting-pot with the Creator as the supreme founder. In speaking of the Creator, he usually referred to Heaven, which is equivalent to God.[38] Occasionally he also referred to the Tao as the Creator. But on the whole, in the writings of Lao Tzu and Chuang Tzu, as in the writings of Confucius, Heaven is God; while the Tao is equivalent to the Power, Wisdom, and Way of God. But as there is no distinction between the attributes of God and God, the Tao or Divine Wisdom can also be called Creator. In speaking of *Yin* and *Yang* as greater than parents, he did not mean that they are parents of the spirit or soul but only of the body. Anyway he never identified *Yin* and *Yang* with either Heaven or the Tao. The whole cosmic process is nothing but an operation of the Tao; therefore, in relation to us, its workings are part of God's Providence.

When Chuang Tzu speaks of a man's transformations after death, he refers only to the physical part of man, not his spirit or soul, which exists beyond time and space, as will be seen from the following illustration:

> On his way to Ch'u, Chuang Tzu saw an empty skull, bleached, but still retaining its shape. Tapping it with his riding whip, he queried it, saying, "Did you, Sir, come to this pass because of your inordinate love of life? Or were you in the service of a perishing kingdom and did you thereby incur death under the axe? Or did you make an end of your life rather than expose some hidden crime to the shame of your parents, your wife, and children? Or did you die of cold and starvation? Or did you die of old age?"
>
> Having finished speaking, he took up the skull and making a pillow of it, he went to sleep. At midnight the Skull appeared to him in a dream and said, "You spoke like a professional orator. But all the questions you asked have to do only with the worries of the living. There are none of these problems after death. Would you like to hear about the dead?" "I would be glad to," said Chuang Tzu, and the Skull resumed: "In death there are no rulers above and ministers below. The workings of the four seasons are unknown. Free and peaceful, our existence is co-eternal with the universe. The happiest king on earth cannot be happier than we." Chuang Tzu could not believe it, and said, "If I could get the Ruler of Destiny to restore your body to life with its bones and flesh and skin, so that you could return to your parents, to your wife and children, and your neighbors and friends, would you like it?" The Skull stared and frowned and said, "How can I cast away my sovereign happiness and enter again into the toils of human life?"[39]

4. Moral Virtues and The Living Fountain

Chuang Tzu was by no means opposed to moral virtues as such. What he deprecated was the moralistic tendency in some of the Confucianists. For him, the ultimate end of man is to be united with the Tao; he looked at moral virtues, such as humanity and justice, as a necessary stage toward this end. The Tao is the living Fountain of the virtues. Once you have attained a union with the Tao, humanity and justice will flow from you spontaneously like a stream from the fountain. They are no longer practiced as onerous duties imposed upon you by an external authority or as a categorical imperative; and in performing them you will feel no sense of being virtuous, but only a deep joy incidental to any act gracefully done. Confucius himself, in his last years, attained this beautiful state in which, as he tells us, "I could follow the desires of my heart without transgressing the limits." This means that what he had been practicing more or less with conscious effort had by that time become part of himself, flowing spontaneously like a stream from the fountain within him. The moral virtues were still there, in substance, but they had been metamorphosed, as it were, into heavenly gifts. The exercise of these gifts involves no deliberate effort; it is rather a pleasure which is practically irresistible. Since it is a pleasure, there can be no more fuss and ado, no more idea of merit, no more sense of virtuousness. As Lao Tzu had put it, "High Virtue is non-virtuous; therefore it has virtue."[40] He had also said, "Strive for the effortless."[41] This was exactly what Confucius had striven for and finally attained.

Whether Chuang Tzu had attained the same state is not as certain as in the case of Lao Tzu and Confucius. But one thing is certain: by dint of his metaphysical genius and mystical gift, he had a clear insight into the wonders of this state. His descriptions of the ideal man are among his greatest contributions to the philosophy of life and mystical literature. Let me reproduce here a few samples:

1. *The True Gentleman.* The Tao covers and sustains all things. It is the boundless ocean in which the true gentleman must wash his heart and his mind. To act without ado is the part of Heaven; to speak from one's spontaneity is the part of Virtue; to love men and benefit all things is humanity; to see unity in diversity is greatness; to avoid the angular and eccentric in one's conduct is catholicity; to possess variety is to be rich; to hold fast to Virtue is to be normal; to be steeped in Virtue is to be established; to follow the leading of the Tao is to be prepared for all occasions; not to let external things dampen the internal ardor is to be perfect. When the true gentleman has thoroughly mastered these ten points, his heart and his mind become all-embracing, and he will be able to enter into the ways of all things. This being the case, he leaves the gold in the hill and the pearls in the sea; he places no value on goods, and keeps aloof from riches and honors; he neither rejoices in longevity nor grieves over

early death; he neither glories in prosperity nor feels ashamed of adversity. To his mind, the wealth of the whole world would add nothing to his own portion, nor would Kingship over the whole empire constitute any glory to his real self. His true glory lies in understanding that all things belong to one treasury, and that life and death are but phases of the same existence.[42]

2. *The Great Man.* Now, grossness and refinement are epithets applicable only to things having forms. That which is beyond the realm of forms admits of no distinctions, just as that which is unlimited cannot be fathomed. The gross aspects of things can be described by words; and even the refined essence of things can be still be conceived by the mind. On the other hand, that which words cannot describe and the mind cannot conceive is beyond grossness and refinement. Therefore, the Great Man, while he does nothing which is not beneficial to others, does not credit himself with charity and kindness. While he seeks for no gain, he does not despise the underlings who do. While he does not strive for goods, he takes no pride in his modesty. While he does not ask help from others, he takes no complacence in his self-reliance and independence, neither does he think contemptuously of those who are dependent and greedy. While he acts differently from the vulgar crowd, he does not plume himself on being eccentric. He conforms as much as possible to the ways of the people, and does not look down upon those who fawn and flatter. No honors and emoluments of the world can move him; and no punishment and humiliation can disgrace him. All this is because he knows that his actions spring from the Tao beyond the human judgment of right and wrong, gross and refined.[43]

3. *The True Man.* (The following words are quoted by Chuang Tzu as coming from the lips of Confucius.) The true men of old could not be moved by the words of the cleverest men, nor seduced by the charms of beauty, nor subdued by the force of the most violent robbers. . . . Life and death are, indeed, weighty matters, yet they knew that even these matters could make no change in their true self, to say nothing of external things like honors and riches. The spirits of such men can pass through the great mountains as though there were no barrier, and descend into the abyss without getting wet. Even if they were placed in the lowest positions of the world, they would feel no affliction. For they are filled with the fulness of heaven and earth, so that the more they give to others the more they have.[44]

4. *The Complete Man.* The sage is versed in the things of heaven but stupid in the things of man. Only the complete man is versed in both.[45]

It should be noted that the different names used to designate the ideal man all point to practically the same reality. Chuang Tzu was not a man to take names seriously and define them exactly. His idea of Perfect Virtue can be summed up by the words which he used in describing the people of the Golden Age:

> They were upright and fair, but not conscious that they were practicing "justice"; they loved one another warmly, but did not deliberately practice "humanity"; they were honest and true, but did not intentionally practice "loyalty"; they fulfilled their promises, but not in order to practice "good faith"; they rendered services to one another out of a spontaneous impulse, but had not the slightest idea that they were doing or receiving a "favor." Therefore their actions left no trace, nor were their affairs recorded.[46]

Sometimes Chuang Tzu spoke of Perfect Love[47] as the Virtue of the Tao, to which all our moral virtues, such as filial piety, fraternal love, humanity, justice, loyalty, good faith, chastity and purity, are subordinated as so many handmaids of the Queen. Isolated from Perfect Love of the Tao, they decay and die. But when linked to Perfect Love, they become integral parts of it, endowed with the dignity and spiritual vitality of the Tao itself.

Sometimes he considered the practice of moral virtues as a stage toward contemplative life.

> Humanity and justice are like the caravansaries the former kings have set up for the wayfarers to lodge in for a night. They are not for you to make your home in. If you are found to tarry, you will be made to pay heavy fines. The perfect men of old borrowed their way through humanity and lodged in justice for a night, on their way to roam in the transcendental regions, picnicking on the field of simplicity, and settling finally in their own home garden, which was not rented from another. Transcendency signifies freedom. Simplicity indicates vitality. Your garden not being rented from another, you are not liable to be ejected. The ancients called it the romance of searching for your true self.[48]

5. Spiritual Life and Human Civilization

For Chuang Tzu, spiritual life is all of one piece, with the inner vision and external activities forming a continuous process. It begins with abandoning the world so as to free oneself from its entanglements. This gives you peace of mind and enables you to practice asceticism quietly and persistently, till you are born to a new life. This brings you near the goal. You are near but you have not arrived. In Chuang Tzu's scheme, the rebirth, resulting from giving up the world and the pleasures of life, only restores you to your original vitality as a human being, and prepares you for the mysterious process of transformation, which lifts you up to the heavenly plane. As he put it, "From the vital force there comes another more vital, and man returns to his origin to be the collaborator of Heaven."[49] From this it is clear that to be restored to your original vitality is one thing, while to return to your origin is quite another thing. The former is the work of man with the help of God, and the latter is entirely the work of God.

Having returned to your origin, it no longer makes any difference whether you remain in retirement or come back to the world to work for the well-being of your fellow men. "You are happy in adversity, and you are also happy in prosperity, because your happiness springs from a source beyond adversity and prosperity."[50] We can go a step further and say that all the works of lasting value in all fields of human civilization and culture have sprung from an internal source.

Chuang Tzu's attitude toward culture and civilization is not easy to define. In some chapters, he does appear to pour out his cynicism on all things human. Probably his sensitivity was wounded by some of the things his uninhibited mind had discerned underneath the veils of convention. The rulers were so far from his ideal king that they must have appeared as supreme bandits wearing crowns, speaking high-sounding words, and making laws to punish petty thieves. This vision must have almost driven him mad. What was worse, he saw learned scholars and so-called sages paying homage to those crowned bandits and helping them in securing their booty. In this way, they made themselves accomplices of the principal criminals. Even the great builders of human civilization in the past were doing nothing but contributing tools and treasures to those supreme robbers for their private enjoyment. Chuang Tzu went to the extent of saying, "Only when the sages have died, will the great Robbers cease to rise. Then only will the world enjoy peace, and troubles disappear." He called a halt to all arts of civilization. For, as he says,

> If pecks and bushels are made for measurement, the great Robbers will steal the measures together with the things measured. If scales and weights are made for weighing, they will steal these also together with the things weighed. If humanity and justice continued to be preached in order to rectify their conduct, even these will be appropriated by them for their own purposes. How do I know this is so? Well, if a man should steal a hook, he would incur the penalty of death by a legal judgment. On the other hand, the man who has stolen a kingdom becomes its prince. And it is exactly at the gates of princes that humanity and justice are most treasured as instruments of government. Is this not stealing humanity and justice together with wisdom and knowledge?[52]

Chuang Tzu therefore proposed to discard wisdom and knowledge, banish humanity and justice, scrap laws and institutions, and destroy all weights and measures, signets and seals, jewels and jades, bows and arrows. He is especially hard on the painters and musicians. Not only were their instruments to be destroyed, but the painters' eyes were to be glued up and the musicians' ears stopped up![53] Just as well that Chuang Tzu did not become a king!

The whole chapter on "Opening Trunks"[54] is a masterpiece of satiric literature. The author was here venting his pent-up feelings; and many a reader must have felt amused and refreshed by it. But certainly it does not represent his mature views on human civilization.

In another noteworthy chapter, the problem of technology is discussed in the light of the ultimate values of life.[55] The discussion is presented in the form of an interesting story. Tzu Kung a disciple of Confucius noted for his utilitarian and pragmatic turn of mind, was traveling in the south, where he came upon an old man watering his vegetable garden by means of a pitcher. He had to draw water from a well and pour it into a ditch, going back and forth without rest. The result was as meager as the labor was great. Moved by compassion, Tzu Kung approached him, saying, "If you had a machine here, you could irrigate in a single day a hundred times your present area. With trifling labor you would accomplish a great deal. Would you not like to have one?"[56] Tzu

Kung then proceeded to describe the machine as a wooden contrivance, heavy behind and light in front, which could draw water up with great ease and in a continuous flow. Instead of being pleased by the suggestion, the old gardener flushed up and said:

> As I have heard from my Master, ingenious contrivances lead inevitably to cunning dealings, and cunning dealings will end by producing a scheming mind. When the scheming mind dwells in one's bosom, his integrity and purity will be impaired, and his spirit become restless. Now, a restless spirit has no place in the Tao. It is not that I do not know of the machine, but I should be ashamed to make use of it.[57]

Taken aback by this unexpected lesson, Tzu Kung remained silent. Then the old man asked him who he was, and he told him that he was a disciple of Confucius. This gave the old man another occasion for venting his mind. He warned Tzu Kung against neglecting self-government while desiring to govern the world. The discourse ended with scant politeness: "Begone! Don't interrupt my work!" Tzu Kung turned pale and went away greatly perturbed. On the way his disciples asked him why he was so deeply affected by the old man's words. In his reply Tzu Kung spoke as though he was completely converted to the old gardener's philosophy. After his return to Lu, he reported the whole episode to Confucius, who, according to our author, said,

> That man is merely a superficial and artificial imitator of the ways of the Penumbral Age. He knows only half of the truth, but misses the other half. He cultivates the inner, but neglects the outer. If a man is really enlightened to the point of transparency, he will arrive at true Purity, and if he is actually non-assertive, he will return to true Simplicity. Embodying perfectly his essential nature, and carrying the spirit peacefully in his bosom, he will move freely in the ordinary ways of the world. If you should meet such a one, would you be disturbed at all? Furthermore, with regard to the ways of the Penumbral Age, what do we know?[58]

By "moving freely in the ordinary ways of the world," is meant that the true man of the Tao would use the instruments as others do without being attached to them. In the following of the Penumbral Age, we must do it in spirit, not in letter. If we are really "penumbral" in spirit, we should not make a clear-cut bifurcation of the inner and the outer. The recluses are only the lower type of Taoists. They are still attached to external surroundings. As for the higher type, they can cultivate the Tao in the court and market as well as in the hills and forests. They are infinitely adaptable to all situations of life, taking care not to attract attention to themselves by any show of eccentricity.

The words which Chuang Tzu put onto the lips of Confucius seem to me to represent his own philosophy in his maturer years. The chapter in question was probably not written by Chuang Tzu, but some of his disciples. Even so, the thoughts must reflect more or less faithfully his teachings. Even if the words were really those of Confucius, as transmitted orally through generations of Confucian scholars, there can be no question that Chuang Tzu was in perfect agreement with them. It seems to me likely that in his later years Chuang Tzu came more and more to assimilate the spirit of moderation of Confucius, just as Confucius in his later years had come very close to the spirit of Lao Tzu, the spirit of *wu wei* or non-assertiveness and spontaneity. Chuang Tzu may be called a God-intoxicated man. Some ancient critics observed that although Chuang Tzu had a penetrative insight into the things of Heaven, he was blind to the things of man. His political philosophy of "Let alone," his denunciation against all civilization, and his advocacy of a radical return to the first age of simplicity and innocence would indeed make him appear like an angel "beating ineffectually against the void." But I do not think that he could have meant them to be taken seriously as practical programs of actions, but only as a graphic reminder to the conventional minded scholars that human traditions must not be mistaken for eternal verities; that many ideas which they held to be sacred and absolute might not actually have a cosmic validity; that ancient sage rulers whom history had canonized might well have been degenerates in comparison with their own ancestors, and surely they were no embodiments of the Tao. What he was trying to do was wash the time-honored traditions with cynical acid. On the other hand, he saw unprincipled and unscruplous States and politicians, whose only god was utility, creating troubles for the people and calling down calamities upon their own heads in spite of, or rather because of, their cleverness and selfishness. With such leaders at the helm of the governments, the people could have fared better if left to themselves. It was against such as these that he directed some of his satires, such as the story of the monkey which, relying upon its own cleverness, did not flee with its fellows into the thicket at the sight of the hunters, and, when it was shot at, nimbly seized the flying arrow with its hand, thus showing off its exceptional skill, which eventually proved to be the cause of its death.[59]

His most valuable contribution to political philosophy is his ideal of "sageliness within and kingliness without."[60] Some of his sayings about the ideal king are among the best spiritual counsels ever addressed to the ruling powers. For instance, he quoted Lao Tzu as saying:

> The enlightened kings, by their wise way of governing, conferred benefits upon the whole world, but they did not seem to consider them as proceeding from themselves. Their transforming influence permeated all things, yet the people were unconscious of it. Completely self-effacing, with no noise or wrangle, they brought it about that all people live happily as though of themselves. At the same time, they were firmly rooted in the Mysterious and found their delight in the Hidden Homeland.[61]

6.   The Mystical Way of Perfection

Man is a conditioned being aspiring to an unconditioned happiness. In the case of Chuang Tzu, the awareness of being conditioned was exceptionally intense, and so was the aspiration to the Unconditioned. From this internal conflict between perception and desire there resulted an agonizing tension, which was the source of all his mental soarings and divings, loiterings and roamings. It cannot be said that his philosophy consists in mere wishful thinking and rationalization. He was too candid and profound a thinker to be deceived by his own make-believe. But it cannot be denied that his intense aspiration to the Unconditioned heightened his perceptive powers so that they were both subtilized and broadened to a degree never reached previously in China nor surpassed in later generations. Of course, even in his case, the perception fell far short of the aspiration, but at any rate it went about as far as the natural lights of man could go in that direction.

But what makes the philosophy of Lao Tzu and Chuang Tzu perennially significant, particularly for the present stage of human culture, is that they were so superlatively perceptive as to realize the gulf between human knowledge and the Tao. They were haunted by the Infinite; but at the same time, they saw clearly the impossibility of fathoming the Infinite with finite intelligence. They would have seen eye to eye with St. Thomas Aquinas when he said: "This is the final knowledge of God: To know that we do not know God."[62] In this light we can understand some of the dark sayings of Lao Tzu, such as:

> To realize that our knowledge is ignorance,
>   This is a noble insight.
> To regard our ignorance as knowledge,
>   This is mental sickness.
> Only when we are sick of our sickness
>   Shall we cease to be sick.
> The Sage is not sick, being sick of sickness;
>   This is the secret of health.[63]

This insight marks the end of knowledge and the beginning of wisdom. One has to enter into the cloud of unknowing if one is to be united with the Tao. One must, in the words of Lao Tzu, "block all the passages" and "shut all the doors."[64] One must disentangle oneself from the tangle of multiplicity, and plunge headlong into the Mystical Whole.[65] Chuang Tzu has illustrated the happy Night by many an intriguing parable. Here is one:

> Once Purity asked Limitless, "Do you know the Tao?" "I do not know," replied Limitless. Then Purity proceeded to ask No-Ado. "Yes," the latter answered, "I know the Tao." "Has it any specific attributes?" "It has." "What are they?" "I know," said No-Ado, "that the Tao has the power to honor and to dishonor, to bind and to loose. From this I know that it has attributes." Purity then repeated the words of both to No-Beginning, and asked, "Now then, between Limitless' 'I-don't-know' and No-Ado's 'I-know,' which is right and which is wrong?" No-Beginning replied: "The 'I-don't-know' is profound, the 'I-know' is shallow. The 'I-don't-know' is internal, the 'I-know' is external." Thereupon Purity lifted up his head and drew a sigh, saying, "So, not to know is to know, while to know is not to know! Who knows the knowledge of no-knowledge?" No-Beginning

replied: "The Tao is inaudible; what is heard is not It. The Tao is unspeakable; what is spoken is not It. If you know that what imparts form to all forms is itself formless, you will understand that it is essentially beyond all names."[66]

Chuang Tzu's symbol for the cloud of unknowing is Hun Tun, the formless Penumbra which existed at the very beginning of the world. He personified it in the following parable:

> Shu was the Ruler of the Southern Ocean; Hu was the Ruler of the Northern Ocean; and Hun Tun was the Ruler of the central zone. Shu and Hu had their frequent meetings on Hun Tun's territory, and Hun Tun treated them with great hospitality. So Shu and Hu, moved by gratitude, consulted together as to how to requite Hun Tun's kindness. They said, "All men have seven holes for the purpose of seeing, hearing, eating, and breathing. Hun Tun alone has none. Let us bore the holes for him." They proceeded to bore one hole in him every day. At the end of seven days, Hun Tun died.[67]

Here, Hun Tun corresponds to the primordial simplicity, the undifferentiated oneness. Other symbols that Lao Tzu and Chuang Tzu employed, were the Uncarved Block, the Newborn Babe, and the Mysterious Feminine. Somehow they were harking back to the beginning of the world when the preternatural innocence of man had not yet been spoiled by the unfortunate advent of the knowledge of good and evil. In Lao Tzu's words, "When the world began to know the goodness of goodness, evil emerged at that very point. When the world began to know the beauty of beauty, lo and behold, there appeared ugliness."[68] This insight permeates the whole philosophy of Chuang Tzu. For him human history is a continuous process of progressive degeneration. Even the sage emperors Yao and Shun, whom Confucius had taken for the paragons of private as well as public virtue, were, to Chuang Tzu, harbingers of worse things to come. When Chuang Tzu brought this philosophy of history to bear upon his views on law and government, it was inevitable that he should tend to a radical anarchism. However, his message may serve as a salutary reminder to the present world that important as technology and knowledge are, wisdom and interior life constitute the foundation of civilization. If the foundation is weak, the more magnificent the superstructure, the greater will be its fall. Let us remember that, while "the pursuit of knowledge consists in daily increase, the practice of Tao consists in daily decrease—decreasing and again decreasing till we reach complete emptiness."[69] For it is only when we are emptied of ourselves that we shall be filled with the Wisdom of the Tao.

When the idea of the formless Penumbra and the cloud of unknowing is brought to bear upon the cultivation of the interior life, it becomes a most fruitful source of mystical insights. For instance, Chuang Tzu's doctrines concerning the "fast of the mind"[70] and "sitting and forgetting"[71] shows that he was an adept of what may be called the *yoga* of Tao, and that he was an expert diver in the depths of the Dark, where, as Lao Tzu had said, is to be found the "Gateway to all spiritual insights." It is an ever-growing wonder to me that the mystics of all ages and all countries seem to talk the same language and point to the same moon. In a recent poem of Chuang Tzu, I am thrilled to find the following lines, which might well have been written by Chuang Tzu himself:

> There is a time to wake, to bypass the feeble ray
> That sparsely flickers in the cell of the mind;
> To enter the depth of darkness, to walk the length of darkness,
> The dark length of the dark passage of darkness—
> In order to learn the exact measure of man, his exact place
> In the turning of the world, in the knotting of past and future.[72]

Chuang Tzu is a mystic through and through. Not only is his notion of Heaven and Its Tao highly mystical, but also his way of perfection is typically mystical. With a remarkable perspicacity he saw the necessary stages one with an aptitude for contemplative life must pass through before one can arrive at the goal. He presents the whole way of spiritual progress by telling how an old Master chose and trained his disciple. Here is the story:

> Nan Po Tzu K'uei said to Nü Yü, "You, Sir, are advanced in years, and yet you still have the complexion of a child. What is the secret?" "Well," replied Nü Yü, "I have been instructed in the Tao." "Can I learn to attain the Tao?" asked the other. "No, Sir," said Nü Yü, "you are not the man for it. In the case of Pu Liang I, he had the potentiality of Sagehood, but he was not acquainted with the Way of Sagehood. In my own case, I know the Way of Sagehood, but I do not have the potentiality for it. I was desirous of teaching him, in the hope that he might actually become a Sage. But it must not be

89

imagined that the job of imparting the Way of Sagehood even to the potential Sage was an easy one. Even in his case, I had to wait and watch for the proper time to start the instruction. After three days of training, he became detached from the world. This accomplished, I watched and guided him for seven days and he became detached from all things sensual and material. Then again I watched and guided him for nine more days, and he became detached from the clinging to life. Now, once a man is detached from the clinging to life, he can hope to be illumined by the clear light of the morning. Illumined by the clear light of the morning, he will be able to see and contemplate the Unique One. By the contemplation of the Unique One, he can transcend Time. Having transcended Time, he is ready to enter into a state which is beyond death and birth (in the physical sense), being in union with the Unique One Who dispenses life and death to all things while He Himself is not born and dies not. When a man is in this state, he becomes infinitely adaptable to external things, accepting all and welcoming all, and equal to all tasks, whether in tearing down or in building up. This is what is called 'Peace in the midst of all trials and sufferings.' How can one maintain Peace in the midst of trials and sufferings? Because it is by trials and sufferings that Peace is perfected.[73]

This is strikingly similar to the teachings of the Gospel and the ways of Christian mysticism. The first three stages, (the threefold deadness to the world, to the lure of things, and to oneself) correspond to the Purgative Way. The fourth (illumination by the dawning light) and the fifth (contemplation of the Unique) correspond to the Illuminative Way. The sixth, seventh, and finally, the eighth stages correspond to the Unitive Way. To transcend in spirit the realm of Time is to rise above nature, to be supernaturalized. To enter into the state beyond life and death is to have an inkling of the eternal life. This corresponds to the beginning of the Transforming Union, leading to its consummation in Peace imperturbable.

"In Thy light we see light," says the Psalmist.[74] It is, frankly, in the light of the Christian Revelation that I have come to discern peoples to the Divine Logos, the True Fountain of Life, to His Sacred Heart, to the Joy of the Cross, to which even the wonderful ideal of "Peace imperturbable" can only serve as a humble usher. Chuang Tzu may or may not have attained all the stages in his own program; but even to have visualized such high things would have been impossible if God had not smiled on this man of rare genius,

90

"the scintillating stars of Oriental mysticism which should lead all " who knew how to soar into the skies and dive into the abysses and who found that the whole universe was but a little finger pointing to the Mysterious Tao, the Eternal Law of God. To my mind, the Tao itself is but a pointer to the Divine Logos.

NOTES

[1] Almost all the materials used in this study are drawn from *The Book of Chuang Tzu* in the Chinese original. There are many editions of this book, but for the purpose of making page reference, I have settled on Wang Hsien-Ch'ien's *Chuang Tzu Chi Chieh* (*The Book of Chuang Tzu, With Collected Annotations*). This work has undergone many editions since its publication in 1908. I am using a popular reprint of it issued by the Chung Hua Book Company in Hong Kong, 1960.

The quotations in this article are my own translations. I have, however, consulted the English translations of James Legge and Herbert Giles, and the French translation of Léon Wieger. Legge's work shows a comparatively more solid scholarship, although occasionally one comes across surprising errors. His translation has recently been reprinted with an Introduction by D. T. Suzuki (New York: Julian Press, 1959). Twelve out of the thirty-three chapters of the book have been translated by Lin Yutang, and included in his anthology, *The Wisdom of China and India* (New York: Random House, 1942). Five chapters, including the last chapter on "The World of Thought," are included in *Sources of Chinese Tradition,* compiled by de Bary, Chan, and Watson (New York: Columbia University Press, 1960).

Of recent Chinese studies, Yen Lin-Fung's *Lao Chuang Yen Chiu* (*Studies on Lao Tzu and Chuang Tzu*), published in Hong Kong, 1959, is worth reading. He has shown that the main ideas of Lao and Chuang had their seeds in the ancient classics. Simon Ting's monograph on *The Mysticism of Chuang Tzu: Its Moral and Religious Significance* (in manuscript) is an intensive study of Chuang Tzu as a man and as a mystic. My reading of it has given me some new ideas about Chuang Tzu.

[2] The data of this section are mainly based upon *The Book of Chuang Tzu* itself and the all too meager and superficial account of Chuang Chou's life in Szuma Ch'ien's *Shi Chi*. His father, Szuma T'an had a deeper insight into Taoism.

[3] See *Chuang Tzu Chi Chieh, op. cit.,* n. 1 (hereafter cited as C.T.), ch. 32, p. 92. Chuang Tzu is there described as living in a miserable hamlet, weaving sandals, with a wizened neck and wan face.

[4] C.T., ch. 18, p. 2.

[5] C.T., ch. 15, p. 96.
[6] C.T., ch. 24, p. 46.
[7] C.T., ch. 17, p. 98.
[8] C.T., ch. 1, pp. 5, 6.
[9] C.T., ch. 4, p. 29.
[10] C.T., ch. 26, p. 62.
[11] C.T., ch. 14, p. 85.
[12] C.T., ch. 32, p. 95.
[13] These words were reportedly said by Pope John XXIII.
[14] C.T., ch. 33, p. 96.
[15] C.T., ch. 33, pp. 101, 2.
[16] *Lien-Lo-Kwan-Min Shu,* Book 9.
[17] C.T., ch. 6, p. 38.
[18] C.T., ch. 22, p. 30.
[19] C.T., ch. 22, p. 29.
[20] C.T., ch. 2, p. 10.
[21] C.T., ch. 6, p. 44 and ch. 13, p. 75. The words quoted in the text are found in both places. In the former reference, the context shows that they refer to the "Creator." In the latter, they refer to "Heaven."
[22] C.T., ch. 24, p. 52.
[23] C.T., ch. 24, p. 52.
[24] C.T., ch. 24, p. 52.
[25] *The Works of St. John of the Cross,* tr. E. Allison Peers (Westminster, Md.: Newman Press, 1949), I, 97.
[26] C.T., ch. 22, p. 27.
[27] *Tao Teh Ching,* ch. 1.
[28] C.T., ch. 12, p. 65.
[29] F. v. Hügel, *The Mystical Element of Religion,* II, 373, 383.
[30] C.T., ch. 23, p. 37.
[31] *Tao Teh Ching,* ch. 48.
[32] C.T., ch. 32, p. 91.
[33] C.T., ch. 2, p. 16.
[34] C.T., ch. 22, p. 29.
[35] C.T., ch. 2, p. 16.
[36] C.T., ch. 2, p. 18.
[37] C.T., ch. 6, p. 41.
[38] Herbert Giles and Lin Yutang render T'ien as "God," and I think that they are right in most contexts. For instance, this: "He who is inwardly straight is a servant of God. And he who is a servant of God knows that the Son of Heaven (the King) and himself are equally the children of God." This is in Giles, *Chuang Tzu,* p. 41. Lin Yutang has adopted this rendering entirely. (See *The Wisdom of China and India,* p. 647.) The rendering is as accurate as it is readable. They have also shown that *T'ien* cannot always be rendered as "God," for in the same excerpt, the term *"T'ien Tzu"* is rendered as "the Son of Heaven," meaning the King. But there can be another way of rendering the passage: "He who is inwardly straight is a co-operator

of Heaven; and being a co-operator of Heaven, he knows in his heart that the king and himself are equally Heaven's children." The meanings of the two versions are practically the same. I have kept to the word "Heaven" because it is the usual rendering for *T'ien*, which means "God" in many contexts, as in this, but in some other context may mean Divine Providence, or Nature (not in the naturalistic sense, but in the sense of God's Art and God's Way).

One more point should be noted. The term *T'ien-Ti*, or "Heaven-and-Earth" means the Universe or the Cosmos; it must never be confused with the term *T'ien* used singly. Used in conjunction with "earth," it becomes a member of the Universe. As a matter of fact, the Cosmic Order has three members, *T'ien, Ti, and Jen*, the Celestial, the Terrestrial, and the Human.

[39] C.T., ch. 18, p. 3.
[40] *Tao Teh Ching*, ch. 38.
[41] *Ibid*, ch. 63.
[42] C.T., ch. 12, pp. 64, 65.
[43] C.T., ch. 17, p. 93.
[44] C.T., ch. 21, p. 25.
[45] C.T., ch. 33, pp. 40, 41.
[46] C.T., ch. 12, p. 71.
[47] C.T., ch. 14, pp. 80, 81.
[48] C.T., ch. 14, p. 84.
[49] C.T., ch. 19, p. 6.
[50] C.T., ch. 28, p. 72.
[51] C.T., ch. 56.
[52] C.T., ch. 10, p. 56.
[53] C.T., ch. 10, p. 56.
[54] C.T., ch. 10.
[55] C.T., ch. 12.
[56] C.T., ch. 12, p. 69.
[57] C.T., ch. 12, p. 69.
[58] C.T., ch. 12, p. 70.
[59] C.T., ch. 24, p. 47.
[60] C.T., ch. 33, p. 96.
[61] C.T., ch. 7, pp. 46, 47.
[62] *Summa Theologica, II-II,* q.8, a.8.
[63] *Tao Teh Ching*, ch. 71.
[64] *Ibid.,* ch. 56.
[65] *Ibid.,* ch. 56.
[66] C.T., ch. 22, pp. 30, 31.
[67] C.T., ch. 7, p. 49.
[68] *Tao Teh Ching*, ch. 2.
[69] *Ibid.,* ch. 48.
[70] C.T., ch. 4, pp. 20-24.
[71] C.T., ch. 6, pp. 45-56.
[72] These lines are, by permission, taken from a long unpublished poem

by Baroness Catherine de Vinck.

[73] C.T., ch. 6, pp. 39, 40.

[74] Psalms, 35:10.

ST. THÉRÈSE
AND LAO TZU:
A STUDY
IN COMPARATIVE MYSTICISM

1. Introductory

(1) *The Paradox of St. Thérèse.* One reason why the teachings of St. Thérèse are such a perennial source of inspiration is that she speaks directly from her heart to your heart. She is so closely united with Jesus that their hearts beat as one. True daughter of Mary, she knows how to keep the words of Jesus carefully in her heart, ruminating on them, and sounding their depths daily by her own experience. She does not teach what she has not *lived*. She has tasted and seen that the Lord is good,[1] and she wants you to taste and see for yourself how good He is. As soon as she has succeeded in introducing you to her Beloved, she retires merrily from the scene, leaving you alone in His adorable company. Her love for Christ is so single-hearted and selfless that she cannot help desiring to make Him known and loved by all. To this end the little bride of Christ is willing to act as a humble match-maker between Him and other souls. Like John the Baptist, she plays the part of the herald in the work of apostolate. *"The friend of the Bridegroom, who stands and hears Him, rejoices exceedingly at the voice of the Bridegroom,"* saying, *"He must increase, but I must decrease."*[2] But the paradox of it is that the more she reckons herself out, the more she finds herself in. It is through complete self-

loss that her self is fully realized. As she would say, "the loser always wins."[3] In fact, her life is in itself a great paradox. A little grain of sand in her own eyes, she was recognized by the great Pius X as "the greatest Saint of modern times."[4] Her little way of spiritual childhood was proclaimed by Benedict XV to be "the secret of sanctity," destined to "increase the number of perfect Christians."[5] Pius XI discerned in her simplicity "an altogether exceptional wisdom,"[6] and viewed her "spirit of childhood" as "inseparable from a real greatness of soul."[7] But no one has presented the living paradox of Thérèse more eloquently than Cardinal Pacelli, destined to be Pius XII. In a discourse delivered on July 11, 1937, as the Legate *a latere* of Pius XI, at the Inauguration of the Basilica of Lisieux, he grew almost ecstatic in reviewing the wonders that God had been working in the Church. After speaking of "the shining genius of Augustine," "the luminous wisdom of Thomas Aquinas," and "the divine poem lived by Francis of Assisi," he said: But a little Carmelite, who barely reached adult years, has conquered in less than half a century countless hosts of disciples. Doctors of Law became children in her school; the Supreme Pontiff has extolled her and prays to her in continual and humble supplication; and even now from one end of the world to the other, there are millions of souls whose interior life has been influenced for good by her little book: *The History of a Soul.*"[8] At the end of the discourse, he addressed himself directly to Thérèse: "Ah! you are great, O little Saint! . . . You are great, O little soul! . . . Little temple of God, you are the vast temple of a humanity conquered by you!"[9]

Her teaching is of one piece with her life; it consists in an endless series of paradoxes.[10] To be empty is to be filled. To be poor is to be truly rich. Suffering is a blessing. To come down is to rise. To be little is to be great. Weakness is strength. Life is exile. To die is to live. To be deprived of joy is true joy. To be homeless is to furnish a home to the Lord. To forget yourself is to be remembered by God. The more you drink, the more you thirst; yet this very thirst has that which can satisfy it. To love the unlovable is true love. Do your duty with all your might, but set no store by it. To give all is to give nothing. To choose nothing is to choose all. To cling to the One is to embrace the whole universe. Indeed, her way comprehends all ways, yet she calls it the "little way."

(2) *Filial Piety, Natural and Supernatural.* The simplest way of understanding the little way of spiritual childhood is to realize the fact that Thérèse took the filial piety of a child towards its parents for her starting point, and applied it, as a child born of the Spirit, in her relations with God. On this point, The Most Reverend Luis M. Martinez has given us an illuminating comment. With respect to God," he said, "the gift of piety inspires us with sentiments of confidence, and prompts us to give ourselves to Him. A child trusts its father, and gives him its heart; a soul under the influence of the gift of piety has complete confidence in God and gives itself wholly to Him. For more than nineteen centuries we have had this sublime thought from the Gospel: 'Unless you . . . become like little children, you will not enter the kingdom of heaven.' (Matt. 18:3.) Yet no one before St. Thérèse of Lisieux so perfectly understood, expressed, and practiced the way of spiritual childhood."[11]

To my knowledge, no one has grasped the "little way" of Thérèse so thoroughly as this late Archbishop of Mexico. What impresses me most is that he should have related the "little way" particularly to the gift of piety. "The unlimited confidence that Thérèse of Lisieux had in God was filial confidence. The absolute surrender by which she put all that she had, all that she was, into the hands of God was the result of the gift of piety."[12]

If we remember that the gift of piety is specially related to the Beatitude of the meek, we should understand why Thérèse should have been attracted so irresistibly by all the virtues and qualities characteristic of the meek. Littleness, weakness, lowliness, hiddenness, docility, self-conquest, consideration for others, patience even with one's own imperfections, cheerfulness in the midst of adversity, simplicity, the capacity to laugh at oneself—all these attributes of meekness flow from the gift of piety.[13]

To me as a Chinese, the most intriguing thing about Thérèse's little way of spiritual childhood is that it is reminiscent, on the one hand, of the Confucian teaching of filial piety,[14] and, on the other, of the Taoistic insight concerning the mystical significance of the little and the low, of the supple and the docile, of the feminine and the new-born.

"The man of true culture," said Confucius, "serves his parents as he would serve Heaven, and serves Heaven as he would serve his parents."[15] It need hardly be pointed out that the nature of filial piety towards God could not have been adequately comprehended before the coming of Christ. But the vision of Confucius can at least be said to foreshadow the Christian vision. As Dom Celestine Lou has observed, the Christian revelation "is the meeting-place of the ways, the unique point where the filial piety which Jesus Christ has shown us, and to which He gives us the right, and which reunites the human creatures with our Father who is in Heaven."[16] Here as elsewhere, Christ has not come to destroy but to fulfill the precepts of natural law.

Now, if we study carefully how Thérèse served God as her Father and Mother, we should be compelled to acknowledge that she has fulfilled the precept of Confucius to a point beyond his dreams. This does not mean that she is by nature more gifted than Confucius. It is only the living example of the divine filial piety of Christ that makes all the difference.[17] What with Confucius was only an adumbrative *desideratum* became a *reality* in Thérèse. But to a Chinese at least, the pleasure of seeing the reality is redoubled by the recalling of the desideratum which has been realized.

2.   The Mystical Way of Lao Tzu

While the Thérèsian spirituality is, in its moral aspects, akin to Confucianism, there is an even more striking similarity between its mystical tone and that of Taoism. In the Taoistic writings one often discerns an unconscious harking back to the beginning of the world; an indescribable homesickness for a lost Age of Innocence and Simplicity. In the eyes of a Taoist, the newborn babe has a mysterious significance, because they look upon it as a living symbol of the Age of Innocence. If we wish to return to the Age of Innocence, we must recover the spirit of childhood, but the way to recover this lies in a passive *docility* to the operations of the

Tao, the Principle of the Universe. The Taoist's symbol for this indispensable *passivity* is the *Feminine*. The fundamental Taoistic intuition is that we can return to Childhood by way of feminine passivity.

With this in mind, we can grasp the meaning of the following mystical poem:

> Know the masculine,
> Keep to the feminine,
> And be the Brook of the world.
> To be the Brook of the world
> Is to move in the path of Constant Virtue,
> And to return to the state of Infancy.
>
> Know the white,
> Keep to the black,
> And be the Pattern of the world.
> To be the Pattern of the world
> Is to be united with the Constant Virtue,
> And to return to the Infinite.
>
> Know the glorious,
> Keep to the lowly,
> And be the Valley of the world.
> To be the Valley of the world
> Is to be filled with Constant Virtue,
> And to return to Primeval Simplicity.[18]

(1) *The Masculine and the Feminine*. Now, all this symbolic language needs some explanation. By "masculine" Lao Tzu meant to symbolize strength and activeness. Nothing can be as strong and as active as the Tao. As Lao Tzu describes it:

> There was Something undefined and yet complete in itself,
> Born before Heaven-and-Earth.
> Silent and boundless,
> Standing alone without change,
> Yet pervading all without fail,
> It may be regarded as the Mother of the world.
> I do not know its name;
> I style it "Tao";

And, for want of a better word, call it "The Great."[19] Tao is, thus, conceived of as the Originator and Sustainer of the universe and all things that be. It is so mighty and creative that even the word "Great" seems to be too lame an attribute to be applied to it. Yet even here he thinks of it in terms of "Mother" rather than "Father." Why? Because, in spite of all its masculine qualities of creativeness, activeness and inexhaustible strength, its *mode* of operation is typically *feminine*. As he puts it, "Tao never makes any ado, yet nothing is left undone. If the ruler can cling to it, all things will grow of themselves."[20] "Tao is hidden and nameless; yet it alone knows how to render help and fulfill."[21] "The highest form of goodness is like water. Water knows how to benefit all things without striving with them. It stays in places loathed by all people. Therefore, it comes near to the Tao."[22] Since the Tao itself is self-effacing and lowly, those who aspire to its greatness and power must adopt its feminine mode of operation. "A great country is like the lowland toward which all streams flow. It is the Reservoir of all under heaven, the *Feminine* of the world. The Feminine always conquers the Masculine by her quietness, by lowering herself through her quietness."[23] So in the pursuit of personal perfection, one must know how to adapt himself to the rhythm of expansion and gathering up: "In the opening and shutting of the door of Heaven, are you able to play the female part?"[24] In one word, if we want to attain real strength and preserve it, if we want to assimilate the true strength of the Tao, we must follow its own mode of maternal tenderness. As Shakespeare would say, "it is excellent to have a giant's strength, but it's tyrannous to use it like a giant."[25]

(2) *The White and the Black.* What does Lao Tzu mean by knowing the white but keeping to the black? It seems to me that "the white" symbolizes the supreme brightness of the Tao as it is in itself, while "the black" symbolizes the darkness of its reflection in our eyes. Herein lies the source of many of his paradoxes, such as "The bright way looks dim"; "High Virtue looks like an abyss"; "Perfect whiteness looks like blackness"; "Great sound is silent"; "Great Form is shapeless."[26] Well knowing that the Tao is infinitely bright and white, yet we must dive into the darkest depths of our soul if we wish to have even the faintest glimpses of it. "Where the darkness is at its darkest, there is the doorway to all

subtleties."[27] These subtleties are so small that they can never be perceived so long as we do not withdraw from all the glittering lights of the world and recollect ourselves in the quiet night of the soul. There alone can we have our secret communings with the Tao. There alone does the Tao sow the hidden seed of its wisdom. In that "subterranean way,"[28] Lao Tzu must have found something like what Thomas Traherne describes in these lines:

> A deep abyss
> That sees and is
> The only proper place of Heavenly Bliss.[29]
> An inward Omnipresence here
> Mysteriously like His within me stands,
> Whose knowledge is a Sacred Sphere
> That in itself at once includes all lands.[30]

By keeping to the dark and the black, by shutting off the distracting lights of worldly knowledge, Lao Tzu found the "Inner Light"[31] whose guidance he followed with a childlike docility. As he wrote:

> Without going out of your door
> You can know the universe.
> Without peeping through the window,
> You can see the Way of Heaven.
> The farther you go,
> The less you know.
> Thus, the Sage knows without traveling,
> Sees without looking,
> And achieves without doing.[32]

(3) *The Glorious and the Lowly.* As to the meaning of *knowing the glorious but keeping to the lowly,* Lao Tzu has illustrated it by this example:

> Humility is the root of greatness,
> The low is the foundation of the high.
> That is why princes and dukes style themselves as
>   "The Helpless One," "The Little One," and
>   "The Worthless One."
> Perhaps, they too realize their dependence upon the
>   humble?[33]
> His symbol for lowliness is the sea:

> How does the sea become the king of all streams?
> Because it lies lower than they.[34]

He knew very well that his philosophy is noble and great. But he was often the victim of mockery and contempt. "All the world says that my Tao is great but queer, being like nothing on earth. But it is just because my Tao is great that it is like nothing on earth. If it were like anything on earth, how small it would have been from the very beginning!"[35] This is how Lao Tzu consoled himself. When the honor of the Tao was involved, he knew how to speak up. "My words have an Ancestor, and my deeds a Lord. Since no one knows him, it is no wonder that nobody knows me. However, the fewer people know me, the nobler are they who follow me. Hence, it is said that the Sage wears coarse garments but carries the jade in his bosom."[36]

It is said that to be great is to be misunderstood, and Lao Tzu is no exception to the rule. His mysticism simply mystified and amused the rank and file of the people. As he himself has testified, "When a wise scholar hears the Tao, he practises it diligently. When a mediocre scholar hears the Tao, he wavers between belief and unbelief. When a worthless scholar hears the Tao, he bursts into a loud guffaw! But if such a one does not laugh at it, the Tao would not be the Tao!"[37] No laughter, no Tao! But the interesting thing about Lao Tzu is that his mysticism was amusing not only to others but to himself as well. If people laugh at him, he could at least smile at them. "All the people strain their ears and eyes: the Sage only smiles at them like an amused infant."[38] Knowing that he had the jade in his bosom, he could afford to wear coarse garments, covering wisdom, as it were, with a coat of folly. He was objective enough to see what a poor figure he was cutting in the world, and he was humorous enough to laugh over his lot. He has given us a self-portrait, with features which mark him down unmistakably as a genuine mystic:

> I have done with learning, and I feel no more vexation. What is the difference between "eh" and "oh"? What is the distinction between "good" and "evil"? Must I be inhibited by other people's inhibitions? What abysmal nonsense!
> All men are seething and beaming, as though feasting upon a sacrificial ox, as though mounting the Spring Terrace. I alone am

placid and give no sign, like a new-born babe which has not smiled. I alone am forlorn as one who has no home to return to.

All men have enough and to spare: I alone appear to have lost everything. Muddled and confused, what a fool's mind is mine! All men are bright, bright: I alone am dim, dim. All men are sharp, sharp: I alone am mum, mum—bland like the ocean, aimless like the wafting gale. All men have something to lean on: I alone am intractable and boorish. *But wherein I am most different from others is in knowing to draw sustenance from my Mother!*[39]

In other words, in Lao Tzu's eyes, the children of the world are lost in their search for the many, while he knows the supreme importance of clinging to the One. As he wrote: "All-under-Heaven have a common beginning. This Beginning is the Mother of the world. Having known the Mother, we may proceed to know her children. Having known the children, we should go back and hold on to the Mother."[40]

In Lao Tzu's time, as in our own age, people had forgotten the one thing necessary but were troubled with many things. Civilization was developing rapidly at the expense of true wisdom. "The court is very clean and garnished, but the fields are very weedy and wild, and the granaries are very empty! They wear gorgeous garments, they carry sharp weapons, they surfeit themselves with food and drinks, they possess more riches than they can use. Such persons are a prelude to outrageous discords. How contrary to the Tao their ways of life!"[41]

It is remarkable that this old philosopher should have compared himself time and again to a newborn child. The keynote of his whole philosophy is that we must recover the spirit of childhood. What is it in the child that captivates the mind of the Lao Tzu? Here is what he says:

One who is steeped in Virtue becomes akin to the new-born babe. Wasps and poisonous serpents do not sting it, nor fierce beasts seize it, nor birds of prey maul it. Its bones are tender, its sinews soft, yet its grip is firm. Not having known the union of the male and the female, it grows in its wholeness, and keeps its vitality in perfect integrity. It howls and screams all day long without getting hoarse, because it embodies perfectly the spirit of harmony.

To know the spirit of harmony is to know the Changeless. To know the Changeless is to have the Inner Light.

To hasten the growth of life is ominous. To drive the passions by the will is to overstrain one's energy. To be overgrown is to decay. All this is against the Tao, and whatever goes against the Tao soon ceases to be.[42]

3. Thérèsian Spirituality

(1) *The Glorious and the Lowly.* Absolutely speaking, only Christ can be said to know the glorious but keep to the lowly, to know the bright but keep to the dark, to know the strong and active but keep to the weak and passive. Let us ponder the words of St. Paul: "Have this mind in you which was also in Christ Jesus, who though He was by nature God, did not consider being equal to God a thing to be clung to, but emptied Himself, taking the nature of a slave and being made like unto men. And appearing in the form of man, He humbled Himself, becoming obedient to death, even to death on a cross."[43] Is this not knowing the pre-eminently glorious but clinging to the utterly lowly? This is truly Divine madness. But it is precisely this madness that intoxicates the soul of Thérèse. As she wrote to Céline, "The one crime charged against Jesus by Herod was that He was *mad* . . . and I agreed with him! . . . . Yes, it was *folly* to seek the poor little hearts of mortals to make them His thrones, He, the King of Glory, Whose presence is mightier than the Heaven can contain! Our Beloved was *mad* to come down to earth seeking sinners to make them His friends, His intimates, to make them *like unto Himself,* when He was perfectly happy with the two adorable Persons of the Trinity . . . . We shall never be able to commit the follies for Him that He has committed for us, nor do our actions deserve the name of folly, for they are in fact most reasonable acts, far below what our love would like to accomplish."[44] Her whole life was a single-hearted emulation of the folly of Divine Spouse. Shortly before her death, she declared, "I will spend my Heaven in doing good upon earth."[45] Knowing Heaven, she clings to earth!

(2) *The White and the Black.* Christ is the Light, the true Light that enlightens every man who comes into the world.[46] But how carefully He hid His light, especially during the Passion! The

Author of life had to go through the valley of death! "There is no beauty in him, nor comeliness: and we have seen him, and there was no sightliness, and we should be desirous of him: despised and the most abject of men, a man of sorrows, and acquainted with infirmity: and his look was as it were hidden and despised, whereupon we esteemed him not."[47] This vision of the suffering Christ forms the basis of Thérèse's devotion to the Holy Face, the keynote of all her spirituality. The Son of God, who is "the radiance of His Father's splendor and the full expression of His being,"[48] is now hidden in the Face which looks misery itself! But Thérèse sees through the veil. "O Blessed Face! more lovely than the lilies and roses of springtime! Thou art not hidden from us. The tears which veil from us Thy *Divine Gaze* are as precious diamonds which we delight to treasure up, and through their infinite value, to purchase the souls of our brethren."[49] Furthermore, the Holy Face is not a mere mask, which can be put on and taken off at pleasure. On the contrary, it is an essential aspect, an integral part, of the whole "radiance of His Father's splendor." The infinite distance between His Celestial beauty and terrestrial "no beauty" is the measure of the immeasurable immensity of His Love for His Father and for mankind. In the Holy Face of "no beauty nor comeliness," Thérèse perceived the *Beauty of Love* and was enraptured. "I too desire to be without comeliness or beauty, 'to tread the winepress alone,' unknown by any creature."[50] As she wrote to Céline, "Jesus is a hidden treasure, a good beyond price that few souls can find, for it is *hidden* and the world loves things that glitter . . . . *To find a thing hidden, we must ourselves be hidden,* so our life must be a mystery! We must be like Jesus, like Jesus whose *look was hidden.*"[51]

In a letter to Sister Marthe of Jesus, we find an illustration of the dialectics of blackness and whiteness. "It is a great trial to see everything *black,* but this is a matter not wholly within your control . . . . Stop worrying, dearest little Sister, in Heaven you won't see everything black, you'll see *everything white.* Yes, everything will be clothed in divine *whiteness* of our Spouse, the Lily of the valleys . . . . Let us make good use of the *brief instant* of life . . . above all, *let us be small, so small that everybody may trample us underfoot,* without our having the least air of noticing or mind-ing."[52] In other words, knowing that we shall be clothed in the whiteness of the Lily, we should be patient with the blackness of the valley.

In her interior life, she was well acquainted with the darkness of the spiritual night. In a letter to Pauline, she said, "I am in a very dark subterranean passage! . . . . I shall consent, if it is His will, to walk all my life the dark road upon which I am, provided that one day I arrive at the goal of the mountain of love . . ."[53] From another letter we are allowed to see that the darkness was not unrelieved by a kind of subdued light. She tells us how during her retreat before Profession she asked her Spouse to choose a road for her to reach the summit of the mountain of love, and "Then," she continues, "Jesus took me by the hand and brought me into a subterranean way, where it is neither hot nor cold, where the sun does not shine, and rain and wind do not come; a tunnel where I see nothing but a brightness half-veiled, the glow from the downcast eyes in the Face of my Spouse."[54] It was in this subterranean passage that her contemplation was purified of all dross and her love purged of all self-gravitated desire for consolation. As she wrote to Sister Marie of the Sacred Heart, "My soul is still in the underground tunnel but it is *very happy* there, yes, happy to have no consolation. For thus I see that its love is not like the love of the world's brides who are always looking at their bridegroom's hands to see if they bear a gift, or at his face in the hope of surprising a smile of love to enchant them."[55] Thus, she had learned to find consolation in desolation and to teach the ethereal joy of no joy. Lao Tzu would call it "savoring the savorless."[56]

As she grew in her interior life, the night of her soul grew darker and darker till it became pitch-black. Even the half-veiled brightness was gone! But by virtue of *blind* trust in the love of God, she was given a peace that nothing could take away from her. About a month before her death, looking out the window, and pointing to a shady part of the garden, she said to Pauline: "See, down there, at the side of the chestnut trees, do you see that black hole wherein nothing is distinguishable? . . . . Well, I am in a place like that, as regards both body and soul . . . . Ah! yes, what darkness. But I dwell there in peace."[57] A week before her death,

Pauline asked her whether she had any intuitions. She replied, "Ah! Mother! about intuitions! . . . If you only knew in what poverty I find myself. I know no more than you know . . . . I divine nothing except what I see and hear. But my soul, notwithstanding the darkness, enjoys a most astonishing peace."[58] As Lao Tzu would say, "All men are bright, bright: I alone am dim, dim."[59] Thérèse knew as well as Lao Tzu that the lights which brighten up the children of the world are false lights, while the true light is to be found only in the dark valley, for in this life, "The bright Way looks dim."[60]

Anyway, were it not for the dark night of her soul, Thérèse could never have arrived at that *blind* faith and *blind* trust in the maternal tenderness of God, which has since become the badge of her glory and a beacon light to wayfarers. Nor could her love have become so pure as to move her to say, "My Jesus, Thou knowest I do not serve Thee for the sake of reward, but solely out of love and a desire to win Thee souls."[61]

(3) *The Masculine and the Feminine.* It seems that all mystics, whether Christian or pagan, Western or Eastern, talk the same language and sing the same tune. For one thing, they prefer the passive way to the active. "Faithful soul," said St. Irenaeus, "It is God Who will operate in you: Offer Him a gentle and docile heart . . . always preserve within you (in the subsoil of your soul) enough humidity not to lose the impress of His divine hands. Do not disturb these successive operations, and you will attain perfection. Whatever within you is imperfect will be covered over and hidden by the wisdom of God. *To act is the property of the goodness of God, to receive belongs to human nature.*"[62] So, Thérèse: "Merit does not consist in doing or giving much, but in receiving, in loving much much."[63] So, Lao Tzu: "In following the natural rhythms of the universe, are you able to play the female role?"[64]

As to discarding discursive reasoning and feeding upon the Mother, Thérèse knows it as well as Lao Tzu. Explaining to Céline how it is not necessary to have an explicit intention for every action of ours, she said, "The infant at the mother's breast takes its nourishment as a matter of course, and without giving a thought to the reason for the action. Yet he thrives on it and it gives him strength and vitality, even though that is not his intention while feeding at the breast."[65] As Céline tells us, "She wanted us to be like little children who possess nothing as their own and who depend entirely on their parents for all their needs. She urged us to live only from day to day without laying by any spiritual store for the future."[66] Is this not what Lao Tzu had in mind when he said, "All men have more than enough: I alone seem to have lost all"?[67]

Lao Tzu said, "Learning consists in daily increase: the practice of Tao consists in daily decrease. Keep on decreasing and decreasing, until you reach the state of complete passivity. Completely passive, and yet you will be completely active!"[68] What could be more passive than the enjoyment of the Beatific Vision in heaven? Yet Thérèse wrote in all seriousness in a letter to a missionary in China, "I am perfectly sure I shall not stay inactive in Heaven, my desire is to go on working for the Church and for souls, that is what I keep asking God, and I am certain He will say yes."[69]

Céline once said, "Oh! When I think how much I have *to acquire!*" Thérèse commented, "Or rather how much you have yet *to lose!* Jesus Himself will fill your soul with treasures in the same measure that you move your imperfections out of the way."[70] Is this not reminiscent of Lao Tzu's "The practice of Tao consists in daily decrease?"[71]

Thérèse often told Céline, "You will never reach perfection if you insist on *climbing* a mountain. What God wants of you is to *go down* to the heart of the valley where you will learn to despise yourself."[72] Lao Tzu had likewise said, "High virtue is like an abyss."[73]

Lao Tzu never tired of praising the "virtues" of water, because it keeps to the low places.[74] Similarly, Thérèse said, "The lowest place is the only spot on earth which is not open to envy. Here alone there is neither vanity nor affliction of spirit."[75] She also pointed out that Jesus is "the Lily of the valleys,"[76] so that if we want to meet Him, we would have to go down to the valleys.[77]

Another reason why Lao Tzu praised water is that it is soft and weak, but "for overcoming the hard and the strong, there is nothing like water."[78] He also said, "When a man is living, he is soft and supple. When he is dead, he is hard and rigid. When a plant is living, it is soft and bending. When it is dead, it becomes stark and dry. Hence, the hard and rigid belongs to the company of the dead, while the soft and supple belongs to the company of the living."[79]

Likewise, Thérèse has taught us the same lesson for our spiritual life. St. Paul's paradox: "When I am weak, then I am strong,"[80] is one of the recurrent themes in her teaching. Here is one passage which almost reads like a graphic commentary on Lao Tzu:

> What does it matter to the *little reed* if it bends? It is in no fear of breaking, for it has been planted on the edge of waters. Instead of touching the earth when it bends, it meets only a pleasant wave which gives it new strength and makes it long for another storm to break over its frail head. It is its weakness that gives it all its confidence. It could not break since, whatever happens to it, it wills to see only the gentle hand of Jesus.[81]

Is this not what Lao Tzu meant when he said, "Bend and you will be whole?"[82]

But Lao Tzu had also said, "Keep empty and you will be filled."[83] This reminds us of Thérèse's advice: "There is but one means of compelling God not to judge us: we must take care to appear before Him empty-handed."[84] But the subtle child knew what she was doing. As she told her sister Pauline, empty-handedness "is precisely that which gives me joy, for, having nothing, I shall receive everything from God."[85]

Again, Thérèse counsels us to lay nothing by, but spend our treasures as fast as we gain them.[86] This is exactly what Lao Tzu said: "The Sage does not take to hoarding. The more he lives for others, the richer he is. The more he gives to others, the more he receives."[87]

It was with Thérèse's approval that Céline chose for the motto of her coat-of-arms "The loser always wins."[88] This would also have been applauded by Lao Tzu who had said: "Truly, one may gain by losing; and one may lose by gaining."[89]

Finally, Lao Tzu said, "He who keeps the Tao does not desire to be full. But precisely because he is never full, he can always remain like a hidden sprout and does not rush to early ripening."[90] Similarly, Thérèse knew that to grow up is to be independent of Our Father. Therefore she said, "I have desired not to group up, because I realized I should never be able to earn my own living, the eternal life of heaven!"[91]

4. The Motherliness of God

We have already seen that Lao Tzu thought of the Tao in terms of "Mother."[92] Thérèse, too, has a special attraction for the maternal tenderness of God. It is true that she called God our Father, but He is *Papa le bon Dieu,* a Father who is more tender than a mother.[93] She repeatedly quoted from Isaias these passages: "Can a mother forget her child? and even if she should forget, yet will I not forget thee."[94] "As one whom the mother caresses, so will I caress you, and shall be comforted in Jerusalem."[95]

Like Julian of Norwich, who actually called Jesus "our Mother,"[96] Thérèse was particularly impressed by His motherliness.

One day, as she was promenading in the garden, supported by her sister, Mother Agnes, she stopped to look at a little white hen sheltering her little ones beneath her wings. Thereupon her eyes filled with tears. "You are crying?" Mother Agnes asked. "I cannot answer you now," she replied, "I am too much moved." Later she said, looking at her sister with a heavenly expression: I have cried on remembering how the good God had compared Himself with a hen in the Gospel, in order to bring home to us His tenderness. All my life He has done just that for me—He has hidden me entirely under His wings. So much so that I could no longer contain myself, my heart overflowing with gratitude and love. Ah! The good God has done well in concealing Himself from me, only rarely allowing me to see, as *through the lattices,* the effects of His mercy. . . .[97]

This little incident throws a flood of light upon the quality of Thérèse's love of her Divine Spouse. It may be said that her heart was so full of Him that every tidbit of her experience reminded her of Him. "Jerusalem, Jerusalem! . . . How often would I have gathered thy children together, as a hen gathers her young under her wings, but thou wouldst not! . . . "[98] What maternal tenderness is revealed in this outpouring of His heart! And what unspeakable anguish He must have felt when He saw that the children themselves would have been only too willing and happy to be gathered under His wings, were it not for "Jerusalem!" "Jerusalem," here, stands for all the forces that conspire to keep away the children from their true Mother—the priests who shut the kingdom of heaven against men, the demon of organization, the tyranny of the group, the formidable barriers of sectarianism and provincialism, the absolutist State bent upon the destruction of the inner sanctuary of man. On one side we see a Mother whose breasts are simply pent up with life-giving milk and who is only too eager to suckle her young ones. On the other side we see hungry children instinctively seeking the breasts of their Mother, but pitilessly prevented from reaching her and feeding upon poison which they are made to believe to be milk. What situation could be more tragic and touching than this?

The reason that Thérèse gave for her tears was her gratitude to God for His tender care of herself. This, no doubt, was uppermost in her mind. But one suspects that deep down in her heart was a yearning of which she might not have been conscious at the moment. The Motherliness of God touched the innermost core of her very being—the *maternal instinct*. She too wished to gather together the children of the world under her wings so that they might become children of God. Her deepest desire is to be a "mother of souls."[99] Recipient of the infinite mercies of God, her cup overflows, so that her practice of fraternal charity is, to her, a necessary relief of her own pent-up love, an additional mercy from God. Thus, in her eyes, giving is actually receiving. With this in mind, we can perfectly comprehend what she means when she says, "Merit does not consist in doing or giving much, but in receiving, in loving much."[100] Her passivity is the measure of her activity. In this way, she can be a contemplative without being a quietist, and an active worker without being an activist. Even the Beatific Vision is no bar to her missionary activities.

She had chosen nothing,[101] and the Lord has given her more than all.

5. Mysticism and Moral Virtues

One of the most famous sayings of Lao Tzu is this: "High virtue is not virtuous, therefore it has virtue. Low virtue never loses its virtuousness, therefore it has no virtue."[102] What did he mean? Could he mean that high virtue is immoral? Certainly not! Lao Tzu prized the practice of virtues as much as any one. As he said, "The Sage is kind to the kind, but he is also kind to the unkind; for Virtue is kind. He is faithful to the faithful, but he is also faithful to the unfaithful; for Virtue is faithful."[103] Elsewhere he said, "I have three treasures, which I hold fast and watch over closely. The first is *mercifulness*. The second is *frugality*. The third is *not venturing to be preferred before others.*"[104] He even said that "Heaven will help the merciful, protecting him by Its own Mercy."[105] It cannot be doubted that these treasures are virtues cherished by Lao Tzu. In saying that "High virtue is not virtuous," he merely meant that a man of true virtue is never self-righteous, as he would attribute his virtues to Heaven and to the operations of the Tao rather than to himself.

How near Lao Tzu's philosophy comes to Christianity will be brought home to us when we compare it with what Therésè said: "A soul is not holy because Our Lord uses it as an instrument . . . We should try to grasp this truth, and attribute nothing of good to ourselves. No one actually possesses the virtues he practices, so let everything redound to the glory of God."[106] In her letter to her eldest sister, Sister Marie of the Sacred Heart, she wrote: "O my dearest Sister, *please* understand your little sister, understand that to love Jesus, to *be* His *victim of love,* the weaker one is, without desires or virtues, the more apt one is for the operations of that consuming and transforming Love. The *desire* to be a victim is enough of itself, but one must consent to stay poor and without strength, and that is the difficulty, for where are we to find the man truly poor in spirit?"[107] Commenting on this passage, Père Lucien-Marie de St. Joseph wrote: "This daring affirmation of the Saint is in line with the severest texts of *The Ascent of Carmel* upon human virtues which are very fine in appearance but Pharisaic, and of which St. John of the Cross proclaims the uselessness (bk. iii, ch. xxvii). In a sense the Saint was 'without desires or virtues.' She did not pique herself upon those which God had gratuitiously put in her hands. She was truly poor."[108]

The language of a mystic is not easy to understand for those of us who are not transcended from a merely human point of view. For example, take these words of Thérèse: "I am happy at the thought of going to Heaven, but when I reflect on these words of Our Lord: 'I come quickly, and My reward is with Me, to render to every man according to his works,' I think that He will find my case a puzzle: I have no works . . . Well, He will render unto me *according to His own works.*"[109] Was she trying to be humorous? At the close of a life of such single-hearted devotion to Our Lord, after having done her level best in serving God and her neighbors in Carmel, to say that she had no works might sound like false humility. But the truth is that she had been lifted to such a height that she had a different outlook from those of us who are still at the foot of the mountain. She did not deny that she had worked for the Lord, but did she therefore *have* or *possess* the works? No, indeed! For every piece of work she had performed had been offered to God, so that she had no more works as far as she was concerned. Besides, did St. Paul not say, *"For it is God who of His own good pleasure works in you both the will and the performance?"*[110] The mind of Thérèse is the mind of Paul. It was Paul who said, "For by grace you have been saved through faith; and that not from yourselves, for it is the gift of God; not as the outcome of works, lest anyone may boast."[111] About himself he wrote candidly that although he had labored more than any of the other apostles, yet, strictly speaking, it was not he that labored, but the grace of God with him.[112] Thérèse saw exactly the same truth. Her most active days were when an epidemic of influenza had broken out among the community at Carmel, and she was one of three who were left on their feet, and had to take care of the sick ones, and arrange for the funerals. When she thought of these hectic days, she had this to say: "God was very good to me in supplying with the strength I needed; I still can hardly imagine how I shrank so little from the work that came my way."[113] I imagine that in Heaven it is those who had accomplished most for the kingdom of God on earth who are the loudest in their expressions of gratitude to Him, realizing as they do with every fiber of their being that all their works were due to His good pleasure.

Thérèse belonged so utterly to God that she simply could not think of anything as belonging to herself. As Sister Marie of the Sacred Heart so keenly observed in a letter to her, "May I tell you? I will: you are possessed by the good God: literally *possessed,* exactly as the wicked are by the devil."[114] Being *possessed* by God, how could she *possess* anything? Even the spiritual riches were "only loans from God."

Like Thérèse, Lao Tzu was *possessed* by the Tao, so that he could not help looking at things from *Its* standpoint rather than from a merely human point of view. That was why he could have given utterance to the lofty idea: "Requite injury with kindness,"[115] which brings him so near to the spirit of Christianity. Confucius was not able to agree with it. When someone quoted the maxim to him, he said that if injury is to be requited with kindness, with what is kindness to be requited?[116] His own view was that we should requite kindness with kindness, but requite injury with justice. It must be admitted that before the Revelation it must have been extremely difficult to say more than Confucius. In this connection, the words that Thérèse once said to Céline come to mind: "Your programme of life seems to be this: I will be kind to those who are kind, and amiable with those who are amiable. Then, naturally you become agitated as soon as someone disagrees with you. In this you are like the pagans spoken of in the Gospel. And Our Lord Himself tells us not to imitate them but rather do good to them that hate you and pray for them that persecute you. To do good to those only who are good to us springs from a wisdom that is merely human: in other words, all for self and nothing for God."[117] How delighted Thérèse would have been to know the philosophy of Lao Tzu!

6.   The Mystery of Incarnation and Suffering

Speaking of the Tao, Lao Tzu observes that "it is just because It does not claim to be great that its Greatness is fully realized."[118]

Speaking of the Sage or Man of the Tao, he says:

> Therefore, the Sage wants to remain behind,
> But finds himself ahead of others;
> Reckons himself out,
> And finds himself safe and secure.
> It is not because he is selfless
> That his self is realized?"

> "He embraces the One
> And becomes a Pattern of the world.
> He does not make a show of himself,
> Hence he shines;

> Does not justify himself,
> Hence he is glorified.
> Does not boast of his ability,
> Hence he gets his credit;
> Does not brandish his success,
> Hence he endures;
> Does not compete with anyone,
> Hence no one can compete with him.

I have quoted all these words because they present a more realistic portrait of the Little Thérèse than I can do with my own words.

Now, as we all know, without Jesus a personality like Thérèse would have been impossible. But the question is, Who could have taught Lao Tzu such wonderful *aperçus* of the truth? The *Divine Logos* who enlightens every man coming into the world![120] The same Teacher of teachers, Who taught Thérèse the wisdom of Love and made her "the greatest Saint of the modern times," had, before His incarnation, sown in the mind of Lao Tzu certain seeds of the same wisdom, and made him the greatest philosopher of ancient China. The revelation has uncovered the hidden meanings of some of Lao Tzu's enigmatic sayings, which were utterances of the unspeakable groanings and yearnings of the Spirit in his soul. He was goaded by the desire of touching the Intangible, comprehending the Incomprehensible, listening to the Inaudible, seeing the Invisible, tasting the Tasteless, and expressing the Inexpressible. He had some glimpses of It, but no sooner had it appeared than it disappeared again. The very hesitations and fluctuations which mark his language earmark the truthfulness of his report. "The Tao appears to be something illusive and evasive. Evasive, and illusive, yet in it is Form. Illusive and evasive, yet in it is Substance. Dim and shadowy, yet in it is Vital Essence. This Vital Essence is supremely real; in it is unfailing Truth."[121] Again: "Look at it and you do not see it: its name is *The Invisible*. Listen to it and you do not hear it: its name is *The Silent*. Reach for it and you cannot seize it: its name is *The Intangible*. These three (attributes) are unfathomable; hence they fuse into one. Its upper side is not bright, nor its under side dark. Continuously the Unnamable moves on, and returns again to the realm of nothingness. We call it the formless Form, the imageless Image. We call it the illusive and the evasive. Confront it and you do not see its face. Follow it and you do not see its back. Yet, equipped with this time-honored Tao, you can harness the present realities. To know the first beginning is the nodal point of the Tao."[122]

How mysterious is the Tao to Lao Tzu! Yet this very fact is a guarantee of the genuineness of his vision. For whatever is real is mysterious, and whatever is not mysterious has nothing to do with Reality.

It was only after *The Word was made flesh*[123] that St. John could say, "I write of what was in the beginning, what we have heard, what we have seen with our eyes, what we have looked upon and our hands have handled: of the Word of Life."[124] This is something Lao Tzu could not have said. Nor could any poet before the Christian era have sung as Francis Thompson did:

> O world invisible, we view thee,
> O world intangible, we touch thee,
> O world unknowable, we know thee,
> Inapprehensible, we clutch thee![125]

However, the Revelation has not done away with the mysterious. In fact, the Incarnation is the Mystery of Mysteries. True, Christ said to Philip, "Philip, he who sees me sees also the Father." But Philip could have answered, "Lord, have I really seen you?"[126] The Revelation has only given us enough to build our faith on. Even the beloved disciple of Christ had to say, "No one has ever seen God."[127] As Dom Paul Delatte says, "God is by nature hidden and invisible, he dwells in light inaccessible. Verily thou art a hidden God, God of Israel, the Saviour." Even when He reveals Himself, He is still hidden: in creation, in the incarnation, in redemption, in the Eucharist. He reveals Himself more and hides Himself more; He is at once God giving Himself, and God incommunicable. And our life, when it is truly the life of Christ, becomes hidden with Him: "Ye are dead and your life is hidden with Christ in God."[128]

For our sake, Christ, God the Son, is still hidden in the Eucharist! Glorious God keeping Himself humble and little! Sitting at the right hand of His Father, He yet continues to immolate Himself at every sacrifice of the Holy Mass! Is this not the supreme exemplar of Lao Tzu's ideal of "knowing the glorious but keeping to the lowly?"[129]

Lao Tzu spoke symbolically of the man of Tao as one "who wears coarse garments, but carries jade in his bosom."[130] This often makes me think of St. Paul's symbol of carrying the treasure of Divine light "in vessels of clay."[131] This is the style of Jesus.

Now, Thérèse loved Jesus so single-heartedly that she wanted to imitate Him in everything, especially in "knowing the glorious but keeping to the lowly," and in "carrying jade beneath coarse garments." She wrote to Céline, "To be the spouse of Jesus, one *must* be like Jesus; Jesus is all bloody, crowned with thorns." What could be more glorious than to be the spouse of the Son of God? Yet, knowing well the glorious, she clings to the humiliations.[132] In order to be like Jesus, she desired to be despised and hidden and accounted for nothing.[133] Further, realizing as she did that "by His bruises we are healed,"[134] she even desired to be a co-victim with Him, that she too might win souls for God by her hidden sacrifices and sufferings in union with His Passion.[135] There was nothing morbid about her desire for suffering. Once we penetrate into her philosophy of suffering, we should see that this desire of hers is as logical and reasonable as a lawyer's desire to win a case. Listen to her: "The end cannot be reached without adopting the means and since Our Lord had made me understand that it was through the cross He would give me souls, the more crosses I encountered the stronger became my attraction to suffering. Unknown to anyone, this was the path I trod for fully five years: it was precisely the flower I wished to offer to Jesus—a hidden flower which keeps its perfume only for Heaven."[136]

To Thérèse, afflictions and trials are sent by God for a two-fold purpose. In the first place, they are meant to perfect us. He allows them "to try our love."[137] "Love these thorn-pricks as so many pledges of love from the Divine Spouse."[138] By accepting them as coming from a loving hand, we are thereby united more intimately with Jesus.[139] In the second place, united with the Passion of Jesus, they acquire a redemptive value. To be a consort of Jesus is to be a mother of souls; and there is no motherhood without birthpangs. For, as Thérèse knows so well, "Only suffering can bring souls to birth for Jesus."[140] Therefore, "do not waste any of the *thorns* that you meet every day; with one of them you can *save a soul.*"[141] The idea of *spiritual motherhood* comes more naturally to a woman than to a man; but every true apostle of Christ, whether man or woman, must be a *mother* of souls. It was not for nothing that St. Paul addressed the Galatians as *"my dear children, with whom I am in labor again, until Christ is formed in you."*[142]

There is a great deal of masculine strength and spirit of initiative in Thérèse; but these qualities only serve to balance and bring to relief her *fundamental femininity.* In fact, her remarkable valiance and impetuosity spring from the typically *feminine single-heartedness* with which she loves her Divine Spouse and His children.

7.   Tao as the Eternal Law

If there is so much coincidence between Lao Tzu and Thérèse in the mode of their feeling, the secret seems to me to lie in Lao Tzu's mystical predilection for the "Eternal Feminine,"[143] which is his symbol for the Tao. Among the virtues he attributes to the Tao are lowliness, patience, hiddenness, mercifulness, flexibility, mellowness, serenity, non-assertiveness, and the generous readiness to benefit others by way of self-sacrifice. All these virtues have been touched upon, except the last one, which seems to come remarkably close to the Christian idea of redemptive suffering. Here is what Lao Tzu wrote:

> To receive the dirt of the country is to be the
> lord of its soil-shrines;
> To bear the evils of the country is to be the
> king of all-under-heaven.[144]

The idea that one must suffer for his own sins is common enough. The idea that one's sufferings are meant to perfect him is much less common; still it can be found in the Confucian classics. Mencius, for example, says: "When Heaven is about to confer a great office on any one, it first exercises his mind with suffering, and his sinews and bones with toil; it exposes his body to hunger, and subjects him to extreme poverty; and it confounds all his undertakings. All this is meant to stimulate his mind, toughen his nature, and supply his incompetencies."[145] But the idea that one can take upon himself the evils of the country so as to ward off calamities for the people, I have not found in any books of ancient China previous to the *Tao Teh Ching,* at least not in such an explicit formula.

Unlike the Confucian notion of Heaven, which is *personal,*[146] Lao Tzu's notion of *Tao* seems to be *impersonal* or *suprapersonal.*[147] Yet the very idea of the efficacy of vicarious suffering seems to suppose a spiritual universe, a moral order, in which all things work together for the good of those who love their fellow beings to the point of self-forgetfulness. Besides, although the whole book deals mainly with *Tao* and *Teh* (*Wisdom* and *Virtue*), the term *T'ien* (Heaven) appears several times in the same sense as Confucius and Mencius used it, that is, a personal God. Let me give a few instances:

> When you have done your work, retire!
> This is the Way of *Heaven.*[148]
> In governing a people and in serving *Heaven,*
> It is best to avoid outward show.[149]
> The merciful are invincible in war,
> And safe and secure in peace.
> *Heaven* will rescue them from peril,
> Surrounding them with its mercy.[150]
> Some things are detested by *Heaven.*[151]
> Vast is Heaven's net;

> Sparse-meshed it is, and yet
> Nothing slips through it.[152]
> The Way of *Heaven* is to benefit, not to harm.[153]

Since *Tao* belongs to Heaven, it is clear that it is not something superior to Heaven. It seems to correspond more to the *Eternal Law,* as understood by St. Thomas Aquinas than to the *Logos* of the New Testament, as denoting God the Son, except in a very remote and vague way. Yet Tao, or Eternal Law, stands in the closest relation to the *Logos,* for "among other things expressed by the *Logos,* the Eternal Law itself is expressed there."[154] Tao is the type of Divine Wisdom; moving all things to their due end. And between the type and the *Logos* there can be no clean-cut demarcation in the mind of a mystic.

It must be noted that in substance Christianity and Taoism belong to different levels. For Taoism is natural wisdom, while Christianity is supernatural wisdom. But God being the Author of both Nature and Supernature, it stands to reason that natural wisdom may serve as a mirror of supernatural wisdom.

Lao Tzu's idea of the Tao is so lofty that he considers It as inexpressible in words, so that all terms we apply to It must be regarded as mere pointers. It is the creative and regulative and constitutive Principle of the universe. It is the first cause and the last end of all things that be. It is the Source of the moral law and the laws of nature, but It is not identical with them. It permeates and sustains all things, but It is nothing in particular.

The *Tao Teh Ching* does not claim to deal with the Tao as it is in itself, only as reflected in its effects. As St. Thomas says, "No one can know the eternal law, as it is in itself, except the blessed who see God in His Essence. But every rational creature knows it in its reflection, greater or less. For every knowledge of truth is a kind of reflection and participation of the eternal law, which is the unchangeable truth, as Augustine says (De Vera Relig. xxxi). Now all men know the truth to a certain extent, at least as to the common principles of the natural law: and as to the others, they partake of the knowledge of truth, some more, some less; and in this respect are more or less cognizant of the eternal law."[155] Now, the *Tao Teh Ching* does not, primarily, deal with the common principles of the natural law, which are known to all;[156] it presents some glimpses of the eternal law, in its effect, beyond the scope of those common principles. With his profound mystical insight, Lao Tzu may be said to be among the best cognizant of the eternal law.

As we have seen, many of his *aperçus* into the modes of operation of the Tao approximate with remarkable closeness to certain parts of the Gospel, just as the moral teachings of Confucius harmonize with some other parts of it. To me at least, they were pedagogues to lead me to Christ; they served as lamps shining in a dark place, until the day dawned and the morning star arose in my heart.[157] They first led me to Thérèse, for they had prepared my mind and my heart to comprehend and embrace her "little way of spiritual childhood." And when I came to find that her little way is but a restoration of Christian spirituality to Christ's own teaching in its purity, I was convinced that what Confucius and Lao Tzu taught about Heaven, Eternal Way, and Goodness (*T'ien, Tao, Jen*) were but pointers to the Blessed Trinity, Father, Son and the Spirit of Love. As St. Augustine has so truly observed, "Even in the time before Christ there were among people those who belonged to the spiritual Jerusalem and lived according to God and were pleasing unto Him."[158]

NOTES

[1] *Psalms,* 33:9.

[2] John, 3:29-30.

[3] Sister Geneviéve of the Holy Face, *A Memoir of My Sister St. Thérèse,* (Kennedy, 1959), p. 31.

[4] See Abbe Andre Combes, *St. Thérèse and Her Mission,* (Kennedy, 1955), p. 3.

[5] Sainte Thérèse de l'Enfant Jesus, *Histoire d'une Ame,* Edition complete, (Lisieux), p. 536.

[6] *Ibid.,* pp. 555-556.

[7] *Ibid.,* p. 557.

[8] *Ibid.,* pp. xxvi, xxvii.

[9] *Ibid.,* p. xxviii.

[10] Although these paradoxes are presented in our own words, they are all based upon her writings, as will be clear in the following pages.

[11] *The Sanctifier,* (St. Anthony, 1957), p. 146.

[12] *Ibid.,* p. 147.

[13] St. Thérèse was richly endowed with all the gifts of the Holy Spirit; but the gift of piety seems to have played a special part in her.

[14] In this essay, we only touch incidentally upon the affinity of her teachings with the ethical philosophy of Confucius. Confucianism and Taoism are essentially opposed to each other. The fact that the spirituality of St. Thérèse can have so much affinity to both without the slightest sign of inconsistency is an indication that Christianity, being higher than both, is capable of reconciling them. But we shall not enter into this in the present paper, which is confined to a comparative study of the mystical ways of Lao Tzu and St. Thérèse.

[15] *Li Ki,* chapter on "The Questions of Duke Ai."

[16] *The Ways of Confucius and of Christ,* p. 114.

[17] Besides, the Sacraments and the sanctifying and actual graces must be kept in mind.

[18] *Tao Teh Ching,* ch. 28.

[19] *Ibid.,* ch. 25.

[20] *Ibid.,* ch. 37.

[21] *Ibid.,* ch. 41.

[22] *Ibid.,* ch. 8.

[23] *Ibid.,* ch. 61.

[24] *Ibid.,* ch. 10.

[25] Shakespeare, *Measure for Measure,* I, ii, 107.

[26] All these paradoxes are in *Tao Teh Ching,* ch. 41.

[27] *Ibid.,* ch. 1.

[28] This expression belongs to St. Thérèse. See *Collected Letters of St. Thérèse of Lisieux,* translated by Francis J. Sheed, (Sheed and Ward, 1949), p. 139. Cited hereinafter as "Letters."

[29] From Traherne's poem on "My Spirit."

[30] "Hymn upon St. Bartholomew's Day."

[31] *Tao Teh Ching,* ch. 27.

[32] Ibid., ch. 47. This is because, as St. Augustine says, "The soul has within itself a hidden abyss, and the things of time and of this world have no place therein, but only what is above them and above all that concerns the body and its activities." (*The Soul Afire,* ed. H. A. Reinhold, Pantheon, 1944), p. 92.

[33] *Ibid.,* ch. 39.

[34] *Ibid.,* ch. 66.

[35] *Ibid.,* ch. 65.

[36] *Ibid.,* ch. 70.

[37] *Ibid.,* ch. 41.

[38] *Ibid.,* ch. 49.

[39] *Ibid.,* ch. 20.

[40] *Ibid.*, ch. 52.
[41] *Ibid.*, ch. 53.
[42] *Ibid.*, ch. 55.
[43] *Philippians,* 2:5-7.
[44] *Letters,* p. 240.
[45] *Sainte Thérèse of Lisieux,* tr. T. N. Taylor, (Burns Oates, 1947), p. 231. Cited hereinafter as Taylor.
[46] John, 1:9.
[47] Isaias, 53:2-3.
[48] Hebrews, 1:3. (Knox).
[49] *Memoir,* p. 113.
[50] *Novissima* Verba, (Kennedy, 1952), p. 83. Hereinafter cited as "N. V."
[51] *Letters,* p. 197.
[52] *Ibid.,* p. 245.
[53] *Ibid.,* p. 138.
[54] *Ibid.,* p. 139.
[55] *Ibid.,* p. 141.
[56] *Tao Teh Ching,* ch. 63.
[57] N. V., p. 117.
[58] *Ibid.,* p. 131.
[59] *Tao Teh Ching,* ch. 20.
[60] *Ibid.,* ch. 41.
[61] Taylor, p. 317.
[62] Quoted in *At the School of St. Thérèse of the Child Jesus,* p. 22, n. 1. So. Father Therg: "In the spiritual life, in the generation of the Word in us, we are 'Mothers,' that is, the passive element." (quoted in Martinez, *The Sanctifier,* p. 35).
[63] *Letters,* p. 189.
[64] *Tao Teh Ching,* ch. 10. See Maritain, *Creative Intuition in Art and Poetry,* (Meridian Books, 1955), pp. 337, 338.
[65] *Memoir,* p. 51.
[66] *Ibid.,* p. 32
[67] *Tao Teh Ching,* ch. 20.
[68] *Ibid.,* ch. 48.
[69] *Letters,* p. 353.
[70] *Memoir,* p. 28.
[71] *Tao Teh Ching,* ch. 48.
[72] Memoir, p. 28.
[73] *Tao Teh Ching,* ch. 41.
[74] See *supra* n. 22.
[75] Taylor, p. 302.
[76] *Letters,* p. 186.
[77] Taylor, p. 342.
[78] *Tao Teh Ching,* ch. 78.
[79] *Ibid.,* ch. 76.

80 2 Corinthians 12:10.
81 *Letters*, p. 104.
82 *Tao Teh Ching*, ch. 22.
83 *Ibid.*, ch. 22.
84 Taylor, p. 310.
85 N. V., p. 23.
86 Taylor, p. 310.
87 *Tao Teh Ching*, ch. 81.
88 *Memoir*, p. 31.
89 *Tao Teh Ching*, ch. 42.
90 *Ibid.*, ch. 15.
91 N. V., p. 88.
92 See *Tao Teh Ching*, ch. 1, 6, 10, 20, 28, 52, 59, and 61.
93 Taylor, p. 139.
94 Isaias, 49:15.
95 *Ibid.*, 66:13.

96 Julian Norwich, *Revelations of Divine Love,* 12th ed. (Methuen 1945), chapters LVIII, LX, LXI, LXIII, pp. 141-159. In her words, "the high might of the Trinity is our Father, and the deep Wisdom of the Trinity is our Mother, and the great Love of the Trinity is our Lord" (p. 145.) The property of Motherhood is Mercy. "The mother may give her child suck of milk, but our precious Mother, Jesus, He may feed us with Himself, and doeth it, full courteously and tenderly, with the Blessed Sacrament that is precious food of my life; and with all the sweet Sacraments He sustaineth us full mercifully and graciously." (P. 150.) So to St. Thérèse "Our Lord is more tender than a mother" (Taylor, p. 138), and "To me He has manifested His Infinite Mercy and in this resplendent mirror I contemplate His other attributes." (Taylor, p. 147.) Similarly, to Lao Tzu, who thinks of the Tao as Mother, mercy is the most precious virtue (*Tao Teh Ching*, chapters 62 and 67).

97 N. V., pp. 17-18 (June 7, 1897).

98 Matthew 23:37.

99 Taylor, p. 201. See also *Autobiography of St. Thérèse of Lisieux*, tr. Ronald Knox (Kennedy, 1958), p. 212. "It's only through suffering we can achieve spiritual motherhood." Cited hereinafter as Knox.

100 See *supra*, n. 63.

101 "I do not prefer one thing more than another. That which God loves best and chooses for me, that is the thing which pleases me most." N. V., p. 122 (Sept. 4, 1897).

102 *Tao Teh Ching*, ch. 38.
103 *Ibid.*, ch. 49.
104 *Ibid.*, ch. 67.
105 *Ibid.*
106 *Memoir*, p. 204-205.
107 *Letters*, p. 289.
108 Journées d'études thérèsienne à Paris, Juillet 1949.

[109] Taylor, p. 328.
[110] Philippians, 2:13.
[111] Ephesians, 2:8-9.
[112] 1 Corinthians, 15:10.
[113] Knox, p. 208.
[114] *Letters*, p. 277.
[115] *Tao Teh Ching*, ch. 63.
[116] *Analects of Confucius*, 14-36.
[117] *Memoir*, p. 133-134.
[118] *Tao Teh Ching*, ch. 34.
[119] *Ibid.*, ch. 22.
[120] John, 1:9.
[121] *Tao Teh Ching*, ch. 21.
[122] *Ibid.*, ch. 14.
[123] John, 1:14.
[124] I John, 1:1.
[125] *The Kingdom of Heaven*.
[126] John, 14:9.
[127] 1 John, 4:12.
[128] Dom Paul Delatte, *A Commentary on the Holy Rule of St. Benedict,* tr. Dom Justin McCann, (Latrobe, Pa: The Archabbey Press, 1950), p. 305.
[129] See *supra,* n. 18.
[130] See *supra,* n. 36.
[131] 2 Corinthians., 4:6-7.
[132] *Letters,* p. 98.
[133] Taylor, p. 125.
[134] Isaias, 53:5.
[135] Almost all her prayers were inspired by the thirst to love God and make Him loved. To this end she was willing to suffer with Christ. See Taylor, pp. 447-454.
[136] Taylor, p. 23.
[137] *Letters,* p. 145.
[138] *Ibid.,* p. 146.
[139] *Ibid.,* p. 145.
[140] *Ibid.,* p. 161.
[141] *Ibid.,* p. 110.
[142] Galatians, f:19.
[143] *Tao Teh Ching,* ch. 6.
[144] *Ibid.,* ch. 78.
[145] *Works of Mencius,* Bks VI, Pt. II, ch. 15.
[146] See Paul K. T. Sih, "The Natural Law Philosophy of Mencius," *New Scholasticism* (July, 1957), 317, 319ff.
[147] Although Lao Tzu calls the Tao "Mother," I think it is more a case of personification than actually conceiving it as a person.
[148] *Tao Teh Ching,* ch. 9.

[149] *Ibid.*, ch. 59.

[150] *Ibid.*, ch. 67.

[151] *Ibid.*, ch. 73.

[152] *Ibid.*

[153] *Ibid.*, ch. 81.

[154] St. Thomas, *Summa Theol.*, I-II, 93, 2, and 2.

[155] *Ibid., in corp.*

[156] On the whole, we may say that Confucianism deals with the common principles of natural law, while Taoism moves beyond them. The former is exoteric, the latter esoteric. But Thérèse, steeped in spirit of Christ, combines the two by transcending both of them. Perhaps, we may say, by adopting the terminology of Jacques Albert Cuttat, that the Confucian outlook is *intra-cosmic,* the Taoistic outlook is *meta-cosmic,* and the Thérèsian outlook is *trans-meta-cosmic.* (See his article on "The Religious Encounter of East and West," in 33 *Thought,* p. 485 ff.) The mentality of many Christians, in spite of their professed supernatural Faith, seems still to belong to the intra-cosmic sphere.

[157] 1 Peter, 1:19.

[158] *Soul Afire,* ed. H. A. Reinhold (Pantheon, 1944), p. 3.

THÉRÈSE AND CÉLINE

It was Walter Pater who said, "All art constantly aspires towards the condition of music."[1] Similarly, we can say that all human relationships aspire towards the state of friendship. Whatever relationship we may look at—whether it be husband and wife, parent and child, brother and brother, sister and sister, prince and minister, teacher and pupil, or even God and man — it merges in its farthest reaches into friendship. The essence of friendship consists in mutual love based upon an intimate understanding and the sharing of a common vision. Between true friends there exists a unity of minds, hearts, and souls.

Who can help admiring the ennobling friendship between David and Jonathan? As the Holy Scripture tells us, "The soul of Jonathan was knit with the soul of David, and Jonathan loved him as his own soul."[2] And upon the death of Jonathan, with what heart-rending words did David lament for him; "How are the valiant fallen in battle? Jonathan slain in the high places? I grieve for thee, my brother Jonathan: exceeding beautiful, and amiable to me above the love of women. As the mother loveth her only son, so did I love thee."[3]

Infinitely more touching, infinitely more illuminating on the nature of friendship, are the words which Christ spoke to his disciples on the eve of His Passion: "Greater love than this no one has, that one lay down his life for his friends. You are my friends if you do the things I command you. No longer do I call you servants, because the servant does not know what his master does. But I have called you friends, because all things that I have heard from my Father I have made known to you."[4]

Christ has actually opened the way for us to become friends

127

of God! This is such a supreme privilege that it bewilders our understanding and baffles our imagination. Yet it is a reality, as Truth has said it and Truth cannot lie. In fact, only friends of God can truly be friends of each other and fully realize the possibilities of human friendship.

Céline and Thérèse were not merely blood sisters, but *friends* in the fullest sense of the word. Theirs is the most beautiful friendship that ever existed between two sisters, as far as I know.

Their mutual affection and devotion found a fitting expression in the last moments of Thérèse. It was Pauline who bore witness to the special friendship between her two younger sisters. To her we owe the faithful recording of this touching and unforgettable scene:

> The death-sweat stood out in great drops on her forehead and coursed down her face. The ever-increasing oppression made her utter feeble, involuntary cries in her efforts to breathe. Thinking to moisten her parched lips, Sister Geneviève of the Holy Face (Céline, her sister) placed a small piece of ice upon them. No one will ever forget the look of heavenly sweetness with which our little Saint gazed upon "Céline" at that moment. It was like a sublime encouragement, a supreme good-bye.[5]

While this represents the crowning point of their friendship on earth, it is to be remembered that, like all friendships, it was not a static entity, but a dynamic process of growth, passing through many interesting metamorphoses in the course of its development while all the time maintaining its essential identity.

Although Céline was almost four years older than Thérèse, they were "fast friends"[6] as early as when Thérèse was barely three years of age. As their mother wrote to Pauline, "Céline and Thérèse are inseparable; you cannot imagine two children fonder of one another."[7] In another letter, she reported an interesting discussion between the two: "The other day Céline said, 'How could God be in such a tiny little Host?' The little one said, 'That is not so strange, because God is almighty.' 'What do you mean by almighty?' 'Why, it means He can do anything He wants to.' "[8] Judging by this, Thérèse must have been precocious and Céline, while not as brilliant as her sister, was at least an earnest seeker after truth. According to their mother, both possessed excellent qualities. As she wrote to Pauline, "Céline never commits the slightest wilful fault. The little one will also do well; she would not tell a lie for all the gold in the world; she has an originality such as I have never seen in any of you."[9] Thérèse herself has summed up her relations with Céline in those early years in these words: "We understood each other very well, only I was much more lively and far less naive than she. Although I was three and a half years her junior, I felt as if we were of the same age."[10]

The second phase of their friendship began from the time when their mother died (August 29, 1877), covering a period of nine years up to the Christmas of 1886, which marked the "conversion" of Thérèse.[11] Thérèse has given us a charming sketch of her intimate relations with Céline during this period, which they spent together in Lisieux, both at home and in school.

> Since our moving to Lisieux, our roles had changed. Now it was Céline who had become the mischievous little imp, and Thérèse was no more than a tame little girl, only excessively inclined to weeping. That did not prevent Céline and Thérèse from loving each other more and more. While we did have an argument now and then, it never amounted to anything serious. Fundamentally we were always of the same mind. I can vouch for it that dear little Céline *never* gave me any pain; she has been for me a ray of sunshine, a continual source of joy and consolation . . . Who will ever be able to tell with what intrepidity she used to defend me at the Abbey school when people taunted me? . . . She took such care of my health that at times I was even annoyed by her solicitude. But what did not annoy me was to watch her at play. She used to set up the whole troop of our dolls in arrays and hold a class for them, in the best school-mistress manner; only she would make it a point that her own "daughters" should always behave well, while mine were often turned out of doors for misconduct . . . She used to tell me all the things she had learned in her class, which amused me greatly, and I came to regard her as a fountain of knowledge. They used to call me "Céline's little daughter," so that when she was angry with me, her most effective weapon of showing disapproval was to say to me, "You are no longer my little daughter, it's finished, and I shall always remember it!" On such occasions what else could I do but to weep like a penitent Magdalen, imploring her to continue to regard me as her little daughter. Before long she would kiss me and promise me that she would not remember the incident any more . . . In order to console me she would take up one of her dolls and say, "My darling, kiss your Auntie." On one occasion, the doll was so anxious to give me a nice hug that it got its two

little arms into my nose, and hung there, to the stupefaction of Céline, who had not expected such a result. It did not take the "auntie" long to dislodge her "niece" from her predicament, and enjoy a hearty laugh over the singular adventure.[12]

Relating how the simplest things could kindle in them the keenest joys, Thérèse commented, "Ah! at that age we were not *calloused;* our hearts had all the freshness and expansiveness of a flower drinking in the morning dew. We were two stalks swaying in the same breeze—what brought joy or grief to the one brought joy or grief to the other."[13] In this connection we may add that Thérèse and Céline never became calloused, for they never lost the "heart of a child."[14]

But it was after Thérèse's "conversion" on the Christmas of 1886 that her friendship with Céline reached the highest point in the first cycle of its development. That "conversion" meant, to my mind, a radical change of Thérèse from being self-centered to being Christocentric. Céline, on the other hand, had never been as self-centered as Thérèse, but to have witnessed at such close range the marvelous transformation in her sister must have given a tremendous impetus to the development of her own spiritual life. Thérèse did not, of course, owe her vocation to Céline, but there is no denying that Céline's hearty approval and constant encouragement did much to confirm it. During the whole year following that Christmas, Céline was her bosom friend at home as well as during their pilgrimage to Rome.

In rendering an account of her relations with Céline during that crucial period of her life, she has given us one of the most beautiful passages in the literature of Christian spirituality. Let us present a tentative translation of it here:

> In those days Céline had become the intimate confidante of my thoughts. Ever since Christmas, we could understand each other perfectly; the barrier of age no longer existed, because I had grown in stature and especially in grace . . . Jesus who wanted to make us advance hand in hand, forged in our hearts stronger ties than those of blood. He made us *sisters in spirit.* In us were realized the words which the Bride uttered to her Lover in *Spiritual Canticle* of St. John of the Cross:
>> In the track of thy footsteps,
>> Young maidens run light-heartedly along the way.

At the touch of a spark,
At the taste of the seasoned wine,
There flows forth the Divine balsam.[15]

Indeed, it was *light-heartedly* that we followed the footsteps of Jesus. The sparks of love which He sowed with open hands in our hearts and the strong, delicious wine which He gave us to drink made transitory things of the world vanish from our eyes, and our lips breathed forth aspirations of love inspired by Him.

How delightful were the conversations that we had every evening up in the belvedere! With our eyes plunged into distance, we watched the pale moon rising slowly behind the towering trees, the silvery rays she cast on a sleeping world, the bright stars scintillating in the unfathomable azure, the fleecy clouds wafting idly along on the soft breath of the evening breeze—all these conspired to lift our hearts towards Heaven, that beautiful Heaven of which the calm sky we saw was but "the limpid *obverse.*"

I may be mistaken, but it seems to me that the opening-up of our hearts which we experienced then was similar to what had happened to St. Monica with her son at Ostia, when they were rapt in ecstasy as they contemplated the marvelous works of the Creator.[16] It seems to me that we received graces belonging to the same high order as those bestowed on the great Saints. As is said in the *Imitation,* God shows Himself to some souls in a braze of light, but to others *"delicately veiled, under symbols and figures."*[17] It was in the latter manner that He manifested Himself to our souls, but how *transparent* and *light* had become the veil with which Jesus was supposed to hide from our sight! There could be no room for doubt; already Faith and Hope were no longer necessary; *Love* enabled us even on earth to find the One whom we sought after. *"Having found Him alone, He greeted us with a kiss: henceforth we need fear no contemptuous looks."*[18]

Many years later, at the request of a Jesuit priest, Céline commented on these conversations as follows:

These conversations on the belvedere have left such a deep and clear impression in my mind that I remember them as if it happened yesterday. What Thérèse wrote about them in her *Autobiography,* far from being exaggerated, seems to me to fall short of the actual reality. We experienced truly some hours of heavenly consolation, of which no words could possibly transcribe. Often we began by repeating with an incredible ardor these words of St. John of the Cross: *"Lord! To suffer and to be despised for Thy sake!"* Yes, this was what we aspired to do with all our might . . . In spirit we were no longer on earth; it was in truth the possession of God in Love. After all these years I can definitely say that the graces we received were not mere accidental flashes of light nor were they the result of some transient outbursts of fervor. No, on the contrary, they produced in our souls a steady and consistent reaching out towards God; we seemed no longer to belong to this earth. Indeed, it could be called *ecstasy*.[19]

There is no question but that it was *ecstasy*,[20] but this does not mean that they had reached the summit of perfection. Each of them had a long way to go before she was to reach the goal as the Lord had destined her to reach. After the Mount Tabor the Calvary![21]

Thérèse was to undergo many trials for her vocation and to spend several years of the most intensive self-discipline and hidden suffering in the Carmel. Céline was yet to nurse her father with a heroic filial love for four years before she was to enter Carmel (in 1894), there to receive the strictest discipline as a novice at the hands of Thérèse, her erstwhile "little daughter."

It was as a mistress of novices that the spiritual potentialities of Thérèse came to full bloom. It was as a novice under Thérèse that the foundation of Céline's remarkable spiritual life were firmly laid. In her sixty-five years of holy living in the Carmel, she may truly be compared to "a tree planted near running waters, which brings forth fruit in due season, and whose leaves do not wither."[22]

Some of those leaves which "do not wither" are to be found in Céline's book, *Ste. Thérèse de L'Enfant-Jesus: Conseils et Souvenirs,* which was published in 1952.[23] An excellent English translation of it, by the Carmelite Sisters of New York, has appeared under the title: "A Memoir of My Sister St. Thérèse."[24] Neither the French title nor the English convey accurately the nature of its actual contents. It is essentially a record of the spiritual lessons which Céline as a novice learned from day to day from Thérèse as her Mistress of Novitiate. Parts of it were written when the Saint was still living, and parts of it were written shortly after her death when the memory was still fresh. The whole book presents a vivid picture of Thérèse *as a teacher*. In composition and in style, it is surprisingly akin to the *Analects* of Confucius which was a compilation of notes made by his disciples of his sayings on different occasions and of their impressions of his personality and conduct.

There are so many similarities between the two great teachers that it would take an interesting volume to present a comparative study of their pedagogies. Let a few examples suffice here. In the *Analects* of Confucius, we find: "The Master's manner was affable yet firm, commanding but not harsh, polite but not easy."[25] In Céline's book we find: "Although our holy Mistress was remarkably sweet in character, she was very firm. She never overlooked anything in the novices which needed correction."[26]

It is well known that Confucius adapted his teaching to the character of each pupil. For example, a disciple of his, Tse Lu, who was noted for his impetuosity, once asked Confucius whether he should make it a rule to carry out immediately whatever lesson he might hear from the master. The master said, "But you have your parents and elders still living; how can you make it a rule to carry out at once whatever you may hear from me?"[27] But when another disciple, Jan Yu, who was inclined to lassitude, asked the same question, Confucius replied, "Yes, you should carry out at once what you hear from me."[28] A third disciple, puzzled by the apparently contradictory answers Confucius had given to the question, asked for an explanation. The master said, "Jan Yu being of a retiring nature, I had to urge him on."[29] Thus, Confucius, who advocated the Golden Mean in all things, applied it also to education. The same is true of Thérèse. As Céline says, "Thérèse was ever on the alert to stem the current of my natural impetuosity which was always in focus in my external activity. I was far too eager about my assignments, and I seemed to be pushed by an irresistible drive to carry out, meticulously, to an exaggerated stage of perfection. Consequently, whenever I did not achieve this, I experienced a sense of frustration."[30] Then she goes on to tell us how Thérèse advised her to be detached from her daily occupations and to cultivate a "perfect freedom of heart."[31] "I remember reading," she told Céline, "that when the Israelites were building the walls of Jerusalem, each laborer while working held a sword in one hand. That is a symbol of the interior attitude we should acquire in the matter of work: that at the point of the sword, we hold off all dissipation of soul in our external labors."[32] On the other hand, as Céline observes, "Thérèse was always careful not to stress this point of utter disinterestedness in the case of those souls who needed a push in the opposite direction, for she could not endure any careless or negligent approach to duty."[33] She did not allow any of her novices "to mistake a casual attitude for the virtue of holy indifference."[34] She never wearied of teaching them that "any negligent performance of our tasks can be just as detrimental to the sacred presence of God as any over-eagerness"; and that "both extremes were to be shunned."[35]

The secret of the striking similarity between Confucius and Thérèse in their ways of dealing with their pupils lies in the fact that both the great teachers were selfless and free from narrow preconceptions, having in mind only the interests and needs of each pupil.

"When you love a person," said Confucius, "can you help being solicitous?"[36] Similarly, Thérèse's solicitude over the spiritual formation of those in her charge sprang from her pure love. She knew that true love does not consist in indulgence, but essentially in sanctifying oneself and helping to sanctify others.[37] She took her duties as the Mistress of the Novices so seriously that she was given the nickname of "the little hunting dog!" She herself took the nickname in good humor, and expounded its connotations in a letter to Céline: "I am the one who runs after the game all day. You know, the hunters . . . are too big to hide in the bushes; but a little dog . . . has a *sharp nose,* and naturally it can *slip* in anywhere!"[38]

As Mother Agnes of Jesus (Pauline) deposed at the Process of Canonization, "Sister Thérèse of the Child Jesus never sought to curry favor with the novices by any trick of human prudence, and this was one of the remarkable features of her direction of the novitiate. Her only desire was to assist the young religious in their struggle for perfection, and for this end she neglected no means in her power, even if it were a question of losing their affection."[39]

Céline has given us another testimony which seems to me to constitute the keynote of their relations in Carmel: She told me confidentially that when she became our Mistress, she had begged God, above all, not to allow the novices to love her with any mere human affection. It was evident that her prayer had been granted, for although the novices all loved her to an extraordinary degree, there was never anything childish or sentimental in our relations with her. We used to have recourse to her simply to satisfy our thirst for truth and not, as is often the temptation with young religious, merely to enjoy the company of the Mistress."[40]

It is to be noted that when Céline entered Carmel,[41] Thérèse had been there already five years, during which time she had become more and more united with God, and grown tremendously in wisdom and grace. Her spiritual state was so far in advance of that of Céline that their conversations inevitably appear like a dialogue, between the voice of grace and the voice of nature. But the very fact that Céline has reported them so faithfully reveals the greatness of her soul. It shows that she was perfectly honest, simple like a child, eager to learn and improve herself, and generously appreciative of her little sister's superior qualities and attainments. She was well aware that Thérése's love for her had in fact grown in depth and in height, in breadth and in length, since their pleasant days at home; that she loved her now with the love of Christ himself. As Thérèse has pointed out, "A heart given to God loses nothing of its natural affection; on the contrary, that affection grows stronger by becoming purer and more spiritual."[42] On Céline's part, too, her love for Thérèse was growing more and more selfless and spiritual under the latter's influence. She tells us in perfect candor how Thérèse initiated her into the mysteries of the Communion of Saints. Once she said to Thèrése, "What I envy in you are your works. How I wish that I, too, could compose beautiful poems to inspire others to love God.!"[43] Thérèse replied: "One must not attach one's heart to such things. One must not set store by books, poems and works of art as a means of doing good to others. Oh no! When faced by our limitations, we must have recourse to the practice of offering to God the good works of others. That is the advantage of the Communion of Saints. Let us never grieve over our powerlessness but rather apply ourselves to the science of love."[44] To reinforce this lesson, Thérèse introduced a thought from Tauler: "If I love the good that is in my neighbor more than he himself loves it, this good becomes mine more than it is his. If, for instance, in Saint Paul, I love all the favors God bestowed on him, all these, by the same title, belong to me. Through this communion, I can become enriched by all the good that is in heaven and upon earth; in a word, by all the good in everyone who loves God."[45]

As far as the works, virtues, and spiritual insights of Thérèse are concerned, I have the impression that Céline soon learned to love them more than she herself did. That is why Céline seems to have taken a great deal of pleasure in recording incidents in which illuminating truths were brought out at her expense. Here is one: "I frequently manifested a desire that others should appreciate my efforts and take note of my spiritual progress. 'When you give in to this desire,' the Saint admonished, 'you are like the hen who, as soon as she has laid an egg, wants all the neighbors to know about it . . . .' "[46]

On another occasion, Thérèse played an impish joke on poor Céline in order to awaken her once and for all from an erroneous conception of the religious vocation. "I was under an illusion," Céline wrote, "that in entering Carmel I was doing something grand and heroic for Jesus. I asked my Little Thérèse, therefore, to write some verses, to the air *"Rappelle-toi,"* which should remind Our Lord of all that I was sacrificing for Him and all that our family had suffered for His love. The Saint received my petition with evident pleasure because, as I was soon to realize, she intended by this means to bring a salutary lesson to me. Consequently, when later I poked over the innumerable couplets of her beautiful poem *"Remember Thou,"* I could find no reference whatever to any sacrifice I might have made for Jesus; each verse was, on the contrary, a telling reminder of all that He had done for me!" This must have been quite a shock to Céline, but it effected a radical transformation in her spiritual outlook, as is evident from her comment on the incident: "I could not help thinking of the Gospel parable of the Pharisee and the Publican. Had I not, like the proud Pharisee, boasted that I have given tithes of all I possessed? This incident also brought home to me the truth that there was no stopping Thérèse in her determination to make me forget self entirely, in order that I might inhale the pure air of love and thanksgiving."[47]

Another incident, which reminds me very much of the way the Chinese Zen Buddhists[48] used to teach their neophytes, is reported by Céline as follows: "One day, during her illness, I was grieving bitterly over a fault that I had committed. 'Take your crucifix,' said Thérèse, 'and kiss it.' I kissed the feet. 'Is that how a child kisses its father? Throw your arms around His neck and kiss His face.' When I had done so, she continued, 'That is not sufficient—*He must return your caress.*' I had to press the crucifix to both my cheeks, whereupon she added, 'Now, all is forgotten.' "[49] This is how the mind of a mystic works. *Perfect love casts out fear,*[50] and unless God returns our caress, fear still remains, *and he who fears is not perfected in love.*[51] But how do we know that God has returned our caress? Because *God is Love,*[52] infinitely more tender than the tenderest mother on earth. So long as our repentance is sincere, God will never fail to return our caress. He will not only forgive our sins, but *forget* them altogether. He is our loving Father, and we are His little children.

Céline must have absorbed this great lesson into her own system. It seems to me that, by nature, Céline was even more childlike and innocent and simple than Thérèse,[53] although she did not seem to possess the latter's spiritual genius[54] and supernatural sensitivity and subtlety. Céline's simplicity is a melody, while that of Thérèse is a symphony. At any rate, when Thérèse expounded to her the *little way* of Spiritual Childhood, it must have found in Céline's heart a spontaneous, not to say instinctive, response. It was not for nothing that Thérèse should have called her "the sweet echo of my soul." In a real sense, Céline may be said to be the co-discoverer of the *little way,* which is ever ancient and ever new. Thérèse used to be moved to tears when pondering over the Lord's prayer: "It is so sweet to call God our Father." According to Céline, her sister "loved God as a child loves its father, with unbelievably affectionate ways."[55] But who could have appreciated this *filial* love of our Heavenly Father better than Céline who had been such a *filial* child of her earthly father? To be a *filial* child of God! To love God as a child loves its father! This is the keynote of their *little way of spiritual childhood.* Nothing could be simpler, yet nothing could be more sublime and more mystical. It is the *whole way.*

The notion of "Spiritual Childhood" is so pregnant with meaning and so all-embracing in scope that it is not possible to enter into a serious discussion of it here. Suffice it to say that, properly understood, it is Christ's own Way, the Way of His filial love for His Father.[56] Through Christ, we too have become children of God,[57] and our whole duty as little brothers and sisters of Christ is to love and serve Our Father as Christ has loved and served Him. In the performance of this filial duty, we need the help and guidance of the Holy Spirit, from Whom we "have received a spirit of adoption as sons, by virtue of which we cry, 'Abba! Father!' "[58] Besides, the Holy Spirit reminds us of what Christ did and said[59] and adapts it to our particular states and conditions of life.[60] As children "born of the Spirit,"[61] we must keep our hearts ever docile "as newborn babes"[62] and ever fresh like "a flower drinking in the morning dew."[63]

However advanced one may be in age and in wisdom, before God he is still a little child ever aware of his dependence on Him. This is why Thérèse said that she had always "desired not to grow up."[64] In fact, in our relations with God, we can never grow up. To grow up is to cease to grow, and to cease to grow is to cease to be. Thus, vis-à-vis God, we must always remain little children.

Many are under the erroneous impression that the *little way* of Spiritual Childhood is only meant for young people and beginners. As a matter of fact, it contains, as Benedict XV so clearly saw, "the secret of sanctity . . . for all the Faithful throughout the whole world."[65] In proclaiming the heroicity of Thérèse's virtues, the Pontiff pointed out that these virtues "spring from *spiritual childhood*."[66] The whole Allocution deserves careful study, but here let me reproduce one passage which seems to me to indicate the essence of the doctrine:

It will be useful to consider the qualities of this *spiritual childhood* both as regards what it excludes and what it implies. Spiritual childhood excludes first the sentiment of pride in oneself, the presumption of expecting to attain by human means a supernatural end, and the deceptive fancy of being self-sufficient in the hour of danger and temptation. On the other hand, it supposes a lively faith in the existence of God, a practical acknowledgement of His power and mercy, confident recourse to Him who grants the grace to avoid all evil and obtain all good. Thus the qualities of this spiritual childhood are admirable, whether we consider their negative aspect or study them in their positive bearing, and we thereby understand why our Saviour Jesus Christ has laid it down as a *necessary* condition for gaining eternal life.[67]

In other words, Thérèse's *little way* is really a timely and fresh rediscovery of Our Lord's own Way. It is the perennial tradition of the Church, the science of the Saints, too often obscured by the complicated writings of certain speculative authors. As Thérèse has so candidly said, "Sometimes, when I read spiritual treatises, in which perfection is shown with a thousand obstacles in the way and a host of illusions round about it, my poor little mind grows very soon weary, I close the learned book, which leaves my head splitting and my heart parched, and I take the Holy Scripture. Then all seems luminous, a single word opens up infinite horizons to my soul, perfection seems easy; I see that it is enough to realize one's nothingness, and give ourself wholly, like a child, into the arms of the good God."[68]

Céline was so deeply convinced that the *little way* of spiritual childhood was the true and universal way of Christian perfection that her interest in the Cause of her sister was solely motivated by her desire to propagate this "secret of sanctity," this way of filial love of God. Before her sister was beatified, the Promoter of the Faith asked her at the Canonical Process, "Why do you desire the Beatification of Sister Thérèse of the Child Jesus?" She announced that "it was solely that her *little way* might become known to the world."[69] The Promoter of the Faith gave her a grave warning: "Once you begin to speak of a special *Way,* the Cause is infallibly doomed; innumerable cases on record bear abundant witness to that."[70] "That is indeed too bad," she replied, "But a fear of hindering the Beatification of Sister Thérèse could never deter me from stressing the only important point that interests me—that her *little way* might be raised with her, so to speak, to the honors of the altar."[71] She held out in spite of the warning. When Benedict XV solemnly approved the Way of Spiritual Childhood, her joy, as she tells us, reached heights never again attained, not even on the days of her sister's Beatification and Canonization.[72] Like her sister, Céline had the true grandeur of soul which has its source in Spiritual Childhood. Blessed are the little ones, for God will clothe them with His own Greatness!

Céline lived to be nearly ninety years of age.[73] To the end of her life she remained a little child of God. Shortly before she died, she said, "I see as clearly as noon-day that it is only the way of Spiritual Childhood which can give true peace of heart, and the grace to be in the Hands of the Good God as a little child."[74] When the Sisters spoke to her of the unique welcome which awaited her from Thérèse and other members of her family, she replied, "The most important thing of all, and by far, will be to see our Dear Lord for the first time, face to face; the family is only secondary."[75] The last word she uttered was "Jesus."[76] Nothing could have endeared her more to Thérèse than just this single-hearted love of Jesus. At that supreme moment of her life, her Spiritual Childhood was consummated, and so was the friendship between the two sisters.

By way of conclusion, let us take another look at their relations during Céline's formative years in Carmel. On Christmas of 1896, Thérèse gave her a letter purporting to have come from the Blessed Virgin, and signed "Your dearest *Mama,* Mary, Queen of little angels."[77] Obviously, Céline was undergoing certain interior trials, feeling utterly dissatisfied with herself. "If you are willing to bear serenely the trial of being displeasing to yourself," the letter runs, "you will be to me a pleasant place of shelter; you will suffer, of course, for you will be outside the door of your own home; but have no fear, the poorer you are, the more Jesus will love you."[78] Here is one of the recurrent themes in Thérèse's teachings, which must have cured Céline of her perfectionist tendencies and launched her full sail into the boundless ocean of confidence and abandonment. But the conclusion of the letter is even more significant: "I am delighted to see you desiring great things, and I am preparing greater still for you: . . . . One day you will come with your *Thérèse* into the beauty of Heaven, you will take your place on the knees of my beloved Jesus, and I too shall take you in my arms and shower caresses upon you, for I am your *Mother.*"[79] Now that they are reunited in Love's eternal Home, their friendship, which began so well on earth, must have grown so much the more beautiful as the seed of grace in their souls has grown into glory. The acorn has become an oak! The Divine Friendship which they share together, far from destroying their little friendship, must have added a heavenly luster to it.[80] For their friendship is a work of God; it is a thing of beauty and a joy for ever.

NOTES

[1] *The Renaissance,* in the chapter on "The School Giorgione."

[2] 1 Kings (1 Samuel), 18:1.

[3] 2 Kings (2 Samuel), 1:25, 26.

[4] John 15:13-15.

[5] *Novissima Verba* (Kennedy, 1952), tr. The Carmelite Sisters of New York, p. 140.

[6] *Autobiography of St. Thérèse of Lisieux,* tr. R. Knox (Kennedy, 1958), p. 47.

[7] Sainte Thérèse de l'Enfant Jesus, *Manuscrits autobiographiques* (Carmel de Lisieux, 1957), p. 23. To be cited hereinafter as *Manuscrits.*

[8] *Manuscrits,* p. 25.

[9] *Manuscrits,* p. 27.

[10] *Manuscrits,* p. 17.

[11] See *Saint Thérèse of Lisieux, The Little Flower of Jesus,* tr. T. N. Taylor (Burns Oates, 1947), pp. 86, 87. Hereinafter to be cited as "Taylor." It would be out of place to analyze the psychology of what Thérèse calls "the priceless grace of my complete conversion." An altogether unexpected rebuff from the lips of her father for her "babyishness" accelerated her process of growing up.

[12] *Manuscrits,* pp. 57, 58.

[13] *Manuscrits,* p. 59.

[14] As Mencius wrote, "A great man is he who has not lost the heart of a child." *Meng Tse* (in Chinese), Chap. IV, par. 2, 12.

[15] Stanza XXV of St. John of the Cross, *Spiritual Canticle.* See St. John of the Cross, *Complete Works,* tr. E. Allison Peers (Sheed and Ward, 1946), Vol. II, p. 321, where the translation is somewhat different from ours in the text. It should be noted that the line which has been rendered as "Young maidens run light-heartedly along the way," is, in the Spanish original "las jovenes discurren al camino," literally: "the youths run along the way." We have added "light-heartedly" because the idea is implicit in the word "discurren," and furthermore the French version that the Saint used reads: "les jeunes filles parcourent *légèrement* le chemin." (*Manuscrits,* p. 115). In fact, in her comment, as will be seen, she emphasized the *light-hearted* mode of following Christ.

[16] See *Confessions of St. Augustine,* tr. F. J. Sheed (Sheed and Ward,

1948), pp. 157 ff.

[17] Thomas à Kempis, *The Imitation of Christ*, III, 43.

[18] *Manuscrits*, pp. 115, 116.

[19] Sister Genevieve of the Holy Face (Céline Martin), *A Memoir of My Sister St. Thérèse*, tr. Carmelite Sisters of New York (Kennedy, 1959), p. 18. I have followed the translation with a few modifications. Herinafter cited as *Memoir*.

[20] As Céline explains it, ". . . this ecstasy did not deprive us of consciousness nor raise us from the ground." *Memoir*, p. 18. What the two sisters did feel was an irresistible *élan* or reaching out toward God, with their hearts melting in spiritual joy. My impression is that their souls felt most at home at the "whistling of a gentle air." (See 3 Kings, 19:12). True daughters of Mary, their intuitions of things Divine take the form of silent communings within the heart.

[21] In a small way all followers of Christ have their days when they feel so near to God that their faith borders on knowledge, and their hearts are full of spiritual joy. They are tempted to say with St. Peter, "Lord, it is good for us to be here." (Matt., 17:4). This is meant to be a preparation for the actual following of Christ, step by step, day in and day out, on the way of the Cross, whether physical or spiritual or both. As Thérèse testifies, "One must have passed through the tunnel to understand how black is its darkness." (Taylor, p. 155). Faith, Hope and Love must be purified in the crucible of suffering before one can become a true child of God. See *Memoir*, pp. 86, 87.

[22] *Psalm* 1:3. It must not be thought that her life was all joy and no suffering. Rather it was "the song of suffering in union with *His* sufferings." (*Letters*, p. 98.)

[23] Published by Carmel de Lisieux. Although this book did not see the light until 1952, it was in substance completed shortly after the death of St. Thérèse. It was only in 1951 that she began to reread the old manuscripts and classify the notes, adding a few reflections. In the preface, she makes this significant remark: "These texts, mostly in the form of dialogue, give, as in *The Imitation of Christ*, the veritable accent of 'the voice of nature and the voice of grace.' And although on some points 'the voice of nature' repeats itself to the point of tediousness, I have thought it best not to suppress anything, in order that the wise responses of 'the voice of grace' might be preserved intact." (P.xvii). Hereinafter cited as *Conseils*.

[24] See note 19.

[25] A. Waley, *The Analects of Confucius* (George Allen & Unwin, 1938), p. 131.

[26] *Memoir*, p. 4.

[27] *Analects*, 11:21. My own translation.

[28] *Ibid.*

[29] *Ibid.*

[30] *Memoir*, p. 100.

[31] *Memoir,* p. 100.

[32] *Memoir,* pp. 100, 101.

[33] *Memoir,* p. 101.

[34] *Memoir,* p. 101.

[35] *Memoir,* p. 101.

[36] *Analects,* 14:7.

[37] Christ Himself has said in His Priestly Prayer: "And for them I sanctify myself, that they also may be sanctified in truth." (John, 17:19).

[38] *Collected Letters of Saint Thérèse of Lisieux,* tr. F. J. Sheed (Sheed & Ward, 1949), pp. 236, 237. Hereinafter to be cited as *Letters.*

[39] *Memoir,* p. 13, n. 7.

[40] *Memoir,* pp. 12, 13.

[41] September 14, 1894. Thérèse had entered Carmel on April 4, 1888.

[42] Taylor, p. 159.

[43] *Conseils,* p. 56.

[44] *Memoir,* p. 71.

[45] *Memoir,* p. 71, n. 5.

[46] *Memoir,* p. 34.

[47] *Memoir,* pp. 97, 98.

[48] See Wu, *Beyond East and West* (Sheed & Ward, 1951), pp. 178 ff.

[49] *Conseils,* p. 49.

[50] 1 John, 4:18.

[51] *Ibid.*

[52] *Ibid.,* 4:8.

[53] Thérèse herself wrote to Céline (August 1894): ". . . if you knew how your *docility* and childlike *candor* charm Him!" *Letters,* p. 238. Their mother had written when Céline was six and one half, "Céline is naturally inclined to be good; as to that little puss, Thérèse, one cannot tell how she will turn out, she is so young and thoughtless. She is a very intelligent child, but has not nearly so sweet a disposition as her sister, and her stubbornness is almost unconquerable. When she has said, 'No,' nothing will make her change . . . ." Taylor, p. 37.

[54] In "The Science of Love" of this book, I wrote, "She is a genius who knows how to hide her genius gracefully." But just because she did not want to show her genius, many people have been taken in. Recently, however, Mrs. Dennis O'Brian has called my attention to Jean Guitton's *The Spiritual Genius of St. Thérèse* (Newman, 1958). So, too, J. C. Eustace, in his *An Infinity of Questions* (Dennis Dodson, 1946), p. 154, writes: "St. Thérèse of Lisieux presents to the modern world a new way of sanctity, which can carry souls to the pinnacle of Divine Love. She combined in herself the genius of natural intuition, of poetic instinct, of a strong and abiding love for nature and earthly beauties, with all the riches of the supernatural life to which she was called, and in which she used all these gifts to the full."

[55] Piat, *The Story of a Family* (Gill, 1947), p. 378.

[56] Cf. Hebrews, 5:7-10.

[57] John, 1:12. "But to as many as received Him He gave the power of becoming sons of God."

[58] Romans, 8:15.

[59] John, 14:26.

[60] Through His gifts, especially the gift of counsel. See Luis M. Martinez, *The Sanctifier* (St. Anthony Guild Press, 1957), tr. Sister M. Aquinas, O.S.U.

[61] John, 3:6.

[62] 1 Peter, 2:2. "Crave, as newborn babes, pure spiritual milk . . . ."

[63] Words of St. Thérèse, *Manuscrits*, p. 59.

[64] *Novissima Verba*, p. 88. Lao Tsu's description of the man of wisdom: "He who keeps the Tao does not want to be full. But precisely he is never full, he can always remain like a hidden sprout, and does not rush to early ripening." *Tao Teh Ching*, chap. 15. The wonderful thing about Thérèse is that she combines the deep moral sense of Confucius with the highest flights of Taoistic mysticism. As Rev. Thomas Berry has so keenly observed, "The finest preparation for reading the Upanishads is to read Parmenides, Plato, Plotinus and Augustine. An understanding of Socrates is an excellent preparation for understanding Confucius . . . ." (*Approaches to the Oriental Classics,* ed. Wm. Theodore de Bary, Columbia 1959, p. 18). I may likewise confess that Confucius and Lao Tzu have helped me to understand Thérèse, who, in turn, has led me to a deeper comprehension of Confucianism and Taoism.

[65] Quoted in August Laveille, *Life of the Little Flower* (McMullen, 1953), p. 263.

[66] *Ibid.*, pp. 263-264.

[67] *Ibid.* p. 264.

[68] *Letters*, p. 332.

[69] *Memoir*, p. 38.

[70] *Memoir*, p. 39.

[71] *Memoir*, p. 38.

[72] *Memoir*, p. 39.

[73] Céline died on Feb. 24, 1959, three days short of ninety.

[74] Obituary sent from Carmel of Lisieux, in mimeograph.

[75] *Ibid.*

[76] *Ibid.*

[77] *Letters*, p. 303.

[78] *Letters*, p. 303.

[79] *Letters*, p. 303.

[80] To Thérèse, not only old friendships will be preserved and transfigured in Heaven, but also there will be new friendships. "Friendship in Paradise will be both sweet and full of surprises, of this I am certain. A shepherd boy may be the familiar friend of an Apostle or of a great Doctor of the Church, a little child may be in close intimacy with a Patriarch . . . . How I long to enter that Kingdom of Love!" (Taylor, p. 302).

TECHNOLOGY AND CHRISTIAN CULTURE: AN ORIENTAL VIEW

The great Hindu, Sri Ramakrishma, once said something which I think is typically Oriental in outlook and flavor:

> Two men went into a garden. The worldly-wise no sooner entered the gate than he began to count the number of the mango-trees, how many mangoes each tree bore, and what might be the approximate price of the whole orchard. The other went to the owner, made his acquaintance, and quietly going under a mango-tree began to pluck the fruit and eat it with the owner's consent. Now who is the wiser of the two? Eat mangoes, it will satisfy your hunger. What is the good of counting the leaves and making vain calculations? The vain man of intellect is uselessly busy in finding out the "why and wherefore" of creation, while the humble man of wisdom makes acquaintance with the Creator and enjoys Supreme Bliss in this world.[1]

In this is revealed the Oriental attitude toward science and wisdom, or technology and human culture. Everywhere in the Far East the traditional view has been that wisdom of life is so much more important than scientific technology that the pursuit of the latter apart from personal cultivation and perfection, which is the one thing necessary, is more a distraction than a help. All the sages of the Oriental world are in full accord with the fundamental philosophy of values taught by Christ and St. Paul. There is no comparison in importance between the way of Mary and the way of Martha; between knowledge that puffs up and charity that edifies. A man can still attain his glorious des-

145

tiny even without any technical knowledge; but a technician would be a mere instrument and therefore not quite a man without a well-cultivated interior life. This is the basic insight from which any discussion of the possible relations between technology and Christian culture must proceed as its starting point. Neither the Oriental sages nor the Christian saints have ever treated technology on the same level as personal perfection. Even Confucius, who was comparatively the most practical and matter-of-fact of the Oriental sages, would say that "a man of self-respect would not make himself a mere instrument." (*Chuin tse pu ch'i.*) The original word which I have rendered as "instrument" is "ch'i," which has also been translated as "a tool," "a vessel," "a utensil." It has the connotation of a particular means to an end, rather than an end in itself.

It is significant that in *The Book of Changes,* which was originally a manual of divination and was later developed into a profound treatise on metaphysics, the word "ch'i" is used as antonymous to the word "Tao," which may be translated as "Wisdom," "Truth," "Way of Life," or "Principle of the Universe," according to the context. There is an important statement in the book which I want to quote: "What is above the visible world is called 'the Tao,' what falls under the visible world is called 'ch'i.'" Thus, the visible world, that is, the world of phenomena, is but a means for attaining the ultimate end of life, which lies beyond the empirical world.

While both Confucianism and Taoism show their definite preference for the Tao over Technology, there is yet a marked difference in their estimates of the usefulness of the latter.

The Taoists were convinced that all the troubles of the world had their origin in the love of knowledge and the employment of artifice. Their basic assumption is that in the beginning man was innocent and lived in harmony with Nature. The knowledge of good and evil, beautiful and ugly, was the herald of all human tragedies.

The ideal country for the Taoists as presented in the *Tao Teh Ching* is as follows:

> Let there be a small country with a small population. Even

though there should be mechanical contrivances requiring ten times, a hundred times less labor, there would be no occasion for using them. Cause the people to love life so that they would hesitate to run the risk of death by moving to far-distant places. Boats and carriages there may still be, but there will be no occasions for riding in them. Weapons of war will lie unused. Let the people revert to the usage of rope-knotting in their transactions. Sweeten their food, beautify their clothes, let peace reign in their homes, and joy and harmony in their social intercourse. Though there be another country in the neighborhood of this, so that they are within sight of each other and the crowing of cocks and barking of dogs in one place can be heard in the other, yet there would be no traffic or communication between the two peoples.[2]

In a later Taoistic classic, *Chung Tzu,* a book of multiple authorship, we find a very interesting story. The author tells us that once the utility-minded disciple of Confucius, Tse Kung, saw an old man watering his garden by means of a pitcher. He had to draw water from a well and pour it into ditch. The result was as meager as the labor was great. Moved by pity, Tse Kung approached him saying, "If you had a machine here, you could irrigate in a single day a hundred times your present area. With trifling labor you will be able to accomplish a great deal. Would you not like to have one?" Tse Kung then described the machine as a contrivance made of wood, heavy behind and light in front, which could draw water up with great ease and in a continuous flow. Instead of being pleased the old gardener flushed up and said, "As I have heard from my teacher, ingenious contrivances lead inevitably to cunning dealings, cunning dealings produce inevitably a scheming mind and when a scheming mind dwells in one's bosom, his integrity and purity can no longer be kept intact, in which case his spirit will be restless. Now, a restless spirit has no place in the Tao. It is not that I do not know of the contrivance you speak of, but I should be ashamed to make use of it."[13] Tse Kung was greatly abashed. When he returned to Lu, he reported to Confucius, who, according to our author, made this comment: "That old man makes a pretense of following the ways of the Embryonic Age (the age of undiversified and undifferentiated wholeness). He knows only half of the truth, but ignores the other half. He regulates what is internal in himself,

147

but neglects what is external to him. What should make you truly marvel is the state of a man whose mind is so thoroughly illumined and enlightened as to return to simplicity, who by following the way of non-activeness is restored to original purity, who, embodying perfectly his essential nature as man and keeping his spirit intact in his bosom, moves freely in the ordinary ways of the world. As to the art of the Embryonic Age, how are we to know it?"

The words used in the story were put into the mouth of Confucius by a later Taoist. They represent the highest peak of Chinese speculation on the problem of other-worldly wisdom and this-worldly technology. We believe that these conversations could not have been written by Chuang Tzu. Even on the face of it we can infer that it was written by one who was primarily a Confucian scholar but who was "baptized" by the teachings of Taoism. If Confucius had really said the reported words, his philosophy could be called a "higher Taoism," which synthesizes Confucian moralism and pursuit of practical knowledge with the metaphysics and mysticism of the Taoists.

This reminds me of some interesting observations of the German philosopher Count Hermann Keyserling. To Keyserling, "Kung Fu Tse (Confucius) and Laotse (Lao Tzu) represent the opposite poles of possible perfection: the one represents the perfection of appearance, the other perfection of significance; the former, the perfection in the sphere of the materialized, the latter, within the non-materialized; therefore they cannot be measured with the same guage."[4] Keyserling could not see eye to eye with the modern Confucian scholar, Ku Hung-Ming, whose "fundamental thesis is that Confucius is the infinitely greater of the two because he understood significance as profoundly as Laotse, but did not retire from the world, but expressed his profundity in his mastery of it." "If Confucius really had been, and had achieved, what Ku asserts of him," Keyserling remarked, "then, of course, he would be incomparably greater. However, this is not so. It would appear to be contradictory to nature that the same man should live altogether in profundity and prove himself, at the same time, to be a mighty organizer of the surface; each one of these problems requires a special physiological organization, and I know of no accredited case in which a man possessed both to a similar degree."[5]

To my mind, these observations by Keyserling are of questionable validity. It is one thing to question whether Confucius had attained that synthesis; it is another thing to deny the very possibility of such a synthesis in the name of human nature. Besides, it is hardly just to call Confucius a mere "organizer of the surface." If one studies the growth of Confucius' interior life, one would see that at least in his old age he did arrive at the sphere of significance. As to Keyserling's denial of the very possibility of such a synthesis, I need only mention men like St. Paul and St. Ignatius of Loyola, who were great organizers precisely because they were so closely united with God and so completely unattached to their works. This question is of vital importance for the future of the world. If really there were no possibility of a living synthesis between the two spheres, then the world has reached a dead end. How, then, could we carry out the command of Christ of working *in the world* and being *not of the world?* But I shall return to this point later. In the meantime, let us study more closely the conversations I have already quoted from the *Chuang Tzu.*

In this interesting story, we find three possible attitudes toward our problem. The first view is represented by Tse Kung, who introduced machinery with the sole purpose of saving labor and promoting efficiency without relating it to the ultimate end of man. This was why he felt abashed by the laughter of the old gardener. In fact, he is reported as having said to his disciples, "That gardener is a man of complete virtue. As to me, I am one of those who are like waves carried about by the wind." The second is represented by the old gardener, who had absolutely no use for technology. The third is represented by Confucius, whose words show that he did not see any incompatibility between true wisdom and technology, whether in the sense of methods of social control or in the sense of mechanical contrivances for mastering the forces of nature.

It would seem that the reported words of Confucius carried a seed or a hint of the true solution of the problem. But for some reason or other, the seed never developed in the history of China, at least along the line of mechanical inventions. Later Confucian scholars concentrated their attention and energy solely upon the technology of controlling human nature to the almost complete neglect of mastering external nature.

This is one of the most puzzling phenomena in the history of human culture. The meagerness of scientific accomplishments in China would not have been due to any lack of intelligence. Potentially, at least, the Chinese people are highly inventive. I need only quote to you some interesting words from an after-dinner speech delivered in London fifty-two years ago in April by his Imperial Highness Duke Tsai Chi: "It is well known that the mariner's compass was invented in China, and to mention no greater results from its extended application in your hands, one very happy result at any rate is that we have been safely navigated to your hospitable shores. Gunpowder and guns had also their origin in China. A very harmless beginning, and there it might have stayed; but on the occasion of our recent visit to Woolsih Arsenal we noticed how greatly our germ had developed; and the idea suggested itself whether it had benefited mankind in making the discovery."[6] We may add that the movable type was also first invented in China, suggesting again the same query as to whether it has greatly benefited mankind, seeing that it has been turned into such an instrument of reckless propaganda rather than the vehicle of truth it was meant to be!

Yet the problem remains why we did not develop the germ ourselves. In his remarkable book, *Science and the Modern World,* A. N. Whitehead wrote: ". . . the more we know of Chinese art, Chinese literature, and of the Chinese philosophy of life, the more we admire the heights to which that civilization attained. For thousands of years, there have been in China acute and learned men patiently devoting their lives to study. Having regard to the span of time, and to the population concerned, China forms the largest volume of civilization which the world has seen."[7] His question was what could be the causes which made it possible for the modern Western world to develop scientific technology to such an extent, while other civilizations have not been able to develop along the same lines? According to him, the habit and tone of definite exact thought, which is the *sine qua non* of the scientific movement, was "implanted in the European mind by the long dominance of scholastic logic and scholastic divinity. When we compare this tone of thought in Europe with the attitude of other civilizations when left to themselves, there seems but one source for its origin. It must come from the medieval insistence on the rationality of God, conceived as with the personal energy of Jehovah and with the rationality of a Greek philosopher."[8] I think that Whitehead has oversimplified the causes. But it cannot be denied that he has pointed out one of the main causes.

My own observation is that the Western mind possesses a greater capacity for abstraction. It is capable of pursuing knowledge for the sake of knowledge, of isolating the means from the end and studying intensively its nature and structure as though it were really independent of the end. In this way it comes to know more potentialities of the means than it would be possible to know if the end were always kept in view. In the Oriental mind, the end seems to dominate. To it, knowledge must minister to Wisdom, so that to pursue knowledge for its own sake would seem to be sheer insanity. The Oriental mind is not at home in drastic distinctions or bifurcations. It thinks and feels analogically and organically. It is more attracted to the final causes than to the efficient causes. Before it undertakes any study, it would ask what it would contribute to the ultimate well-being of man. It looks at life as a journey toward a goal, whatever it may be. This Oriental tone of mind finds a typical expression in what Gandhi wrote of himself: "My national service is part of my training for freeing my soul from the bondage of flesh; I have no desire for the perishable Kingdom of earth. I am striving for the Kingdom of Heaven, which is Moksha. To attain my end, it is not necessary for me to seek the shelter of the cave. I carry one about me if I would but know it. My patriotism is for me a stage in my journey to the eternal land of freedom and peace. Thus it will be seen that for me there are no politics devoid of religion. Politics bereft of religion are a death trap, because they kill the soul."[9] In fact, all professions should be looked at in the same light. Our profession cannot be separated from our religious faith. The question for us Christians is how does our profession contri-

151

bute to our sanctification, or more plainly, how can we make our profession a special means and mode of expressing our love of God and our neighbor?

If we treat technology as a means of serving God and mankind, as a phase in the process of our sanctification, no conflict can enter between the two. Our Lord Himself has told us to be "wise as serpents, and guileless as doves."[10] Does technology not help us in becoming "wise as serpents"? But the important thing is to be at the same time "guileless as doves." Besides, the intensification of technological development threatens to submerge our personality in the mass, to crush our soul under the very weight of matter. This situation presents a tremendous challenge to us Christians. If we must become anonymous in the mass, let this very anonymity be our cloister in which we live our hidden lives only to God, let us permeate the very mass with the spirit of Holy Mass. Are we surrounded by dangers on all sides? Then, let us, with St. Paul, be "well-assured that everything helps to secure the good of those who love God, those whom He has called in fulfillment of His design."[11] If Brother Lawrence could turn his "little omelette in the pan for the love of God,"[12] what prevents us from turning every beat of our heart into a *Deo Gratias?* Pope Paul VI, when he was Archbishop of Milan, in one of his Pastoral Letters, had this to say: "A mechanic, in the presence of his machine, must say, with satisfaction, thoughtfully: I have discovered more than I have invented . . . . This has been for me an unexpected meeting with God. If in the past nature was the intermediary between Him and the human mind, why should not the work of technology or art be the intermediary today?" The only difference, perhaps, is that while nature is God's child, technology is His grandchild. The good Archbishop predicted that "the dawn of this new spirituality is not far off."[13]

To the Oriental, the cultivation of Science and Law can serve as "a bath of purification" for the soul bent upon its own deepening. For both Science and Law follow a slow, orderly, disinterested procedure, requiring for its fruitfulness the continuous mortification of selfwill, wishful thinking, and wandering fancies.[14] For a constant preoccupation with the end without attending sufficiently to the means will result not only in a failure to attend the end but in cramping the soul in a self-imposed inclosure. On the other hand, absorption in the means without a necessary awareness of the end may mean the wrecking of our souls in the midst of our journey without ever reaching the destination.

The East and the West must learn from each other in order to progress together in the pilgrimage of life. If the East cares for nothing but eating the mangoes and will not count the mango-trees, and learn how many mangoes each tree will bear, she may indeed satisfy her hunger this year, but be starved next year. Besides, what is the pleasure of eating mangoes all alone by yourself? The mango will taste better if others will eat with you. It is true that every one of us can only enjoy the mango by eating it with his own mouth. I cannot enjoy the mango that you are eating, but I can enjoy your enjoyment of it. Thus we can enjoy the mango and at the same time rejoice to see others enjoying the mango. But if we really want to share our mangoes with others, what could be more practical than to count what might be the approximate price of the whole orchard? This is what the East should learn from the West. But the West must also learn that the most foolish thing is to regard a mere means as the end; to possess more than you can enjoy, or, even worse, to gain the whole world but lose one's soul; or to pity others for their dirty streets while being perfectly complacent in one's own dirty thoughts; or to call others atheists who perhaps have a nobler idea of God than one's own narrow conceptions of Him.

In trying to convert the East to Christianity, we Christians should take care not to think that we alone possess God while the pagans have no knowledge of God at all. The truth is that we are all fellow seekers after God. Lay apostles especially, who have not sufficient grounding in Theology, must avoid the temptation of appearing to the pagans as though we could teach the catechism as a book of Geometry; as though we could communicate in language all deep things of our Religion in a technological way. In this connection, I have come across some very profound reflections in Don Delatte's *Commentary on the Rule of St. Benedict*: "St. Benedict's master thought is that we should *seek God*. There are only two legitimate attitudes towards God: to enjoy Him when we possess Him, to seek Him as long as we do not possess Him fully. God is by nature hidden and invisible; He dwells in light inaccessible. 'Verily thou art a hidden God, God of Israel, the Saviour.' (Isa. xiv. 15.) Even when He reveals Himself, He is still hidden: in creation, in the incarnation, in redemption, in the Eucharist. He reveals Himself more, and hides Himself more; He is at once God giving Himself, and God incommunicable."[15]

Christ alone fulfills eminently in His humanity all the good qualities of the East and the West, of the North and the South.

When I hear Him say, "Behold the birds of the air, for they neither sow, nor do they reap, nor gather into barns: and your heavenly Father feedeth them. Are not you of much more value than they? . . . . Consider the lilies of the field how they grow: they labor not, neither do they spin. But I say to you, that not even Solomon in all his glory was arrayed as one of these?" my Oriental heart utters a cry of joy like a lark singing in the morning sky. When I hear Him say, "Martha, Martha, thou art careful, and art troubled about many things. But one thing is necessary. Mary hath chosen the best part, which shall not be taken away from her"; I begin to see the moon which all the Chinese Taoists and Indian mystics were trying to point at like so many fingers. But when I hear Him say, "Consider, if one of you has a mind to build a tower, does he not first sit down and count the cost that must be paid, if he is to have enough to finish it?" my Occidentalized mind responds with a ready accordance to the irresistible logic and supreme good sense of the Divine Logos. And when I hear Him say to Peter, "Put your sword to its sheath; shall I not drink the cup the Father has given me?" I perceive here the perfect union of the strength of the North with the tenderness of the South. Indeed, in Christ "are hidden all the treasures of wisdom and knowledge." It is only by following His humanity that we can hope to be partakers of His divinity. The crying need of this critical age of ours is a true Christian humanism, which embraces all the values capable of being realized by redeemed men. The highest in the hierarchy of values are, of course, the theological virtues of love, faith and hope. The natural virtues of humanity, justice, temperance, fortitude and prudence, though lower in the scale, are nevertheless indispensable. Technology, too, has its place in the totality of values; but it is an instrumental value, appended to the virtue of prudence. It is only when people exalt it above the virtues that it loses its value even as an instrument and becomes a grave danger to our well-being. Technology is a good servant, but a bad master. So long, therefore, as we keep it resolutely to its place as a handmaid of the virtues, more particularly, as a vessel of charity, technology can be of help even to our sanctification.

In short, ever since the Renaissance in Europe, the history of the West has, on the whole, been a continuous centrifugal movement, from the standpoint of Christianity. In many quarters, even Christianity itself has become, so to speak, completely *humanized*. Man's self-dependence has grown steadily, and his dependence on God has been on the wane. The extraordinary technological development is, in some sense, a by-product of this centrifugal movement. Now, I am Confucianist enough not to remonstrate with what is past. I even think that the Lord, who alone is capable of drawing good out of evil, has permitted certain separatist movements to keep His Church constantly watchful and vital. It is also probable that the weakness, worldliness, and even corruptions of some of our human elements were partly responsible for driving members of people to seek after false gods. But, whatever may have been the causes, the centrifugal movement seems to have brought us to a point where a new decisiveness is imperatively demanded of us Christians to live up fully to our professions. Only in this way can we make this critical point of human history a real turning point. And I believe we are bound to succeed, not because we can depend upon our own efforts, but because we are members of the Church of God, against which, as Truth Himself has told us, the gates of hell cannot prevail. Everywhere I see encouraging signs of a revival of spiritual life. We are living in a new apostolic age, in which a tremendous centripedal movement is dawning. If in the past few centuries, Christianity has been *humanized,* the oncoming centripedal movement will *re-Christianize* humanism. This alone wll be able to turn a potential monster into a potent friend of mankind. In the meantime, let us thank God together for the ineffable privilege of living in this age and working for the deepening and spreading of His Reign in the hearts of men.

NOTES

[1] F. Max Müller, *Ramakrishna: His Life and Sayings,* p. 130.

[2] ch. 80.

[3] ch. 12.

[4] *The Travel Diary of a Philosopher,* II, p. 108.

[5] *Ibid.*

[6] *London and China Telegraph,* 17 April, 1906, quoted in Herbert Giles' essay on "The Mariner's Compass," in his *Adversaria Sinica,* p. 107.

[7] P. 6.

[8] P. 13.

[9] Quoted by M. S. Sundaram in his paper, "The Natural Law in the Hindu Tradition," in 5 Natural Law Institute Proceedings, 1951, p. 86.

[10] Matt., 10:17.

[11] Rom., 8:28.

[12] *Practice of the Presence of God,* p. 49.

[13] See quoted in Second World Congress for the Lay Apostolate: Basic Text "B," p. 24.

[14] Friedrich von Hugel, *The Mystical Element of Religion as Studied in Saint Catherine of Genoa and Her Friends,* II, 373, 383.

[15] P. 305.

CHRISTIANITY, THE ONLY SYNTHESIS REALLY POSSIBLE BETWEEN EAST AND WEST

I

Strictly speaking, John the Baptist was the only Precursor of Christ:

> The voice of one crying in the desert,
> "Make ready the way of the Lord,
> Make straight his paths.
> Every valley shall be filled
> And every Mountain and hill shall be brought low,
> And the crooked way shall be straight,
> And rough ways smooth;
> And all mankind shall see the salvation of God."[1]

But in no part of the world was Our Lord without heralds who, to speak analogically, sowed the "seeds of the Logos" in the hearts of men before *the Word was made flesh*. Unlike John the Baptist, those heralds were not aware of their mission, and yet God endowed them with wisdom and the moral courage to teach others doctrines pointing, nostalgically, as it were, to the Eternal Word soon to be incarnated, the Redeemer and Teacher of mankind. Among such heralds were Socrates, Plato, Aristotle, and Cicero in the West, and Gautama Buddha (b. ca. 563 B.C.), Confucius (551-479 B.C.), Lao Tzu (who was an elder contemporary of Confucius), Mo Ti (who flourished in the fifth century B.C.), and Mencius (371-289 B.C.), in the East.

It is no small wonder that these men of exceptional wisdom, whose influences on human minds are still alive today, should all have been born and flourished within six centuries immediately preceding the Birth of Christ. Their doctrines, it is true, are not unmixed with errors, and even where they were not erroneous they were inadequate and left the human mind at an *impasse*. But this very *impasse* underlined the necessity of the Revelation; while the grains of truth that they contained and shared in common were faint intimations of the Gospel, in whose light alone we can perceive their real significance. In other words, what the pagan philosophers had uttered as desiderata are seen as reality in the Person of Christ.

We Christians must constantly remind ourselves that Christ is not only the Founder of Christianity, but also the Divine Word, the True Light that *enlightens every man who comes into the world*.[2] Thus, the natural wisdom of man, the moral truths that every man discovers in his conscience, the laws written in his heart, come from the self-same Word Who was "conceived by the Holy Ghost, born of the Virgin Mary," suffered in redemption of mankind, and founded the Holy Catholic Church. To know this as an abstract truth is one thing, but to realize it as vibrant reality and to rejoice in the Spirit that it is so, is a quite different thing. Since Christ is the Light of the whole world, the East as well as the West, whatever differences there may be between East and West can only be in the accidentals, not in the essentials; and we may be sure that such differences and varieties as we can find are permitted to exist that they may express the infinite glory of God to the fullest extent possible on earth.

In maintaining, therefore, the theme that Christianity is the only possible synthesis between East and West, our necessary starting point must be the Person of Christ. Christ is the One Reconciler, reconciling men to God and at the same time reconciling men with one another under the Fatherhood of God. In the words of St. Paul, "For it has pleased God the Father that in Him all His fullness should dwell, and that through Him He should reconcile to Himself all things, whether on the earth or in the heavens, making peace through the Blood of His Cross."[3] This is the fundamental Reconciliation, out of which springs the brotherhood of all men. "For He Himself is our peace, He it is Who has made both one, and has broken down the intervening wall of the enclosure, the enmity, in His flesh."[4] This reconciliation flows like a river from the fountainhead of Redemption.

Our present theme can only be viewed against the background of the double reconciliation that Christ has achieved on the Cross. Essentially all true Christians are *new men* in Christ, no more Jew or Gentile, East or West. What we have to synthesize are only certain qualities and modes of thinking and feeling acquired by the peoples of the East and the West in their different courses of history and perhaps also from their respective natural environments.

But before we deal with the theme, a formidable obstacle presents itself to our minds. What do you mean by the East and the West? Each of these terms covers such a wide sphere and includes such a variety of peoples and cultures that any generalizations about them are bound to be contradicted by realities. When you look at a people from outside, you are likely to think that all its members are about the same in character as they are in appearance. But the more intimately you come to know them, the more differences and variations you will discover among them. All types of personalities are to be met with in both the East and the West; in all parts of the world you will find that some are contemplatively-inclined and others actively-inclined; some materialistically-minded and others spiritually-minded; some quick-tempered and others slow-tempered, and so forth.

All comparisons between the East and the West cannot be more than impressionistic, and must be taken as such. My own impression is that on the whole the Occidental mind works more methodically than the Oriental. The former goes step by step, while the latter jumps at conclusions. The former relies upon ratiocination, while the latter trusts in the intuition. The former sees more readily the distinctions where the latter

159

sees only the analogies. The former is more attracted by what is regular, the latter by what is exceptional. The former relies more on one's own effort, the latter more on Providence.

Bishop Fulton Sheen has made a generalization, perhaps as accurate as a generalization can be: "It is apt to be an error of the Eastern World to think that God does everything and man does nothing; it is apt to be the error of the Western World to believe that man does everything and God does nothing. The Oriental thus ends in Fatalism and the Occidental in Pride."

This observation furnishes much food for thought to both of the worlds. Only in Christ is the reconciliation between predestination and free will fully accomplished. The same is true, to a lesser extent, of the Christian saints. The East and the West will not meet except in the bosom of Christ.

Another interesting contrast between East and West is to be found in Father Gerald Vann's book, *Saint Thomas Aquinas*. I suspect that in his desire to call his Western readers' attention to the importance of the interior life, Father Vann has attributed a little too much spirituality to the East. However, the contrast is thought-provoking, and his conclusion that the East and the West are complementary to each other is truly encouraging and illuminating. I take liberty therefore to quote his words at some length, because, except for the idealizing tendency I have mentioned, his words represent my own thoughts, only in a much more beautiful form:

As Father Vann sees it, the East is to the West what Mary is to Martha:

> What, ultimately, is this radical difference of outlook which cuts us off from the east, from antiquity as whole? We shall find its deepest roots revealed to us in the story of Mary of Bethany. People of the west are accustomed to despise the east for its inertia, its lack of enterprise, its inattention to what they regard as progress, the fact that the centuries have not made its streets any cleaner, its sanitation more efficient. They want it, in a word, to be busy about many things. But the east is ready with its retort. *Unum necessarium:* one thing is necessary; and the western world in its hustling concern for material things, its worship of material efficiency, its tendency to think of greatness in terms of captains of industry and grandeur in terms of

material aggrandisement, has forgotten the better part. It is shallow, and vulgar, and meretricious; it is busy about many things but they are the least important things.[5]

All this may be a caricature, but it is one that brings into sharp focus a real difference of outlook on life.

Father Vann further develops his theme by the analogy of the masculine and the feminine:

There is a useful analogy to be drawn between the divergent psychological tendencies of west and east on the one hand, and the male and female types of mind on the other. There are perhaps few people who are psychologically speaking wholly male or female; in the genius the characteristics of both types are united. But in theory at least the two are easily distinguishable. In the male mind there is predominance of reason, concern with the active, the practical, the doing; direction is centrifugal, looking to external achievement. In the female mind there is predominance of intuition, receptivity, concern for being rather than doing; direction is centripedal, the well-being of the object of love rather than the well-doing of other external things. And beneath this confrontation of reason and intuition, action and contemplation, there lies a deeper difference. The active, practical mind tends both to superficiality, that 'externalization' of the mind against which the mystics warn us, and also to self-sufficiency and egocentricity, to absorption in the question, "What am I going to *do*?" The intuitive, contemplative mind, on the other hand, tends rather to despise the just claims of the superficial in its absorption with deeper things; it tends also to forgetfulness of self, it tends to find its happiness precisely in self-loss, to make its chief question, "What is *he* going to *be*?" Consequently, in terms of religion, it is the active mind that tends to moralism, to reduce the relationship of creature to Creator simply to accurate drawing up and observation of rules of conduct; while the contemplative mind puts before these things the quest for self-loss which is on an entirely different plane from ethical unselfishness, and in which indeed it sees the ultimate reason for ethical unselfishness.[6]

But what delights me most is Father Vann's insight that these types not only may but *must* be fused if we are to be full Christians. To quote him once more, "It follows that, as each of these types of mind has its own specific richness and its own dangers, the soundest, fullest, and deepest life is to be found in the fusion of both. There are individuals who achieve this fusion in their own personality; for others it is found in the fusion of two personalities in one, the cleaving of two in one flesh which love effects. And as either in isolation is normally likely to lack balance and completeness, so east and west in isolation are incomplete, and need one another, complement one another."[7]

All this does not really present anything new from the standpoint of the Christian tradition. Who could have been more active than St. Paul? As the Apostle of the Gentiles, he was the pattern of all later missionaries. How full of toil and moil was his life! From what is recorded of his activities in the Acts, and from his own epistles, one can easily see that from the time of his conversion, or at least after his return from his retreat in Arabia, there was not a moment of rest for him, right up to his martyrdom in Rome. In modern parlance, we can say that his missionary works were extremely practical and efficient and successful. But what was the secret of his sanctity and his lasting fruitfulness? To my mind, it was his intensely contemplative life, his close union with Christ, his mystical wisdom, and his spirit of love. In his second epistle to the Corinthians, he revealed his internal landscape in a moment of self-forgetfulness in these words: "For if we were out of our mind, it was for God; if we are sane, it is for you."[8] In my Chinese version of the New Testament, I have rendered this pregnant utterance in words which are more intelligible to the Chinese readers: "If we are inebriated, it is for God; if we are sober, it is for you." But the important point is that if Paul did not love God unto folly, if he had not attained to what Plato had called "divine madness," he could not have been so perfectly sane and sober in his dealings with the world for the sake of the faithful. Only when our interior life has moved beyond reason can we conduct ourselves with perfect reasonableness in the world of human relations. Only when we love God without measure can we fulfill our duties toward men in the full measure.

All the difficulties incidental to the Christian apostolate arise from the fact that we have to live and work in the world, while all the time we are *not of the world*.[9] The realization that we are not of the world but belong to another Kingdom must be the hidden spring of all our activities in the world, if they are to be of any supernatural significance, if they are not to degenerate into sheer activism, which is but materialism in action.

Of course, Love is the bond of perfection; but Love must be purified and sanctified in the truth before it can truly work wonders in one's own soul and in the souls of others. If Love is not adequately illumined and guided by the true doctrine, it is liable to produce bitter fruits. If, for instance, we should go to a pagan country, with all the good intentions in the world, but with the wronghanded idea that its culture belongs to the Devil, then even if we should make a great number of converts, they would not be converts to Catholicism, but rather to Provincialism. This is one extreme to be avoided. The other extreme is for a missionary to become so enamored of a pagan culture that he is in reality no longer a priest of Christ but only a student of ethnology. Both these extremes, with infinite gradation between them, come from the fact that they are not adequately prepared to be missionaries, not having delved deep enough into the inexhaustible heritage of Christian wisdom. This heritage is all comprehensive; it contains all that is true and good and beautiful in the East and in the West. We need only to look at the galaxy of the Doctors of the Church to realize what a variety of types are represented therein. Among them are supreme masters of dogmatic, moral and mystical theology. But due, partly at least, to the unbalanced development of the modern technical civilization, mystical theology does not seem to have received half of the attention that it deserves. St. Thomas is important, but so are St. Bernard, St. Bonaventure, and St. John of the Cross. It is precisely because I am a Thomist that I regret deeply that the other Doctors' writings, especially those of St. John of the Cross, are so little known even among the priests.

But frankly I cannot imagine how anyone can go to the East without being steeped in the mystical theology of our Church as well as in the dogmatic theology. How is one to cope with natural and pantheistic mysticism without being armed with true Christian mysticism? If we want to convert the East, we must first find the real East in ourselves, and I venture to think that the real East is securely in the bosom of the Christian heritage, but we do not realize it, because we seldom probe deep enough into the hidden riches of our Church, and all too often we live on the circumference of the spiritual life.

In the great Encyclical Letter "Evangelii Praecones," Pope Pius XII has summed up all the necessary directives for apostolic works, whether of missionary priests or of missionary laymen. Just as St. Augustine and St. Thomas and others "baptized" Plato, Aristotle, and the Stoics, so we must know how to "baptize" the pagan philosophers of the ancient East and the modern West. As our Holy Father says, "The Church from the beginning has always followed this wise practice: let not the Gospel on being introduced into a new land destroy or extinguish whatever its people possess that is naturally good, just, or beautiful. For the Church, when she calls a people to a higher culture and a better way of life under the inspiration of the Christian religion, does not act like one who recklessly cuts down and uproots a thriving forest. No, she grafts a good scion upon the wild stock that it may bear a crop of more delicious fruit." The Holy Father further says, "Human nature, though owing to Adam's fall it is tainted with original sin, has in itself something naturally Christian; and this, if illumined by divine light and nourished by God's grace, can eventually be changed into true and supernatural virtue. This is the reason why the Catholic Church has neither scorned nor rejected the pagan philosophies. Instead, after freeing them from error and all contamination she has perfected and completed them by Christian revelation."

The whole Encyclical Letter must be studied and pondered and faithfully followed. For our present purpose these quotations will suffice to define the true meaning of "baptizing" the pagan philosophies and cultures.

II

On the whole the mind of the East is more intuitive than the mind of the West. Even Confucius, who is comparatively the most matter-of-fact and scholarly of Oriental sages, goes more by intuition and aesthetical sensibility than by logical reasoning. His doctrine of names, for instance, is really not a logical doctrine, but an axiological philosophy. He thinks in pictures, not in abstract terms. When he says that a father must be a father, he does not analyze "fatherliness" but rather imagines an ideal father who would act in this and that way toward his son. This image is a mixture of the *a priori* and *a posteriori,* of the ideal and the actual. In all his recorded sayings, I cannot find a single definition. All of them contain a judgment of what is appropriate and fitting in a concrete situation of life. He does not try to formulate in definite words the principles underlying his moral judgments. It is only by reading and re-reading his collected conversations that you are able to see directly into his mind.

He kept his mind untrammeled by hard-and-fast rules, so that it could respond freely to the demands of each particular individual. An instance may serve to elucidate further this point. In the time of Confucius, the official music masters were chosen from the blind. One day such a music master called. Confucius went to the door to receive him. When they came to the steps, Confucius said, "Here are the steps." When they came to the mat for the guest to sit down, he said, "Here is the mat." When all were seated, he said, "So and so is here; so and so is there." After the music master had gone, a disciple asked, "Was that the way of conducting an interview with a blind master!" "Yes, indeed," said Confucius, "it is the way to guide a blind master."[10]

As a matter of fact, the way was the result of moral intuition responding directly to the exigencies of the situation.

Now, of all Oriental sages, Confucius is comparatively the nearest to the West, but even he seems miles away from the systematic and methodical ways of the West. However, the average westerner can easily see eye to eye with Confucius in most of his moral judgments. The same cannot be said of the other sages of the East like the Taoists and the Buddhists. Their seemingly wild and trackless speculations are likely to mystify the practical intellect of the West.

For instance, I have heard a learned Western priest say that some of the Taoistic paradoxes in the *Tao Teh Ching* were "nonsense." The truth is that the typically Western mind moves in straight lines, while the typically Eastern mind moves in circles. I shall give some samples of the paradoxes of Lao Tzu:

> Bend and you will be whole.
> Curl and you will be straight.
> Keep hollow and you will be filled.
> Grow old and you will be renewed.[11]

> Truly, one may gain by losing;
> And one may lose by gaining.[12]

> The greatest perfection seems imperfect,
> And yet its use is inexhaustible.
> The greatest fullness seems empty,
> And yet its use is endless.

> The greatest straightness looks like curve.
> The greatest skill seems like clumsiness.
> The greatest eloquence sounds like stammering.[13]

Taoism is not easy to understand. Its emphasis is on the indefinability of the Supreme Reality. It proceeds by the *via remotionis,* while Confucianism proceeds by the *via excellentiae.* Buddhism reenforced Taoism in its full exploitation of the *via remotionis.* The two ways, the one active and moral and the other passive and mystical, were never brought into a real synthesis in the soul of any Chinese, so far as I can judge. They were suffered, as it were, to co-exist in the same soul as a result of compromise, but without any vital unity. Po Chu-i (772-846 A.D.), the most representative poet of China, though not the greatest, summarized his philosophy of life as follows:

> Outwardly conforming to the moral laws of the world,
> Inwardly, I am free from the ties of life.

Like practically all Chinese intellectuals since the coming of Buddhism, Po Chu-i was officially a Confucianist, but at heart sceptical of the cosmic validity of human virtues.

Thus, there is a schism, an unhealing wound, in the soul of

every Chinese. Instead of achieving a true detachment, we have landed in a certain dichotomy inevitable in such a dual view of life.

Only the Christian saints have really synthesized the *via excellentiae* and *via remotionis*. On the one hand, they have lived in this world and loved their fellow men and performed duties of their station with as much earnestness and sincerity as Confucius could ever have desired. On the other hand, they have been as free from the ties of life as the Taoists and Buddhists could ever have hoped for. What is the secret of this marvelous achievement? *The Incarnation of the Word of God, and their union with Him.* The Incarnation is the central event of the universe; human destiny hinges on this one event. This alone makes it possible for us to live in the world and yet have our being in God. This alone unites the Transcendent and the Immanent, and clothes every thought, action and word of ours with an eternal significance. The Incarnation is the only Bridge between the *via excellentiae* and *via remotionis*.

In His earthly life, Christ has taught us by example and precept the way of perfection. This way contains eminently all the best qualities of the East and the West.

When an Oriental reads the Gospel, it is probable that his heart will first be touched by the ineffable tenderness of Christ toward all sinners, except the self-righteous ones. Our Lord combines an eminently feminine heart with an eminently masculine intellect. How many times He must have wept in pity of the infirmities and miseries of men! Even as recorded in the Gospel, He wept in sympathy with the sisters of Lazarus;[14] again He wept "when He drew near and saw the city" of Jerusalem.[15] One of the most touching passages is what Our Lord addressed to Jerusalem:

> Jerusalem, Jerusalem! thou who killest the prophets and stonest those who are sent to thee! How often would I have gathered thy children together, as a hen gathers her young under her wings, but thou wouldst not! Behold, your house is left to you desolate. For I say to you, you shall not see Me henceforth until you shall say, "Blessed is He Who comes in the name of the Lord"![16]

In this connection, neither St. Matthew nor St. Luke says

explicitly that Our Lord wept, but who can help feeling that every word of the whole passage is a crystal of tears? To my mind, it is most significant that Our Lord should have compared Himself to a "hen" rather than to a cock. His Sacred Heart is the heart of a mother. This is borne out by what God Himself had declared through the Prophet Isaias: "Can a woman forget her infant, so as not to have pity on the son of her womb? And if she should forget, yet will I forget thee."[17] Again: "Shall not I that make others bring forth children, myself bring forth? . . . . As one whom the mother caresseth, so will I comfort you, and you shall be comforted in Jerusalem."[18]

One of the most vital things, therefore, that Christianity has revealed to us is the tenderest *maternal* love and care of God for the children of man. The soul of the Orient, if I may judge by my own feelings, is most easily captivated by this attribute of Divinity. Speaking for myself, it was the reading of the autobiography of St. Thérèse of Lisieux that opened my heart to the warm sunshine of Divine grace. The saint of Lisieux knew the motherly Heart of God so intimately and presented it so vividly that my own little heart vibrated violently in response to the mighty waves of Divine Love. There was nothing sentimental about my conversion. On the contrary, it was because the saint focused my interior eye upon the *true* nature of God's love that my heart began to open like a flower to receive the balmy breath of Heaven.

As to the eminently masculine intellect of Christ, I need not enlarge upon it. In my last book, *Fountain of Justice,* I have attempted to expound His philosophy of law from many angles. I have tried to show how infallible is His scale of values, how perfect His logic, how consummate His art of judging, how divinely appropriate His analogies and distinctions. He is the Sun of Justice, Who is to judge the living and the dead. The King of kings, He is also the Judge of judges. What men of genius, what men of science, can ever fathom the infinite profundities and riches of the Wisdom of Christ? All that the saints have thought and written, all that the Church has taught, have been drawn, with the help of the Holy Ghost, from the inexhaustible Fountain of Wisdom, The Word of God.

There is nothing that the human mind has discovered or can discover which is not already in the Fountain of Wisdom in an eminent way. So far the East is more at home in the inexpressible, while the West is more at home in the expressible. But both the inexpressible and the expressible belong to the same Fountain, and the Holy Ghost alone can help us attain a living synthesis, because He alone knows the Mind and the Heart of the Father and the Son.

It was not without reason that the Psalmist should have been inspired to write:

> Clouds and darkness surround Him,
> Justice and right are the foundation
> His throne.[19]

This couplet must never be separated in our contemplation of God, for it presents a whole view. Without clouds and darkness, justice and right, the clouds and darkness would have no foundation.

But there is no denying that the spirit of the East likes to dwell in the clouds and darkness, being afraid that an over-sharp delineation of justice and right might be a futile attempt to confine the Infinite in the finite. On the other hand, the spirit of the West dares not even to lift up its eyes to the clouds and darkness, still less to plunge itself into them, lest its clear-cut notion of justice and right might be lost. The modern West is daring and progressive in everything in the spiritual life. *except*

The only cure for both these groundless fears is to hold fast to the Mystery of Incarnation. If only the Easterner would see that True God has actually lived as True Man; that True God and True Man is one and the same Person, and that it is precisely because He is Infinite that He could be made flesh; then he will understand that our only hope of perfection and divinization lies in the faith in the Divinity of Christ coupled with a whole-hearted followng of His human example. In other words, the Easterner should remember that True God is also True Man. On the other hand, the modern Westerner should remember that Christ is not only True Man but also True God, and being True God, His words and actions during His human life must be envisaged in

169

the light of His Divinity.

In conclusion, let me say that in order to convert the East, we must know how to "baptize" the Eastern culture and philosophy of life. But since the most representative Eastern sages are all mystically inclined, we shall not be able to "baptize" them unless we first delve into a much neglected part of our Christian heritage, the inexhaustible mine of Christian mysticism. To lead the East to Christ, we have to plunge ourselves into "the cloud of unknowing;" we must pray to the Holy Ghost to set our souls free from bondage to the material civilization and technical habits of the modern times. With absolute obedience to our Holy Mother, the Church, as our ultimate safeguard, let us aspire to the liberty of the children of God. The work of the apostolate presupposes on our part an earnest desire to be sanctified in the Truth and to progress without cease in our own spiritual life. It is providential therefore that at the present juncture both the East and the West are challenging us to lead a more interior life: the East, in that we must show it that the kingdom of God within us is the reality of which all its past philosophies have been but foreshadowings; the West, in that only by developing our interior life in proportion to the material civilization can we transmute the deadening weight of matter into a vessel of the Spirit.

If the East does not find the West in Christ, it will never meet the West and love it. If the West does not find the East in Christ, it will never meet the East and love it. If the East is westernized, it becomes worse than the West. If the West is easternized, it becomes worse than the East. If the East and West are married outside of Christ, the union will not last, being the result of momentary infatuation, which will only produce monsters. Only when they are united in the bosom of Christ will they love each other with the love of Christ, and the union give birth to *the new man.*

NOTES

[1] Luke, 3: 4, 6.
[2] John, 1:9.
[3] Colos. 1. 19, 20.
[4] Eph. 2.14.
[5] *St. Thomas Aquinas,* 1940, pp. 4, 5.
[6] *Ibid.,* pp. 5, 6.
[7] *Ibid.,* p. 6.
[8] 2 Corinth, 5:13.
[9] John, 17: 14.
[10] *Ibid.,* 15:16.
[11] ch. 22.
[12] ch. 13.
[13] ch. 14.
[14] John, 11:35, 36.
[15] Luke, 19:41, 44.
[16] Matthew 23:37-39.
[17] Isaias, 49:15.
[18] *Ibid.,* 66:8, 13.
[19] Psalms, 96:2.

WATER AND WINE:
CHINESE ETHICS AND
THE CHRISTIAN FAITH [1]

A beautiful affair was the wedding feast in Cana. Our Lady was there, and so were Jesus and His disciples. Festiveness was in the air, and who can blame the guests if they drank more than usual? Perhaps they should have remembered that the newly wedded were of moderate means. But to remain temperate on such a happy occasion would be an instance of immoderate moderation. The Oriental temper would not have allowed it.

But the fact remains that the supply of wine failed when the spirits of the guests were running high. You can hardly imagine what a terrible embarassment it was for the bridegroom and bride. Our Lady, herself an Oriental, knew what a serious "loss of face"[2] such an untoward event would mean for the new couple. It would remain on their memory like an unsightly scar, thus marring their marital happiness.

Impelled by her unbounded human sympathy, Our Lady rose to the occasion. Knowing that only her Son could save the situation, she approached Him in the lady-like manner so characteristic of her, not by making a direct request, but by passing on to Him an information pregnant with suggestion: "They have no wine."[3] Our Lord gave her a gentle rebuff. "Woman," He said, "what is it to me and to thee? My hour is not yet come."[4] This was the fore-echo, as it were, of that heart-rending prayer He was to utter three years later in the garden of Gethsemani: "My Father, if *it* be possible, let this chalice pass from me."[5]

True Man as He is, how could he help feeling afflicted even at the start of a journey which was to lead to the Calvary? Did His Mother realize this as clearly as He did? I wonder. But being *True God,* could He help being divinely pleased by His Mother's marvelous spirit of charity, which, unimpeded by the barriers of sin, flowed out spontaneously from her Immaculate Heart toward all children of man, especially the poor and needy.[6] Nor was she discouraged by His rebuff; she went ahead to tell the waiters, "Whatever He shall say to you, do ye."[7]

Now, it happened that there were six waterpots standing there, as the Jewish custom of ceremonial washing demanded. They were of stone, holding two or three firkins apiece. Jesus, accommodating Himself to what was already there, said to the waiters, "Fill the waterpots with water."[8] After they had filled each of them up to the brim, Jesus said to them, "Draw out now, and carry to the chief steward of the feast,"[9] which they did accordingly.

In the meantime, the water had been transformed into wine, and when the chief steward tested it, not knowing whence it had come, he called the bridegroom and said to him, "Every man at first setteth forth good wine, and when men have well drunk, then that which is worse. But thou hast kept the good wine until now."[10]

Liturgically, the mystery of water and wine has been made to symbolize human nature and Divine grace. I need only to remind you of the prayer at the Offertory: "O God, Who in a wonderful manner didst create and ennoble human nature, and still more wonderfully hast renewed it; grant that by the mystery of this water and wine, we may be made partakers of His divinity Who vouchsafed to become partaker of our humanity . . . ."

For the purposes of my present discourse, the six waterpots stand for the six cardinal relations of men, as the Chinese ethical tradition has presented them. Confucius and other sages of old China have filled them almost to the brim with the water of natural wisdom, waiting only for us to do the rest and for Christ to turn it into wine. Today I consider myself as one of the humble and willing waiters standing at the beck and call of Our Lord. You will have to play, tentatively at least, the part of the chief steward of the feast. It is hoped that what I carry to you will be wine rather than water. We must remember that today Our Lord and Our Lady are in the midst of us. Our Lady knows only too well that my supply of wine has failed.

Now, what are the six cardinal relations of men according to the natural philosophy of the Chinese sages? Ordinarily, only five relations are mentioned explicitly, namely, father and son, elder brother and younger brother, husband and wife, friend and friend, prince and minister. But in reality there is a sixth, which is implicitly assumed when the Chinese scholars speak of human relations; and that is the relation between the teacher and the pupil. In fact, this last relation was regarded as of transcending importance. To quote from a Confucian classic, "The drum has no special relation to any of the five musical notes; but without it they cannot be harmonized. Water has no special relation to any of the five colors; but without it they cannot be displayed. Learning is not specially related to any of the five senses; but without it they cannot be regulated. The teacher lies outside of the five degrees of mourning; but without his guidance human relations would be devoid of the appropriate affection."[11] The teacher, therefore, may be compared to the conductor of the whole symphony of human relations. It would take too long to enlarge upon the functions of the teacher. I shall confine myself to the other relations.

1. Father and son. In the Chinese classics, very little can be found on the duties of parents toward their children, the emphasis being on the duties of children toward their parents. In no other culture to my knowledge has the philosophy of filial piety been so well developed as in China. Herein lies both the strength and weakness of the Chinese culture.

Confucius himself had a rather balanced conception of filial piety. On one occasion he is reported to have said to a ruler, "A man of true humanity serves his parents as Heaven, and serves Heaven as his parents."[12] But later Confucianists, beginning already with his disciple Tseng Shen, have developed the first part of the remarkable statement to the point of hypertrophy, leaving the second part to atrophy almost completely. In the system of Confucius, filial piety was the starting point of all virtues, with humanity (*jen*) as the ultimate virtue embracing all the others.[13] He himself was a filial child of Heaven, to whose will he became more and more docile as he grew in years. That is why he said that at fifty he had begun to know the will of Heaven, and at sixty his ears had become attuned to the biddings of Heaven.[14]

When we come to the teachings of his disciple Tseng Shen, we find an altogether different atmosphere. Tseng Shen was a good man with a narrow mental outlook. His outstanding virtue was that of filial piety toward his parents. But his ethical philosophy lacks the catholicity and balance and palpitating richness which we find in that of Confucius. He makes filial piety not only the starting point, but also the sum-total of all virtues. Thus, in his system, filial piety takes the place occupied by humanity in the system of his master.

Tseng Shen's philosophy of life, like his character, has the charm of a rugged simplicity. He derived all virtues from filial piety. The underlying reason of our duty of filial love and gratitude toward our parents is that we owe our very bodies to our parents, and therefore we must hold the body as a sacred trust from them. In Tseng Shen's own words, "The body itself being something transmitted to us from our parents, how dare we be careless in the employment of our legacy?"[15] From this fundamental intuition follow all our other duties, such as self-respect, loyalty to the ruler, faithfulness to our friends, conscientiousness in discharging our public functions, in a word, assiduous self-cultivation in all things; for all our attainments and achievements will redound to the glory of our parents, as surely as our failing and lack of character will cast discredit on them.

As you can easily imagine, this was a very practical and down-to-earth philosophy of life, which anyone with average intelligence and strength of character could grasp and make his own. It is little wonder that throughout the later generations up to the beginning of this century this philosophy should have been the dominating feature of the mental landscape of Chinese scholars in general. It furnished the main motive to all their actions; it instilled a meaning to their existence and made life worth living for them. I know this from my personal experience. I was born just early enough to be brought up as a child under this time-honored tradition. I need hardly say that I was not a model child, but the fact that I was not worse was mainly due to the powerful influence of this pivotal principle, which operated both positively and negatively: positively as a stimulus to good actions and negatively as an inhibition of the graver wrongs. I aspired to be a good student in the hope that I might pass not only the school examinations but also the state examinations, for that would bring honor to my parents. I refrained from fighting with my school-mates, because if I inflicted injury upon another, it would bring shame on my parents, while if I was injured, it would bring grief to them.

All this would seem to work very well. On the whole, I must say, juvenile delinquency was practically unknown in those days in China.

But this family-centered philosophy of life has its serious drawbacks, if it is not balanced by the idea of brotherhood of men under the Fatherhood of God. Catholicism preserves the sound kernel of the idea of family solidarity, but at the same time it does not make a god of the family head, as Confucianism has tended to do. In other words, Christianity, while emphasizing also the duty of filial piety, does not allow it to degenerate into clannishness. The teachings of Christ and St. Paul subordinate filial piety on the natural plane under that higher Filial Piety which we owe to the Father of all. Christ's filial love for His Mother lasted up to the very end of His life on earth. I need only remind you of His words spoken from the Cross to St. John: "Behold, thy mother," and to His Mother: "Behold, thy son."[16] How tenderly He loved His Mother! But this did not prevent Him from attending to His "Father's business."[17] and fulfilling His supreme Mission of Redemption of mankind. Nor did Mary's motherly love prevent her from being the willing Co-Redemptrice.

Those of us who have a son with the vocation to be a priest or a daughter with the vocation to be a sister, must sometimes feel *something* of the joys and sorrows of the

177

Blessed Virgin. Usually such a son or daughter is among the most filial of children. Supernaturally you are infinitely grateful to God for deigning to pick up one of your own blood and flesh. You will be saying, "How have I deserved to be the parent of a priest of Christ, or of a spouse of the Divine Bridegroom?" So you will be shedding tears of gratitude and joy. But *naturally,* you will be shedding tears of sorrow, the sorrow of parting, the sorrow of loneliness, and the sorrow of anticipation in the sense that if your child is any good as a priest or as a sister, he or she must follow the Way of the Cross. This natural weakness keeps us humble and the pains we offer to God make us share in the vocation of our children. Our life would be incomplete if we were only blessed with the "Joyful Mysteries," without being graced by the higher blessing of the "Sorrowful Mysteries."

The affection between parent and child increases a hundredfold, when both of them share a whole-hearted love of God. They can strengthen each other in the virtues of faith, hope, and love; they can even correct each other's faults in the spirit of charity. Thus a merely temporary relationship is transformed by grace into an eternal friendship in the Bosom of Our Father.

But I do not wish to be understood as maintaining that the Chinese cultivation of filial piety has nothing to contribute to the lives of many Christians. It does not add anything new to Christianity, but to modern Christians it should serve as a reminder of the fourth Commandment, which, as St. Paul pointed out in special emphasis, "is the first commandment with a promise: That *it may be well with thee, and thou mayest be longlived upon the earth.*"[18] One wonders if the individualistic philosophy of the past few centuries in the West has not eclipsed this important commandment in the lives of the Christians. The Communists have gone a step further. In the words of a leading Chinese Communist, "Filial piety is the first of all evils." I know from this that it will not be well with them, and that their ideology cannot last long upon the earth.[19]

In their practice of filial piety the ancient Chinese went

to heroic lengths. They may have gone a little too far. But some of the moral intuitions uttered by Confucius in this regard belong to the perennial philosophy of mankind. Let us be contented with a few instances. When a disciple asked Confucius how to serve one's parents, the master answered, "According to the modern ideas, filial piety consists in providing the parents with enough to eat. But even dogs and horses are cared for to that extent. If there is no feeling of respect, where is the distinction between the two?"[20] Another disciple asking the same question, Confucius said, "The difficulty is with the countenance. Merely to toil and labor for the old folks and to furnish them with wine and food is not the sum-total of filial piety. Is it?"[21] But why did he lay such stress on the "countenance"? Because the countenance is the index to the interior feeling. The interior feeling is the kernel, but the kernel must grow into a complete fruit. In another classic, we find an elucidation of this point: "When the love of a filial son goes really deep, he will naturally possess a spirit of harmony; when he has the spirit of harmony, he will naturally shed an atmosphere of gladness; when he has the atmosphere of gladness, his countenance and manners will radiate a spontaneous charm and grace."[22] The moral system of Confucius is as practical and matter-of-fact as the Rule of St. Benedict.[23]

Sometimes I think that if only we Christians could serve God with as much sincerity and preparation, as much love and reverence, as many of the Confucian scholars have served their parents, we should really be saints. The greatness of Dom Célestine Lou lay precisely in this, that he had absorbed the whole spirit of filial piety as taught by Confucius and applied it, with the help of the grace and example of Christ, to the serving and loving of our Heavenly Father.[24] In the meantime, he continued to love his country and his parents, not in place of God, but in Him and through Him. Whenever I think of Don Lou, I remember something that St. Thérèse had said: "A heart given to God loses nothing of its natural affection; on the contrary, that affection grows stronger by becoming purer and more spiritual."[25]

By "father and son," the Chinese really meant "parent and child," thus including the mother and the daughter. In the history of China I do not know how many great men owed their upbringing to their mothers. The mother of Mencius, for instance, believed that the education of a child should begin in the womb, and she acted upon her belief.[26] She was the Chinese counterpart of St. Monica, who wept for the sins of her son more bitterly than other mothers weep for the bodily deaths of their children.[27] In the end he became doubly her child, the child of her blood and of her tears.

2. From the relation of parent and child, we pass on to that of brothers. A Chinese regards his brothers as members of his own body. The elder brother normally exercises a protective love over the younger, and the latter looks to the former with a kind of deferential affection. Of course, even in ancient China there were quarrels between brothers. But on the whole I believe that there was a greater sense of solidarity between brothers in China than in any other countries. Let me quote a realistic stanza from an ancient song:[28]

> Within the walls brothers may fight
> But insults from without
> Will their forces and hearts unite
> The common foe to rout.

Even after brothers had married and established families of their own, they usually made frequent visits to each other. The commonest feeling has been expressed by a well-known couplet:

> Every time we see each other we have grown older,
> How many more years can we remain brothers?

The idea is that one lifetime is hardly enough in which to enjoy being brothers and to develop fraternal love. A most famous pair of brothers were Su Tung-po and Su Tse-yu.[29] Both of them were consummate writers, whose essays are still found in contemporary anthologies. They uttered together a joint wish: "May we remain brothers throughout all the future transmigrations of our souls!" This is indeed a beautiful wish based upon the Buddhist faith. The faith may be illusory, as I believe it is, but who will gainsay the intensity of affection as expressed by the tremendous wish?

All this is very beautiful, but I have come to know some

Christian pairs of brothers, whose story is even more beautiful. A few years ago I was thrilled in receiving a letter from a seminarian in Loyola Villa in Wisconsin. I take the liberty of quoting a few lines from it: "I am a Jesuit of some four years now. My vocation came after I had completed my college and had already embarked on my chosen calling, the Law. I accredit this *volte-face* (not really that the vocations are incompatible, but rather the one incorporates the other) to the prayers of my twin brother who entered the year previous." I usually do not quote from private letters, but this event is too joyful to be kept to myself. How deeply these brothers must love each other! The Lord had predestined them to be twins for all eternity. They are closer to each other than the Siamese twins; and theirs is a closeness that does not impede in any way their freedom of locomotion. The Siamese twins may be separated some day, but these twins never. Physically, they may be separated by continents and oceans; spiritually, they will always be united. They are two corpuscles in the Sacred Heart of Christ. We Chinese, as I have said, considered brothers as members of our own body; but alas! how long will our own bodies last? It is only when brothers become in addition the members of the Mystical Body of Christ that they are brothers indeed and for aye.

But let me tell you another story, more wonderful still. Just as I was beginning to prepare this paper, I was favored with the visit of a Jesuit missionary, Father Narciso Irala, S. J. who had just come to America from Formosa. In introducing him, a mutual friend of ours, Mr. Theodore Langen, incidentally mentioned that Father had a twin brother in Rome, also a Jesuit. My curiosity being excited, I pressed the Father to tell the story about their vocations. They were born in Spain. Their mother died when they were three. When they were in their early teens, their father sent them to France to study at a school run by the Christian Brothers. By the time they were fourteen, Narciso began to think seriously of studying for the priesthood. He wanted to be a missionary, and wished to join the Society of Jesus. Tremblingly he confided this secret to his twin brother Antonio. What was his surprise when he heard Antonio say, "I have been thinking about exactly the same thing, and have reached the same decision."

So they went back together to Spain and were admitted into the House of St. Ignatius in Loyola. At nineteen, they took vows together, with their father attending. It was only then that he revealed a tremendous secret. "The first time you were in this house, you were in the womb of your mother, who offered you to God through St. Ignatius!" She thought she was offering one child, but the Lord accepted two from her.

It seems as though St. Ignatius of Loyola specialized in the vocations of twins! But who can tell how many miracles of grace have been due to the prayers and tears of holy mothers!

I know of another pair of brothers, who are at least twins in spirit. The older brother is Monsignor John McNulty, the President of Seton Hall University, and the younger brother is Bishop James McNulty of Paterson, New Jersey. You may be interested to know that both John and James were students at Louvain, and were ordained together in 1925. And their mother is still living.*

But not all brothers need to be twins or priests in order to feel the redoubling of their affection. When Our Lord used me as an instrument for the conversion of my elder brother and my elder sister, I felt, in addition to the natural fraternal affection, a kind of maternal tenderness for them. I told Our Lord, "Now I have borne you some big children, haven't I?" When I converted some of my elder children, I felt that now I was not only their father but also their mother. Sometimes I feel like a younger brother of my children when my faults are discovered by them.

3. From brothers let us pass on to an even more interesting relation, husband and wife. The marriage ceremony of old China was perhaps the most solemn outside of the Catholic Church. But I remember what an old Confucian scholar said to me after attending my eldest son's Nuptial Mass in Shanghai. Archbishop Paul Yupin was the celebrant, and the late Father Beda Chang gave a sermon. The old Confucian scholar was so deeply impressed by the solemnities that he remarked, "This is exactly what our old marital rites had foreshadowed!" In other words,

---

* Monsignor John McNulty died in 1959; Bishop James McNulty is now Bishop of Buffalo: their mother died in 1962. (Editor).

the seeds that Confucianism had sown came into flowering in the Sacrament of Marriage.

In China the good wishes of our friends at our marriage were expressed in some such phrases as: "Wish you two grow old together and live to see grey hairs on each other's head!" "Wish you two to see your children and grandchildren fill your hall!" "This union is made by Heaven!" "May you always love each other like a pair of mandarin ducks!"

All these sentiments and ideals are embodied in the Catholic Liturgy. The two are to "have and hold" each other "from this day forward, for worse, for better, for richer, for poorer, in sickness and in health, till death us part," and they plight their troth to each other, right in front of the Altar. At the exchange of the rings, the Priest calls down blessings of God upon them and prays that they may "ever live in mutual charity." In the Form of Blessing is found this prayerful wish: "May you see your children's children even to the third and fourth generation, and may you attain to a happy old age." In the Nuptial Mass, we find: "Thy wife shall be as a fruitful vine on the sides of thy house."

From this we may perceive that all that man by nature could legitimately wish and desire has a place in the liturgy of the Church. One thing noteworthy is that the Church liturgy seems to be more matter-of-fact than the Chinese counterparts. For the Chinese did not like to mention such things as "death," "sickness," or even "poverty" at such an auspicious occasion as marriage. In fact, "grow old together" was the limit of proprieties, for it was a euphemism for death. The Church could afford to call a spade a spade, because of the assurance of higher hope.

Two things are missing in the Chinese ceremony. One is "What therefore God hath joined together, let no man put asunder." As you know, in certain cases, the old Chinese law permitted a husband to put away his wife, although this privilege was but rarely exercised. The other element which is missing in the Chinese ceremony is the most significant factor of a Christian marriage; it is bodied forth in this expression: "O God, who has hallowed wedlock by a mystery so excellent that in the marriage bond Thou didst foreshadow the union of Christ with the Church." This is the keynote that makes the Christian marriage a Sacrament. The Catholic couple are not only one flesh but one spirit. They are two hands folded together in eternal adoration. The Church, it is true, employs the expression: *"till death us do part."* She has to be very prudent in the use of her language. If she should say "till death us truly unite," it would be absolutely right in the supernatural sense; but it may be misconstrued by the carnally-minded to mean that the couple will remain husband and wife through all eternity. But who can doubt that after a lifetime together of mutual help in their pilgrimage through the valley of tears, of daily Communion and Rosary, of redoubled single-heartedness in the love of Our Lord, or generous co-operation in the rearing of children to the wholesome members of His Mystical Body, and after habituating themselves in the contemplation of the marriage bond as foreshadowing the union of Christ and His Church, who can ever doubt that their souls will be united in eternal friendship in the Bosom of Our Father?

A Chinese proverb runs: "So long as husband and wife love each other, what if they are beggars together?" This saying has a ring of truth about it; its originator must be speaking from his actual experience. But if the natural affection between the two could have such a wonderful effect, how much more wonderful their life would be if they can love each other in God, for God, and through God? Such life would really be like heaven beginning on earth. I am well aware that human endurance has its limits; and that happiness on earth cannot be entirely immune from the stings of fortune. But, as St. Paul has so truly said, the Lord will never try us beyond our strength, and even if great trials should come, He will always increase our strength. Ultimately, sanctity is a matter of trust, of boundless trust, of unquestioning trust, of child-like trust, in God. Without complete trust, the Lord's hands are tied, for even He cannot pour His endless blessings into a closed vessel. On the other hand, if your trust is boundless, His blessings are infinite. If a couple are equally endowed with the virtue of trust, they will encourage each other, whether the weather be foul or fair, in exercising this virtue, with the result that they will grow daily in love and joy, and, even in straitened conditions, they will enjoy in the glorious freedom of God's children.

In the normal marital life in old China, the man and wife did not know each other, at least not intimately, before their wedding; but gradually as they had children their hearts were more and more united by a common love; and finally they became lovers as their friendship grew. This is the direct opposite of the modern romantic love. Nowadays, when two young persons meet and court each other, their love immediately reaches the boiling point. Then they marry and discover each other to be only human beings full of frailties and perhaps selfishness. When an illusion is broken, there comes disenchantment. From disenchantment comes resentment. In such a state, one is most vulnerable to new illusions, whose false splendors make the realities appear even more miserable. The "archangel" becomes a hideous monster; and the "goddess" becomes a female devil. To the romantics, marriage is, in theory and in practice, the "grave of love." Many nominal Christians are romantics in actual practice if not in theory. But the true Catholic philosophy of love is similar to the Chinese philosophy in that it considers wedding as the starting point of love and marital life as a school of love. Only it is far superior to the latter because the common love in a Catholic family is not only of the children but of God. Furthermore, while good Catholics would consult their parents on the choice of their spouses, the final decision rests with them, and not with parents, who only do the counseling. Only those young folks who have ears need to hear.

But even outside of the Church, marital love is meant to be a life-long romance, when things go in the normal way. I have seen a number of old couples in China living happily like pairs of nuthatches sticking together till the end. The sight of such a couple often reminded me of an old "Cockerow Song,"[30] which sang of the wife's joy at the return of her wayfaring husband:

Cold is the wind, chill the rain.
The cock crows *kikeriki*.
Now that I have seen my love,
Peace has returned to me.

The wind whistles, the rain drizzles.
The cock crows *kukeriku*.
Now that I have seen my love,
My sickness is healed too.

The wind and the rain darken the day.
The cock continues to crow.
Now that I have seen my love,
My joy ceases not to grow.

This is the pure water of wedded happiness. But let us have a taste of the wine that Christ has made of the water. Since I came to America, I have had the consolation of seeing many a happy couple; but none is happier than a Belgian couple, Baron and Baroness José da Vinck. They have graciously shown me a sheaf of poems writen by the Baroness. With their permission I take liberty to quote a lovely poem addressed to her husband, José who is an artist:

I love you in the rain and in the wind,
And I dance for you the dance of love
For this short time we are on earth together.
But I love you better than for close and mortal joys,
For the healthy wheat of children we bring forth
As prayers rising toward God.
I love you more than for your gifts and for your peace;
I love you for the One you bear, so radiant and clear,
I love you for the One who carries us
In His unending love.
I love you even now
As my companion of eternity.

What Nature was yearning in unutterable groanings, Christ has made it possible for us to articulate and realize. He comes not to destroy, but to fulfill and transfigure.

4. The relationship of friendship. So far we have been dealing with family relations, strictly so-called. But all human relations aspire to friendship just as all arts aspire to music.

In the history of China there have been innumerable instances of exemplary friendship between man and man.[31] But not the least beautiful is the friendship between Po Ya, the most famous lute-player of ancient China, and his great *connoisseur* Chung Tse

Ch'i.[32] Although Po Ya was admired by the whole world, yet no one else knew the inward vision that inspired his art. On one happy occasion, Chung Tse Ch'i was among his listeners. As he played on the lute, his mind roamed to the high mountains. At the end of the performance, Chung Tse Ch'i exclaimed, "O how sublime! The music soared to the sky like the mountain ridges!" When Po Ya played the next piece, his thoughts were wafted to the flowing streams. Chung Tse Ch'i again exclaimed, "O how beautiful! The sound has ended, but the music goes on like an ever-flowing river!"

Other people appreciated the sound of the music; Chung Tse Ch'i alone saw the inner landscape of the musician. They became bosom friends. But unfortunately, Chung Tse Ch'i died shortly afterwards. Po Ya felt the bereavement so keenly that he cut off the strings and broke the lute. He never played again for the rest of his life.

This touching story portrays the Chinese idea of friendship. In fact, up to now, we speak of a friend as "chi yin," which means "the *connoisseur* of our music." It is to our friends that we pour out our hearts in full strains. For, as Christ Himself has told us, it would be foolish to "cast your pearls before swine, lest perhaps they trample them under their feet, and turning upon you they tear you."[33]

The minimum condition of friendship is that two hearts must meet somewhere. If your heart is set on heavenly things and mine on the things of the world, then we keep our treasures in different places, and there can be no meeting of minds between us. There is a hierarchy of friendships. The lowest order is one which is based upon a common material interest. Much higher is one based upon common moral principles. Still higher is one based upon the sharing together of noble vision.[34]

Of all his students, Confucius had a very special friendship for Yen Hui, because their hearts were perfectly united in a common philosophy of values, and their minds in a common vision.[35] First of all they shared in a sincere love of wisdom. Confucius spoke of himself that "in a hamlet of ten houses, there must be some who are just as loyal and faithful as myself, but there is none who loves learning and wisdom as I do."[36] Of Yen Hui he once told a friend that among his students there was only one true lover of learning and wisdom, Yen Hui, but that unfortunately he was dead. Because they loved wisdom for its own sake, and not as a means to worldly riches or position, they did not mind being poor. Confucius was deeply impressed by Yen Hui's detachment from such things. He once exclaimed, "What a virtuous man is Hui! A single bowl of millet, a single ladle of soup, living in a mean alley! Others felt sorry for him, but Hui himself remained as cheerful as ever! What a remarkable man!"[37] Speaking of himself, Confucius said, "With coarse food to eat, water for drink, and a bent arm for a pillow, I could find happiness even in such a state. As for wealth and honor improperly obtained, they are to me like a fleeting cloud."[38]

But most important of all, they had in common a child-like confidence in providence. Once as Confucius was traveling with a group of his students in a foreign state, they were surrounded by threatening forces sent by the ruler on account of some misunderstanding. Confucius continued to play his lute and sing as if nothing were happening. Everybody was scandalized by his spirit of *insouciance,* but not Yen Hui.[39] Confucius called them one by one and put to each of them the same question, as a test: "An old ode has it: 'We are no rhinoceroses, we are no tigers. How is it that we find ourselves roaming the wilds?' Now, tell me, is it because our Way is wrong? Why has it brought us to this pass?" After receiving a few answers, which showed how little the pupils saw eye to eye with him, he called in Yen Hui and put to him the same question. Yen Hui said, "Your Way is extremely great. That is why the world cannot contain it, but this is no cause for worry. Precisely because the world cannot contain and tolerate our Way, we are assured that it is a noble Way. The trouble is with the world, not with the Way." Confucius smiled affably and said, "Is that so? Oh, son if you were a rich man, I would like to be your butler."[40] Yen Hui was to Confucius what Chung Tse Ch'i was to Po Ya.

We are all pilgrims on earth. We too need like-minded friends to strengthen our faith, to share our joys and sorrows, to encourage each other on the way of perfection. In the meantime, our friendship must be supernaturalized and sealed by a higher

Friendship. Who is the Supreme Friend whom we share in common? Who else could it be but Christ? "Greater love has man none than this, that a man lay down his life for his friends."[41] To whose blood do we not owe our true life? It was neither Paul, nor Appollo, nor Peter, nor all the martyrs combined, which gave birth to the new man in us. Christ alone has redeemed us with His Blood; and the Holy Ghost alone understands us perfectly, not only our conscious intentions, but also our unconscious groanings, unknown even to ourselves. Ultimately all our friendships, to be of value, must spring from God and return to Him.[42] Therefore, no human friendship can be closer than the friendship between the saints. In spirit all of them have leaned "on the bosom of Jesus." (John, 13: 23 and 25.) All of them have listened to the music of His Heart, and perceived more or less clearly His internal landscape. To the extent that they are friends of Christ, to that extent they are friends of each other. Their mutual affection is preserved and constantly renewed by their common love.

I need hardly tell you what beautiful friendships have existed between the saints. The Blessed Virgin and St. Joseph represent the summit of human friendship. There are other friends like St. Ambrose and St. Augustine, St. Francis of Assisi and St. Clare, St. Thomas Aquinas and St. Bonaventure, St. Theresa of Avila and St. John of the Cross, St. Aelred and the holy Simon, St. Francis of Sales and St. Jane Frances of Chantal—it would take too long to talk about the mutual help and encouragement they received from each other in their journey of life. But the unique privilege of a Catholic, in this regard, is to find friends even in the Blessed ones.[43]

One of the qualities of friendship on which the Chinese sages have laid the greatest emphasis is that of constancy and permanence in the face of the vicissitudes of life. Here again we find the fulfillment in Christ, Who, having loved His own during His life on earth, "love them unto the end."[44] What is more, the end is only a beginning. Let me quote some words from Father J. P. Arendzen's essay on "Heaven, or The Church Triumphant:"

> Among the Blessed themselves there will be the fellowship begotten of mutual respect, admiration, and intimate intercourse. Moreover, human nature is still human nature, however glorified. There will be

ties of friendship between the saints. St. Augustine has met St. Ambrose and rejoiced. St. Francis has met St. Clare, and found delight in converse with her. We also shall find among the saints in heaven our friends whom we loved and venerated on earth. Christ on earth formed friendships, though he possessed the Beatific Vision. He loved John, Mary and Martha and Lazarus. So, too, among the Blessed friendships will persist . . . . The unbroken comradeship with those of our own nature and race is part of the complete development of our manhood. In the center of this fellowship is Christ in his human nature, for the Incarnation remains forever the link by which men are bound together. In Christ we are all brethren, not merely on earth, but throughout eternity.[45]

Here the yearning of the "soaring mountains" and "flowing streams" is fulfilled beyond all dreams. Here, what "the world could not contain" finds ample room in the house of many mansions. Like all human relations, friendship finds its consummation only in Christianity.

It is important to point out that there is nothing static or exclusive about friendship. No, it is dynamic and expansive. In the end, friendship merges into the Confucian virtue of humanity, which is the natural counterpart of the Christian charity. Confucius described the virtue of humanity in these terms: "Being established yourself in the way of truth, you wish to help others to be likewise established. Having thoroughly understood the way of truth, you wish to help others to attain the same understanding. To be able to explain it by drawing analogies from things near at hand is a part of the art of humanity."[46]

Now, this comes pretty close to the Christian initiative in the making of friends. It has been said that the only way to make a friend is to *be* one. A true apostle, whether priestly or lay, offers his friendship to every man. He is everybody's friend without becoming "nobody's friend." The secret is that having the Friendship of Our Lord, he loves all men as He does, but does not rest his happiness upon being understood and loved by them. If the Lord gives him some friends, he is consoled and grateful for it. But if the Lord takes them away, he would not break the lute, because he can still play to the Lord. Only in this way can you be a true friend of anyone who would accept your friendship. What is more, a Christian apostle not only makes friends for himself but causes others to be friends with each other. Like St. Francis, he will sow love where there is hatred, sow pardon where there is injury, sow faith where there is doubt, sow hope where there is despair, sow light where there is darkness, sow joy where there is sorrow. He is so utterly overwhelmed by the supreme consolation of the Divine Friendship that in his intercourse with others he can afford to seek not so much to be consoled as to console, not so much to be understood as to understand, not so much to be loved as to love. All that he desires is to share Christ with others.[47]

This is the summit of the Christian ideal of life. But before we reach the summit, there is a great need of friends who can help each other in the climb. There is a touching scene between two disciples of Confucius, which may edify us. Tse Hsia lost his son and was so overwhelmed by grief he lost his eyesight. Tseng Sheng came to condole with him, saying, "As I have heard, when a friend loses his eyesight, we should wail for him."[48] As Tseng Sheng started wailing, Tse Hsia also wailed and in a moment of anguish he said, "O Heaven, wherein have I offended?" Upon hearing this complaint, Tseng Sheng was moved to anger, and said, "Sheng, how can you say that you have not offended? You and I served the Master between the two streams, Chu and Hsi, but after his death you retired and grew old in the neighborhood of the Western River, where you made the people compare you with the Master. This was one offense. When you lost your parents, people heard nothing about it. This was your second offense. When you lost your son, you mourned so much that you lost your eyesight. This is your third offense. And yet you say, 'Wherein have I offended?'" Tse Hsia threw down his staff and bowed, saying, "I was wrong, I was wrong. It is a long time since I isolated myself from the community of my friends and lived all alone here."

Such sincerity on one side and readiness to admit fault on the other are possible only when both of them shared the same principles and the same object of love and devotion. We find the Christian counterpart of such sincerity and generosity in the friendship of St. Peter and St. Paul.[49]

Such friendships are absolutely necessary if we are to perfect ourselves, and to prosper in our apostolic work. You cannot comb hair aright without a mirror. Nor can you see your faults without the mirror of your friends. It is especially important for missionaries and native priests to enter into close friendships. Due to their diverse cultural backgrounds, their ways of thinking and doing things are bound to be different. They should therefore seek to associate with each other as much as they can, so that they can see each other's strong points and weak points. When they have sufficient mutual affection, they should not hesitate to speak to each other with absolute frankness. In the meantime, they should practice the utmost humility and generosity toward each other. If a man is not capable of rising above nationalities, he is not fit to be a Christian, much less a priest or a lay apostle. On the other hand, if you go to a foreign country as a missionary and love its people as your own, the people will love you and love the Lord Who has made such great love possible. Nay, more, they will also love the country which is capable of producing such a great lover. Then you are a true patriot, for by seeking the kingdom of God even before your own country, you render honor to your country in the eyes of the nations. This leads us to our next topic.

5. Prince and minister. On this relationship hangs a whole system of political philosophy. I can only touch upon one of its problems here, namely, the foundation of political authority. With all his respect for authority, Confucius was no positivist or absolutist. To him, political authority is not based upon force, but upon virtue. Theoretically, he justified this doctrine by the logic of names or concepts. But in reality his logic is saturated with ethical connotations. For example, he declared that the prince, to be worthy of the name, should behave like a true prince, and the minister, to be worthy of the name, should behave like a true minister.[50] He held that the root of all evils in his time was that the prince is not like a prince, the minister not like a minister, the father not like a father, the son not like a son. This way of employing names or concepts as rule and measure of realities is akin to St. Paul's way when he wrote to Timothy to "honor widows that are widows indeed," for "she that liveth in pleasures is dead while she is living."[51]

In other words, the mere physical fact that a person held the position of a prince is not enough to make him a prince in the proper sense of the term. A prince, properly so-called, must possess princely virtue. Confucius was emphatic on this point. To be a ruler, one must be straight in oneself. A ruler who is not straight is a contradiction in terms. Confucius could be very brusque in his dealings with political superiors. Once, a powerful officer who was noted for corruption, came to consult Confucius as to how to cope with the rising tide of robberies and thefts. The answer of Confucius was: "If you yourself, Sir, were not greedy, the people would not steal even for a reward."[52]

Throughout the ages, the Confucian scholars have seldom failed to maintain their moral dignity vis-à-vis the sovereign and other political superiors. They were guided by the principles of justice and rectitude, sanctioned by their age-long tradition. They believed in the existence of an immutable moral law ordained by Heaven and therefore superior to the will of the king.[53] For them, kingship and public offices were instituted for the well-being of the people, not for oppressing the people. Once a king asked Mencius whether it was true that certain ancient kings were banished and overthrown by their ministers or subjects. Mencius answered, "So it is in the histories." "May, then, a subject put his sovereign to death?" asked the king. Mencius' reply was: "He who outrages humanity is called a robber; and he who outrages justice is called a ruffian. The robber and ruffian we call a mere fellow. I have only heard of executing a mere fellow for his monstrous crimes, but I have not heard of murdering a monarch in these instances."[54] To him, "The noblest element in a country is the people; next in order come the Protecting Spirits of the land and grain; the lightest in the scale of importance is the ruler."[55] In a memorable interview with King Hsuan of Ch'i, Mencius expounded his philosophy of government as a trust which may be withdrawn when the trustee has proved unequal or unfaithful to his duties.[56]

The Confucian scholars were respectful toward their sovereigns, but when moral issues were involved, they would sooner sacrifice their heads than compromise their principles. There have been a goodly number of martyrs of principle throughout the history of China. Let one instance suffice. In 1402, a famous

Confucian scholar, Fang Hsiao-ju, was executed for refusing to draft rescripts for a usurping emperor. "You can kill me, but cannot make me draft the rescripts." He threw the brush on the ground.[57]

The philosophic faith which furnished the moral backbone to the Confucianists is presented in a nutshell in the words of Lu Ku'en (1538-1618): "There are only two things supreme in the world: One is Reason, the other Authority. Of the two, Reason is the more supreme. When one gives voice to Reason in the Imperial Court, even the Emperor cannot suppress it by his authority. And even when Reason is temporarily suppressed, it will always triumph in the end and will prevail in the world throughout the ages."[58]

This reminds us of a fine passage which R. W. Chambers has written in his book on Thomas More, who "died for the right of the individual conscience, as against the State."[59] I quote:

> The problem of what is due to the individual conscience, what to the State, is indeed an eternal one, and not a few people have been surprised and distressed to find it emerging in Europe today, as much alive as ever it was. 'Wherefore our battle is immortal, and the gods and angels fight on our side, and we are their possessions . . . . And the things that save us are justice, self-command, and true thought, which things dwell in the living powers of the gods.' (Laws, bk. X.). So wrote Plato, naming three of the four Cardinal Virtues on which Utopia is founded—Fortitude is the fourth. Plato's fine words do not solve the problem for us; every man at need must do it for himself, for the ability to weigh two duties, and balance them against each other, is the measure of human worth and dignity. It rings through the *Antigone* of Sophocles as it does through the *Apology* of Socrates, and nowhere will it be found more clearly than in More's writings in prison. It was as one of a mighty company that on Tuesday, 6, July 1525, he spoke on the scaffold his last words and told them that they should pray for him in this world, and he would pray for them elsewhere, protesting that he died the King's good servant, but God's first.[60]

We find the same philosophy, the same faith, and the same Spirit working in the modern martyrs in Asia[61] as well as Europe. Let one instance suffice. Father John Tung, in opposing the Communist campaign to isolate the Catholics in China from the Mystical Body of Christ, declared, in a public speech, among

194

other things, "I am today required to attack the representative of the Holy Father. Tomorrow I shall perhaps be forced to attack the representative of Jesus Christ, the Holy Father. The following day why should I not then be constrained to attack God Himself?" He further said, "If I live by deceit and fear death, I become a completely untrustworthy man, of use to no one. . . . I am a Catholic and desire to love both my country and my religion. I do not wish discord between the two, but if the government cannot work harmoniously with religion, persecution will follow and many victims will be demanded from among Catholics. In such an event it is better that I die right now."

Father Tung, like St. Thomas More, was the country's good citizen, but the Kingdom of God's first.

But there is a passage in Father Tung's speech which is peculiarly Chinese in flavor. "Gentleman," he said, "I have but one soul, which I cannot share with you, but I have a body which may be divided. So it seems to me the best thing for me to do is to offer my soul in its entirety to God and His Holy Church, and my body to the country. If she should desire it, I will not refuse it to her. Good materialists, who deny the existence of the soul, cannot but be satisfied with the sacrifice of my body." The spirit is the spirit of a Christian martyr; the mode is the mode of a Chinese scholar. With Father John Tung, the waterpot has been filled to the brim, and Christ has made it into wine. There is a prophetic note in Father Tung's speech, when he declared: "A Christian who is capable of denying his God, will be only too ready to betray his Church and his country. The Communists have a saying: 'For one man who falls ten thousand will rise.' And could a Catholic forget that the blood of martyrs is the seed of Christians?"

During the last fifteen years, I don't know how many holy priests and good Christians have been martyred in my country and elsewhere, and how many are still waiting for their turn in jail. Truly this is the worst persecution that our much persecuted Church has ever suffered. But just as the persecution has been terrible so the harvest will be terrific. Of the conversion of my country there is absolutely no doubt in my mind. The important thing is for us survivors to live in the spirit of the martyrs, and to

195

put every ounce of the energy into the great mission of spreading the reign of Christ in the hearts of all men. This is an age in which in order to remain Christians we have to become saints.[62] This is the age of the Holy Spirit, Who alone can form the living image of the Son in us, to the greater pleasure and glory of Our Father. Let us beseech Our Lady to hasten again the hour of Our Lord. In the meantime, we must fill our water-jars to the brim, that Christ may change the water into wine. For it is only by developing our humanity as fully as we can, that we may hope to be partakers of His Divinity.

Even before the Incarnation of His Son, God had created human nature and ennobled it by endowing it with the natural moral law appropriate to it. It is to the discovery and elaboration of this natural moral law that the Chinese philosophers have dedicated all their attention and energies. Their findings have not been entirely free from errors and exaggerations, but their efforts have not been in vain. If the Greeks excelled in speculative philosophy, and the Romans excelled in jurisprudence, the Chinese have developed an ethical philosophy which is second to none outside of the Revealed Religion.

A. N. Whitehead, in his *Science and the Modern World,* has traced the marvelous development of the modern scientific civilization to its origins in the medieval Scholasticism. According to him, the habit of definite exact thought which made the scientific movement possible "was implanted in the European mind by the long dominance of scholastic logic and scholastic divinity."[63] "When we compare this tone of thought in Europe with the attitude of other civilizations when left to themselves, there seems but one source for its origin. It must come from the medieval insistence on the rationality of God, conceived with the personal energy of Jehovah and with the rationality of a Greek philosopher."[64]

Speaking of the Chinese civilization, Whitehead, while pointing out the lack of the above-mentioned tone and habit of thought as the principal cause of the meagerness of its scientific achievements, has nevertheless expressed a high appreciation of its other aspects. "For example," he wrote, "the more we know of Chinese art, Chinese literature, and of the Chinese philosophy of life, the more we admire the heights to which that civilization attained. For thousands of years, there have been in China acute and learned men patiently devoting their lives to study. Having regard to the span of time, and to the population concerned, China forms the largest volume of civilization which the world has seen."[65]

Time has come for Christian scholars to explore systematically the rich mine of natural wisdom of life in the culture of China and other countries in the Orient, in order to "baptize" them as our medieval predecessors did with the Greek and Roman cultures.[66] As Bishop Fulton Sheen has so well said, "The distance from nature to grace, from sin to salvation, from doubt to Faith, is the same for a Western soul as for the Eastern soul, for only Christ's grace can bridge the distance. From this point of view, Confucius can be just as good a starting point for the discovery of Our Divine Lord as Aristotle. It is conceivable that he may even be better, at least to the extent that his ethics is more personal, more intimate and existential. It would be a great mistake for our Western world to feel that the East must study Aristotle, before it can come to the Faith."[67]

To this I wish only to add one more word. Although grace does not dispense with nature, nature can fulfill its destiny only by receiving the blessings of grace and the leavening of the Spirit. Without the supernatural uplift any natural system of ethics, however high it may be, tends inevitably to degenerate and to decay and die. As the chief steward of the feast so candidly put it, ordinarily people serve the better wine first and when the guests have well drunk they begin to serve the worse kind. Partly because of this inherent tendency of all things human, and partly because of our contact with the secularized part of the West, Chinese ethics has been rapidly decaying for more than a century. In the sage words of Celso Cardinal Costantini, we can only "conserve and deepen the ancient national Chinese culture by giving it the rejuvenation of Christianity."[68] In so doing we are at the same time helping Christianity to fulfill its historical mission in the whole world.[69]

NOTES

[1] This paper is an extension of a discourse delivered on May 25, 1958, at the World Conference on Christian Humanism, in Brussels.

[2] The Chinese expression "loss of face" demands some explanation. "Face" is not as superficial as is commonly supposed. The word corresponds exactly to the Latin *"persona"* which originally designated a mask but gradually took on the meaning of the human person. So the word "face" actually means dignity of a man in his social relations. The "loss of face" implies that one does not play his role well as a member of society. Thus, the wine running short on such an occasion as a wedding would indicate that the host fell short of his role. Such an event would be remembered and talked about for a long time. At any rate, that is what would have happened in China, and I have no reason to doubt that it is the same with the Jews. It was, therefore, for a serious reason that the Blessed Virgin saw fit to intervene.

[3] John, 2:3.

[4] John 2:4.

[5] Matthew 26:39. The *total humanity* of Our Lord is one of the strongest proofs of our faith. As St. Paul says, "For we have not a high priest who cannot have compassion on our infirmities, but one tried as we are in all things except sin." (Hebrews, 4:15.)

[6] There is in each of us an inexhaustible fountain of sympathy and empathy. The purer we are, the more intense is the fire of charity. As the Blessed Virgin was purity itself, her compassion is without limits.

[7] John, 2:5.

[8] *Ibid.*, 2:7.

[9] *Ibid.*, 2:8.

[10] *Ibid.*, 2:10.

[11] *Li Chi* (The Book of Rites), in "Hsueh Chi" (On Education).

[12] *Li Chi,* in "Ai Kung Wen" (The Questions of Duke Ai).

[13] "Humanity" signifies the perfect realization of the nature which man has received from God. All other virtues and qualities are satellites of Humanity.

[14] *Analects,* 2:4.

[15] *Li Chi,* "Chi-i".

[16] John, 19:26, 27.

[17] Luke, 2:49.

[18] *Ephesians,* 6:3.

[19] One of the songs that the Communists in China have taught the people to sing is:

> I don't want papa,
> I don't want mama
> I want only Kuo chia.

[20] *Analects,* 2:7.

[21] *Ibid.,* 2:8.

²² *Li Chi,* "Chi-i" (The philosophy of sacrifice).

²³ The Rule of St. Benedict has it: "The twelfth degree of humility is that the monk, not only in his heart, but also in his very exterior, always shows his humility to all who see him." Dom Paul Delatte comments: "If humility be really in the heart it will be like a new temperament, a nature made in humility replacing the old. This external manifestation is a thing natural and necessary; it is the very consequence of our oneness of being." *The Rule of St. Benedict: A Commentary by The Right Reverend Dom Paul Delatte,* tr. Dom Justin McCann (Latrobe, Pennsylvania, 1950), p. 127.

²⁴ Dom Célestine Lou, *The Ways of Confucius and of Christ.* (London: Burns Oates, 1948).

²⁵ *The Story of a Soul,* ch. 9.

²⁶ See Albert R. O'Hara, S.J., *The Position of Women in Early China.* This book deserves to be better known.

²⁷ Cf. St. Augustine's *Confessions: A New Translation,* by Francis J. Sheed, p. 42.

²⁸ *Shih Ching* (Book of Songs), in "Minor Odes," poem 4.

²⁹ Lin Yutang has produced a monograph on *Su Tung-po: The Gay Genius.* The Su lived in the 12th century, and formed one of the most illustrious families in the literary History of China.

³⁰ *Shih Ching,* in "Kuo Fung," the Poem is called "Fung Yu" (Wind and Rain).

³¹ In old China, noted friendships existed only between men. A friendship between a man and a woman, outside of the family circle, was inconceivable, because it was against all social conventions. On the other hand, in the West there have been many instances of a profound friendship between a man and a woman, especially among the saints.

³² *Lü-shih Ch'un-ts'iu,* 14.2 Little is known of these friends except that they were contemporaries of Confucius.

³³ Matthew, 7:6.

³⁴ There is a hierarchy of visions. As St. Thomas has pointed out, "According to philosophers, the entire system of the cosmos, complete with all its causes, may be delineated at the soul. This, they maintain, is the last end of man. We, however, set it in the vision of God, for, as Gregory remarks, for those who see him who sees everything, what is there they do not see?" Disputations, 11 de Veritah, 2. (In Gilby, *St. Thomas Aquinas: Philosophical Texts* Oxford, 1951, p. 391.)

³⁵ It seems to me that Confucius had only one friend, in the proper sense of the word, among his numerous disciples, and that was Yen Hui. While other disciples had a perception of some of the Master's qualities, Yen Hui comprehended his personality as a whole. Yen Hui once said with a deep sigh, "The more I gaze up to his wisdom, the higher it soars, The harder I bore into it, the more impenetrable it becomes. I see it in front, and suddenly it is behind. The Master knows how to lead me on step by step. He has broadened me with arts and letters, and restrained

me with moral precepts and rites. Even if I wished to stop, I could not. After I have exhausted all my resources, there still looms something overtoppingly before me which prevents me from following him further." (*Analects,* 9:10.) It was because Yen Hui had such a profound comprehension of the personality of his Master that he began to perceive its transcendental dimension. But the very recognition of the wall is the beginning of the break through. True friendship borders on mysticism, which understands by not understanding. You know your friend as intimately as you know yourself; and just as you are a mystery to yourself, so is your friend. This is because in the deepest core of every person is a divine spark, which defies all human understanding.

[36] *Analects,* 5:27.

[37] *Ibid.,* 6:11.

[38] *Analects,* 7:15.

[39] See *Kung Tzu Chia Yü,* ch. 12

[40] *Ibid.*

[41] John, 15:13.

[42] In his essay on "Friendship," Emerson says, "The condition which high friendship demands is ability to do without it." To my mind, this condition is completely fulfilled only in the cases of two souls that love God more than they love each other.

[43] Although all the saints in Heaven are our friends, yet each of us has a special psychological conditioning which impels him to have a predilection for certain saints. Jacques Maritain, for instance, has a special friendship for St. Joseph Labré.

[44] John, 13:1.

[45] Canon George D. Smith, *The Teaching of the Catholic Church,* II, p. 1264.

[46] *Analects,* 6:28.

[47] In this sense, we can say that the more we share the Lord with others, the more profound will be His friendship with us.

[48] *Li Chi,* ch. 3.

[49] Galatians, 2:11, 21. 2 Peter's Epistle, 3:15, 16.

[50] *Analects,* 12:11.

[51] 1 Timothy, 5:6.

[52] *Analects* 12:18.

[53] Paul K. T. Sih's article on "The Natural Law Philosophy of Mencius," in *New Scholasticism,* 317-337; and my own essay on Mencius in this volume.

[54] *Mencius,* Bk. 1, Part 2, ch. 8.

[55] *Ibid.,* Bk. 7, Part 2, ch. 14.

[56] For this interview cf *Ibid.,* Book 1, Part 2, ch. 6. and see also p. 27 of this book.

[57] "Life of Fang Hsiao-ju" in *Ming Shih* (The History of Ming Dynasty).

[58] Shen Yin Yü, Livre I, Part 1.

59 Chambers, *Thomas More*, p. 400.

60 *Ibid.*

61 See Monsterlcet, *Martyrs en Chine;* Cary-Elwes, *China and the Cross;* Jean Lefevre, *Shanghai: Les enfants dans la ville* (Paris: Casterman, 1956.) Father John Tung, ordained at Fribourg, was a priest of the archdiocese of Nanking. (Editor: The latest news about Father Tung is that he is still alive somewhere in West China.)

62 The challenge of our age is so great that we are faced with the necessity of a new decisiveness. Either we accept the challenge wholeheartedly or we hold up our hands and surrender. More than ever are the words addressed to the Church of Laodicea appropriate now: "I would that thou were cold or hot." (*Apocalypse*, 3:15).

63 Whitehead, *Science and the Modern World*, p. 13.

64 *Ibid.*

65 *Ibid.*, p. 6.

66 See Thomas Berry, "Our Need of Orientalists" in *World Mission,* 1956, 301-314.

67 Bishop Fulton Sheen, in his generous "Introduction" to my pamphlet, *From Confucianism to Catholicism.*

68 See John C. H. Wu, *Beyond East and West.*

69 See *Evangelii Praecones.* An excellent comment on this encyclical is to be found in Bishop Stanislaus Lo Kwang, "La culture chinoise et l'encyclique Evanvegelii Praecones," in *China Missionary Bulletin,* (March, 1952), pp. 167-173.

THE SCIENCE
OF LOVE*

1. Love and Science

Shortly before his death, Goethe said to Eckermann, "Let mental culture go on advancing; let the natural sciences go on gaining in depth and breadth, and the human mind expand as it may —it will never go beyond the elevation and moral culture of Christianity as it glistens and shines forth in the Gospel!" Since these words were uttered, more than a century has passed during which the natural sciences have made tremendous progress, and psychology has probed deep into the darkest nooks and corners of the human mind. But have we gone beyond the elevation and moral culture of Christianity? No. Christianity still continues to shine as the Morning Star and will continue to shine to the end of time. In fact, as Pope Pius XI pointed out, "It might even be said that a knowledge of Nature will serve as an introduction to what is of far greater value, an understanding of things supernatural. The more science grows, the nearer we shall be to a living Faith. Material civilization is a welcome fuel to the fire of love. If the fire is weak, it may be smothered by the fuel. But if the fire is strong, the more fuel it has to feed on, the brighter will be its flame."

I have just read a love song of ancient China:

> A quiet girl,—oh, she is charming!
> She gave me a roseate flute.

---

* First published in *T'ien Hsia Monthly*. Vol. X, No. 4. April, 1940. (Editor).

Oh, how splendid are the colors of the flute!
How they chime in with the beauty of the girl!

From the pastures she brought me rush-wool,
Beautiful and rare indeed!
Oh, rush-wool, you would not be so lovely,
If you were not the gift of my love.

I wonder what a modern girl would present to her lover. Instead of a roseate flute, she might give a motor-car or a radio set. Instead of rush-wool, she might give a piece of brocade or even a gorgeous rug. The important thing is love, and so long as love is there, what difference does it make how it happens to manifest itself. If there is any difference at all, one would prefer a radio to a roseate flute, and brocade to rush-wool. Love has nothing to lose and everything to gain by the continual progress of civilization. And how can science ever supersede Christianity, which is the Religion of Love par excellence?

To my mind, the most beautiful exposition of the philosophy of Love is that of St. Paul. Let me present it in my own paraphrase:

Love is patient. Love is kind. Love is free from envy, free from vanity, free from pride, free from ambition, free from self-seeking, free from anger, and free from resentfulness. Love finds no joy in the errings of others, but is gladdened by goodness and truth. Love bears all things, believes all things, hopes all things, and endures all things. Love is a living fountain that never dries up.

No one is more gifted than St. Paul, and no one knows better that all gifts are of no account if they are not lit up by the flame of Love. He expresses this perfectly when he says:

I may be able to speak all the languages of men and of angels, but if I have no love, I am no better than a noisy gong or a clanging cymbal. I may be able to prophesy, I may fathom all mysteries, I may possess all knowledge, I may even have such faith as would move mountains, but if I have no love, I am nothing. I may distribute all my goods to feed the poor, I may even offer my body to be burnt, but if I have no love, there is no virtue in these actions.

The whole trouble with modern civilization seems to me to lie just in this: There is too much love of science and too little science of love.

"The science of love!" exclaimed little Thérèse. "Ah! sweet is the echo of that word to the ear of my soul! I desire no other science than that. For the sake of love, having given all my riches, like the spouse in the Canticles, I feel as though I had given nothing. There is nothing except love which could render us agreeable to the good God. This is so plain to me that this love has become the sole treasure upon which I set my heart."

To give all and to reckon it as nothing—that is the acme of love!

2.   Some Types of Saints: Martha and Magdalen

Now, to Christians, there is no other way of loving God than by loving Jesus His Son, for it is through Jesus that God has revealed Himself to man. The Word took on flesh in order that all flesh might take on Divinity. The incarnation of the Word has humanized the relation between the Creator and the creature. For human purposes, to love Jesus is the same as to love God, for Jesus is God.

But what exactly is God to us? Is He our Father? Yes, He is our Father, but He is more than that. Is He then our Mother? Yes, He is also our Mother, but He is more than that. He is, besides, our Friend, our Brother, our Sister, our Spouse, our Lord, our Minister, our All! His relation with us is so all-embracing that it includes all the five relations of men and something infinitely more. We may call Him this or that; but all these names are used analogically, for human language has its limits, beyond which it can no longer denote anything definite and can at best only hint. So long as we use them only as hints, all names of human relations can be applied to God, and with equal appropriateness.

Do you remember the question of Jesus, "Who is My mother and who are My brethren?" Pointing to His disciples, He said, "Behold My mother and My brethren. For whosoever shall do the will of My Father that is in heaven, he is My brother, and sister, and mother." So Peter, the rugged fisherman, was to Him not only brother, but sister and mother as well! This is how God uses human language, which is intrinsically so poor that there is no adequate term to designate our relation with Him, with the result that He Himself has to resort to figures of speech, to borrow, as it were, from human relations.

Now, of all relations, the dearest and the most fundamental is, at least according to the Chinese way of thinking, that between man and woman. It is, then, no accident that many saints, and among them some of the greatest, purest and sweetest, speak of their relation with God in terms of the Bridegroom and the bride. This is the highest offering that human speech can make to God. What more fitting language can we use towards Him than what we find in the Canticle of Canticles? "Let him kiss me with the kiss of his mouth: for thy breasts are better than wine, smelling sweet of the best ointments." "I found him whom my soul loveth. I hold him: and I will not let him go till I bring him into my mother's house, and into the chamber of her who bore me." "My soul melted when he spoke."

All saints have one thing in common, their love of God; and yet there are saints and saints. Some love Him primarily as their Father, some as their Lord, some as their Friend, some as their Brother, and some as their Lover. From these initial differences in their ways of loving Him arise different types of saints, for whom He provides many mansions in His House. In the home in Bethany, for instance, Martha loved Him in one way, while her sister Mary loved Him in another way. St. Luke has given us a very vivid account of these sisters:

> Now it came to pass as they went, that He entered into a certain town: and a certain woman named Martha received Him into her house. And she had a sister called Mary who, sitting also at the Lord's feet, heard His word. But Martha was busy about much serving, and she stood and said: "Lord, hast Thou no care that my sister hath left me alone to serve? Speak to her therefore, that she help me." And the Lord, answering, said to her: "Martha, Martha, thou art careful, and art troubled about many things. But one thing is necessary. Mary hath chosen the best part, which shall not be taken away from her."

Both Martha and Mary are saints, but the former served Jesus as her Lord, while the latter loved Him as her heart's adored. In the Feast of Life there are many dishes, and each of us will have to choose for himself, but there is no question that Mary chose the best dish.

What a great lover Mary Magdalen was can be gathered from another account of her in St. Luke's Gospel:

One of the Pharisees asked Him to dinner, and entering the house of the Pharisee He reclined at table. Now there was a woman in the town who was a sinner, and when she found out that Jesus was at a table in the house of the Pharisee, she brought an alabaster flask of perfume and stood behind Him at His feet in tears; as her tears began to wet His feet, she wiped them with the hair of her head, pressed kisses on them, and anointed them with the perfume. When his host the Pharisee noticed this, he said to himself: "If He was a prophet, He would know what sort of woman this is who is touching Him: for she is a sinner." Then Jesus addressed him. "Simon," He said, "I have something to say to you." "Speak, Teacher," he said. "There was a money-lender who had two debtors; one owed him fifty pounds, the other five. As they were unable to pay, he freely forgave them both. Tell me, now, which of them will love him most?" "I suppose," said Simon, "the man who was most forgiven." "Quite right," He said. Then turning to the woman He said to Simon: "You see this woman? When I came to your house, you never gave me water for my feet, while she has wet My feet with her tears and wiped them with her hair; you never gave Me a kiss, while ever since she came in she has kept pressing kisses on My feet; you never anointed My head with oil, while she has anointed My feet with perfume. Therefore I tell you many as her sins are, they are forgiven, for her love is great; whereas he to whom little is forgiven has but little love." Jesus appreciated the love of Magdalen so deeply that after His Resurrection it was to her that He made the first recorded appearance!

But why have I dwelt so long upon Magdalen? Because she is the prototype of Thérèse of Lisieux. She knew the art of love. Having given all, she feels as though she had given nothing. Thérèse herself has said: "Most of all do I imitate the behavior of Magdalen, for her amazing—or rather I should say her loving

—audacity, which delighted the Heart of Jesus, has cast its spell upon mine."

3.   Love: Natural and Divine

Like Magdalen, Thérèse loves Jesus as her Betrothed. With touching candor she writes: "Eight days after I had taken the veil our cousin Jeanne was married to Dr. La Néele, and at her next visit I heard of all the little attentions she lavished on her husband. I was greatly impressed, and I determined it should never be said that a woman in the world did more for her husband than I for my Beloved. Filled with fresh ardor, I strove with increased earnestness to please my Heavenly Spouse, the King of Kings, Who had deigned to honor me by a divine alliance." In a letter to her sister Céline, she says: "Let us make of our heart a garden of delights, where our sweet Saviour may come for repose; let us plant therein beautiful lilies of purity, for we are virgins . . . and then let us not forget that 'virginity is a complete indifference to all earthly cares; not only to useless cares, but to all cares . . . .' " Elsewhere she says: "The great saints have worked for the glory of God, but I, who am only a very little soul, I work for His pleasure alone. I wish to be, in the hands of the good God, a floweret, a rose of no use, but of which the sight and fragrance will nevertheless be to Him a refreshment, a little joy superadded." One seems to hear the voice of Magdalen herself.

It often occurs to me that a woman's love, as a rule, is deeper and more constant than that of a man. For, as Laurence Housman so fairly puts it:

> O! a man's love is strong
>   When fain he comes a-mating.
> But a woman's love is long
>   And grows when it is waiting.

Woman is not only more patient, but has also a greater capacity for suffering and self-sacrifice. No one has depicted her lot better than John Masefield:

> I know a woman's portion when she loves,
> It's hers to give, my darling, not to take;
> It isn't lockets, dear, nor pairs of gloves,
> It isn't marriage bells nor wedding cake,
> It's up and cook, although the belly ache;
> And bear the child, and up and work again,
> And count a sick man's grumble worth the pain.

If only a woman would turn her natural capacity for unselfish love from man to God, she would already be at the very portals of Heaven.

Thérèse was born with a genius for love, extraordinary even for a woman. Her affection for her parents, her sisters, her cousins, and her neighbors, was as deep as it was strong. Her sympathy for the poor, her compassion for sinners, revealed itself early in life. She had a heart on fire with love, and she was destined to be united with God. Even as a child, she was conscious of her high destiny, but she was not proud, because she knew that her high destiny was a free gift from her Lover. She was as humble as she was gifted. Nature and grace conspired together to make a great saint of Little Thérèse, for nature prepared her to be a great lover, and grace led her to love the Holy Face. It was not Jesus transfigured on the Mount of Tabor, it was Jesus on His way to Calvary, that especially captivated her soul. As she said: "My devotion to the Holy Face, or rather all my piety, has been based on these words of Isaias: 'There is no beauty nor comeliness in him; we have seen him, and there was no sightliness in him . . . . Despised and most abject of men, a man of sorrows, and acquainted with infirmity; his face was as it were hidden and despised, whereupon we esteemed him not.' I too desired to be without glory or beauty, 'to tread the winepress alone,' unknown by any creature." This confession is of paramount importance, for it seems to me to constitute the keynote of her character. I even think that there is a tinge of chivalry in her love of Jesus. "For many serve Him when He gives them consolation, but few consent to bear Him company when He sleeps on the storm-tossed waves, or when He suffers in the Garden of Gethsemani. Who, then, will serve Jesus for Himself? Ah! it shall be Thérèse." What a gallant lover this woman was!

It was St. Francis de Sales who said: "Love equalizes lovers," and I have a suspicion that Jesus appreciates loving audacity much more than cold courtesy on the part of His friends. Thérèse called her Divine Spouse a thief, a fool, a blind lover who is ignorant of arithmetic; and Jesus loved her all the more, because on the lips of little Thérèse, they were terms of endearment. How deeply she felt for Jesus can be inferred from a little anecdote. Someone gave her a crucifix. She kissed it with tenderness, and said: "He is dead. I like it better when He is represented as dead, because then I think that He suffers no more." Only a woman could have felt that way.

4.   Sincereity as the Soul of Love

Thérèse loved her Divine Spouse for His own sake, not for the sake of His diamonds. All that she desires is to rejoice the Heart of Jesus. She wins Him by her secret caresses, for she knows that He is a bashful Bridgegroom who would blush at caresses too dramatically performed. She gently insinuates herself into His Heart, until she knows all its ins and outs. The wise serpent that she is, she bores sinuously into the deepest recesses of the Sacred Heart of her Beloved, and yet she never wearies Him by overloading Him with attentions. She holds Him by not using any ropes or "hoops of steel." She even confides this to Mother Mary:

> All that He hath given me may Jesus take again,
> O tell Him, Mother, ne'er to feel in aught constrained with me;
> He may hide Him if He will, in peace shall I remain
> Till the Day that knows no setting, when faith shall cease to be.

This was written when she felt Jesus was far away from her. But love has hopes unknown even to faith. She knew Him too well to fear that He would ever desert her. The subtle child wrote to her sister Pauline: "The glory of Jesus, that is my whole ambition; my own I abandon to Him, and if He seems to forget me—well, He is free to do so, since I am mine no more, but His. He will weary sooner of making me wait than I of waiting for Him!" Not that she relies upon her own charms, but that she has a boundless confidence in His goodness. The Almighty is incapable of being unfaithful to His lovers. Just because the little Thérèse did not want any reward, how amply He has rewarded her! She did not want to shine like jades and resound like bells. She wished to be an obscure grain of sand, too small to be trodden upon even by the feet of men; she wished to remain a hidden flower whose fragrance is for Him alone. But He is not to be outdone in generosity. He has transformed the grain of sand into a radiant star gleaming with a thousand fires; He has filled the whole universe with the fragrance of the little fugitive flower. One wonders what she feels now. I should think that she would still feel as she did when she was on earth, "I am but a tiny soul whom Almighty God has loaded with His favours—still I cannot boast. See how this evening the tree-tops are gilded by the setting sun. So likewise my soul appears to you all shining and golden because it is exposed to the rays of Love. But should the divine Sun no longer shine, it would instantly be sunk in gloom." Is this false modesty? No, she is only telling the Truth and nothing but the truth. Any one who knows the power and love of God as intimately as she does, any one who has a glimpse into the infinite greatness of God and his own nothingness, simply can no longer boast, even if he would.

5. God as a Lover

I sometimes think of God as a Lover who knows how to tease. For it frequently happens that if you want a thing He will purposely hold it back from you, and if you do not want a thing, He will purposely give it to you. Like all true lovers, He wants to know whether your love for Him is genuine and pure. But unlike other lovers, He can never be deceived by any insincere manifestations of love. If He really seeks you out, He will send trial after trial until you are completely emancipated from all earthly ties and worldly desires. But Thérèse was such a teachable child that for her a whispered hint was enough where for others God would have had to send thunderous warnings, if not hailstorms. She turned every little experience of her brief life to good account. Her mind was like an extremely sensitive film that records the slightest movement of grace. No lesson was lost on her. She was so thoroughly saturated with the Holy Spirit that everything became for her a parable of the Truth and a symbol of Love. In twenty-four years she learned more about God than mankind has been able to do in twenty centuries. Indeed, as she says: "Love can take the place of a long life." "It seems to me that the good God has no need of years to accomplish His work of love in a soul; one ray from His Heart can, in an instant, cause His flower to blossom for eternity." How many of us, for instance, have been emancipated from the dominion of that hydra-headed monster called Public Opinion? But little Thérèse killed the monster at the very first encounter when she was sixteen. Here is what a sister records about her:

It often happened that painful remedies had to be applied to her side, and one day, having suffered from them more than usual, she was resting in her cell during recreation, when she overheard a sister in the kitchen saying: "Soeur Thérèse will not live long, and really I wonder sometimes what our Mother Prioress will find to say about her when she dies. She will be greatly puzzled, for though the little sister is very good she has certainly never done anything worth speaking about." The infirmarian, who had also overheard what was said, turned to the saint and remarked: "If you relied on the opinion of creatures you would certainly be disillusioned to-day." "The opinion of creatures!" she replied, "happily God has given me the grace to be absolutely indifferent to it. Let me tell you something that showed me once and for all how much it is worth. A few days after my clothing I went to our Mother's room. 'Mother,' remarked a lay-sister who happened to be there, 'this novice certainly does you credit. How well she looks! I hope she may long be able to observe the Rule.' I was feeling really pleased at the compliment when another sister came in, and looking at me, said: 'Poor Soeur Thérèse, how very tired you look, you quite alarm me. If you continue like this I am afraid you will not be able to keep the Rule very long.' I was then only sixteen, but the incident made such an impression on me, that I never again set store on the variable opinion of creatures.

Confucius once said: "He who feels no irritation when others misunderstand him—is he not a gentleman?" But this is easier said than done. Only when one is completely attached to God can one achieve a complete detachment from the world and from one's self. Little Thérèse, whose great passion was the love of God, could afford to disregard all other things. All her virtues are streamlets flowing from one living Fountain. Happy souls who could say: "Our Lord's Will fills my heart to the brim, and if anything else be added it cannot penetrate to any depth, but, like oil on the surface of limpid waters glides easily across. If my heart were not already brimming over, if it needed to be filled by the feelings of joy and sadness that follow each other so rapidly, then indeed it would be flooded by bitter sorrow; but these quick-succeeding changes scarcely ruffle the surface of my soul, and in its depths there reigns a peace that nothing can disturb."

6.   The Martyrdom of Love

The more I study the character of Thérèse, the more she fascinates me, and the more I adore that supreme Artist of Souls, Jesus. What a remarkable girl she must have been who could write at fifteen words like these: "Love can do all things. The most impossible tasks seem to it easy and sweet. You know well that Our Lord does not look so much at the greatness of our actions, or even at their difficulty, as at the love with which we do them. What, then, have we to fear?" This reminds me of a Chinese proverb: "So long as man and wife love each other, what if they are beggars together?" For the sake of her Divine Spouse, she was willing to suffer any form of martyrdom and reckon it as nothing. To her, life becomes a continual martyrdom, a great bundle of little sacrifices. She wants to be a martyr without appearing to be one. Her heroism reaches such a height that it no longer seems heroic but quite ordinary. She has, by precept and example, deepened, subtilized, and broadened the idea of martyrdom, and she has achieved it for herself and for other souls by subordinating everything to Love."Far from being like to those great souls who, from their childhood, practice all sorts of macerations, I made my mortification consist solely of breaking my will, keeping back a word of retort, rendering little services without making much of

them, and a thousand other things of this kind." With her, martyrdom is not simply to be beheaded or to face the firing squad, or
even to jump into boiling oil. Such opportunities are, after all,
very rare, and given only to the privileged few. But there is the
daily life to live; and as love feeds on sacrifices, it would be starved
to death if we should wait for chances of making big sacrifices. In
her hands, our everyday life acquires a new dignity and a new
meaning. What George Herbert had sung she put into practice:

> Who sweeps a room as for Thy laws,
> Makes that and th' action fine.

For God really does not need our sacrifices, they are useful only
as proofs of our love for Him. If we love Him with a burning passion and single-hearted devotion, everything we do or refrain
from doing, every word we speak or refrain from speaking,
becomes a little sacrifice, which may be likened to a fragrant
flower, because we offer it with a cheerful countenance and a
sweet smile that captivate the Heart of God.

There is a Chinese saying: "If you fail in painting a tiger, the
result is liable to turn out a dog; whereas if you fail in carving a
swan, the result may at least resemble a duck." It is safer for
little souls to imitate little Thérèse, than to imitate the giant saints
of yore. For the swan and the duck are birds of one feather;
while the tiger and the dog, according to our Chinese notion,
belong to entirely different orders.

And after all, is our blood so valuable that it can add anything
to the Blood of Christ? What does a tiny little drop mean to an
infinite ocean? And yet, when necessary, our blood is useful as a
humble token of our love for God, but only as a token and not as
an end in itself. In other words, the Martyrdom of Love absorbs
all other forms of sacrifice and mortification and adds something
new, over and above. "Many make themselves victims to Justice,
while none think of making themselves victims to love." Needless
to say, she was not the first to practice this form of martyrdom.
All saints are more or less martyrs of love. But there is no denying
that she, or rather the Holy Spirit working in her, brought this
fundamental aspect of Christian doctrine to a more intense focus
and clearer articulation.

Sanctity is like a pyramid. The higher the apex, the broader the base, and the larger the bulk. The pyramid of Thérèse has Love for its apex, nature for its base, and all the circumstances of our everyday life for its bulk. With her the greatest simplicity goes hand in hand with the greatest diversity. By embracing the One, she embraces all!

In a truly remarkable essay on "What Religion Means to Me," Madame Chiang Kai-shek has presented the nature of Christian simplicity in a nutshell. "Life is really simple, and yet how confused we make it. In old Chinese art, there is just one outstanding object, perhaps a flower, on a scroll. Everything else in the picture is subordinated to that one beautiful thing. An integrated life is like that. What is that one flower? As I feel it now, it is the will of God." I quote these words, because they seem to fit the life of Thérèse like a glove.

7. "A Baby Who is an Old Man"

Her life was not a simple melody, but a marvelous symphony. If she is a child, she is a subtle one. If she is as simple as a dove, she is also as wise as a serpent. Her little way of spiritual childhood is really the most mature way, and she seems to be aware of it. During her serious illness, she once said: "Let God play the part of Papa; he knows what is best for baby." Her eldest sister Marie asked her: "Are you a baby?" Thérèse looked serious and said: "Yes—but a very wise baby! A baby who is an old man." Is she then proud? No, no one realizes better than she where all her wisdom comes from. "My special favorites in Heaven are those who, so to speak, stole it, such as the Holy Innocents and the Good Thief. There are great saints who won it by their works. I want to be like the thieves and to win it by stratagem—a stratagem of love which will open its gates to me and to other poor sinners. In the Book of Proverbs the Holy Ghost encourages me, saying: 'Come to Me, little one, to learn subtlety!'" The charming thing about it is that it is an open theft. God allows her to steal into Heaven because she allows God to steal herself. "How willingly would I help the 'Divine Thief' to come and steal me. I see

Him in the distance, and I take good care not to cry out: 'Stop, Thief!' On the contrary, I call Him, saying: 'This way, this way!'" Lao Tzu said: "Established Virtue looks like a thief." I suspect that there is something thievish, illusive or paradoxical about the Spirit of Truth, and perhaps that is why all His children are, as Paul says, "as deceivers and yet true; as unknown and yet known: as dying and behold we live: as chastised and not killed: as sorrowful, yet always rejoicing; as needy, yet enriching many; as having nothing and possessing all things." The subtlest truths can only be felt or experienced, but cannot be reasoned about, still less talked about. Thérèse the subtle child knows it. "It is related in the Lives of the Fathers of the Desert that one of them converted a public sinner whose misdeeds had scandalized the entire country. Touched by grace, this sinful woman was following the saint into the desert, there to do rigorous penance, when, on the first night of her journey, before she had even reached the place of her retreat, the links of life's chain were broken by the vehemence of loving contrition. The holy hermit at the same time saw her soul borne by angels into the bosom of God. That is a most striking illustration of what I would express, but these things are beyond words." Her mind is truly like Providence in a watchful state. It is not she, but the Holy Ghost that is speaking through her.

The progress of psychology in our age has made man self-aware to a degree never before reached. The remedy is not to return to unconsciousness, which is impossible, but to go a step forward until we find God in the most secret chamber of our heart. To cure ourselves of urbanity, it is useless to dream of returning to the country. Even if we should go to the country, we would still carry the city with us. We have already gone too far to retrace our steps. We must be so urbane that we become citizens of the City of God, which exists before both the city and the country ever did. My only wish is to see people so thoroughly sophisticated as to be aware of the utter worthlessness of their sophistication, so thoroughly sceptical as to be able to doubt their own doubts, and so thoroughly disillusioned as not to fall in love with their own disillusionment, but with something greater than themselves.

216

J. W. N. Sullivan says in his *Limitations of Science:* "Certainly the most significant factor in the development from amoeba to man seems to us to have been the increase in consciousness. "The great artist, painter, poet, or musician, makes us aware as we have never been aware before. He extends and subtilizes certain elements of our experience and so gives us greater knowledge and mastery of life." To my mind, Thérèse is so significant to the spiritual life of our age, precisely because she is a saint fully aware of her mental states. She is charmingly subtle and subtly charming. She is ingenuously ingenious, and ingeniously ingenuous. She is as humorous as she is holy. She is as complicated as she is simple. She is delicately audacious, and audaciously delicate. She has the head of a witch, and the heart of an angel. She is as flexible as water, and as passionate as fire. She is a genius who knows how to hide her genius gracefully. She knows the masculine, but keeps to the feminine. She is as sharp as a two-edged sword, but she always keeps her sword in its scabbard. She was a precocious child, but she pasteurized her precocity by always remaining like a hidden sprout and not rushing to early ripening. Even now, after she has become a veritable prodigy of miracles, she is still a hidden sprout at heart; and, in spiritual things, as we know, a sincere disposition of heart is all that matters. I think that now more than ever she has realized the truth of what she said before she had shed her mortal coils: "It is Jesus who does all, and I . . . I do nothing."

I suppose that Lao Tzu would have said: "It is the Tao (the Word) that does all, and I . . . I do nothing." But the Tao is such an impersonal entity that it appears to me to be of the ice, icy: whereas Jesus is such a living flame of love that He enkindles every fibre of my heart. To me as a Chinese, the great thing about Christianity is that it combines the profound mysticism of Lao Tzu with the intense humanism of Confucius. It differs from Taoism in that the Tao or the Word has taken on flesh and a warm pulsating heart. It differs from Confucianism in that it is the Word, and nothing short of the Word, that has done so. The Confucian idea of God is personal but narrow, while the Taoistic idea is broad but impersonal. In my humble opinion, God is more than a Person, and for that very reason He is capable of assuming a

Personality. Those who think otherwise seem to place themselves above God. They presume that they alone can possess personalities, but not God. Only Christianity can satisfy my mind completely, because its idea of God is at once broad and personal. And it is Thérèse who has confirmed my faith in my religion, for her mind is as subtle and detached as that of Lao Tzu, while her heart is as affectionate and cordial as that of Confucius.

8. Emancipation Through Love

By choosing to be a willing captive of Love, she becomes as free as a bird in the air. As she grew more attached to her Bridegroom, she became more and more detached from everything else. From her early childhood she possessed a deep insight into "the hollowness of things that pass away." "Was Jesus not my only friend?" she wrote about her early days: "To Him alone could I open my heart. All conversation with creatures, even on holy subjects, wearied me. True, sometimes I felt sad because of the indifference shown me, but I would console myself by repeating this line from a beautiful poem Papa often recited for us: 'Time is thy barque and not thy home.' "
Thus, she looked at the world *sub specie eternitatis* (in the light of eternity). This general outlook on life prepared her for detachment from particular things, however much she might be affected towards them in her heart. She detached herself successively from dependence upon creatures, from love of the beauties of nature, from the allurements of art, and from the possessive instinct, not only in regard to material things, but also in connection with what she calls "spiritual riches." "If I had been rich, it would have been impossible for me to have seen a poor hungry man without giving him straightway something of my goods. So also in the measure that I gain my spiritual treasure, I at the same instant think of those souls who are in danger of falling into hell, and I give them all I possess, and I have never yet found the moment in which I could say: 'Now I am going to work for myself.' " A novice has recorded a little anecdote about her: "I was regretting a pin which I had been asked for, and which I had

found most useful. 'How rich you are,' she said; 'you will never be happy!' " What volumes of meaning are contained in this gentle reproach! A person may be rich with a pin, but poor with a million. So long as one is not spiritually detached from matter, the possession of a single pin would bar him from the highest Heaven. On the other hand, if one regards matter as only a means of helping others, the possession of even the whole world could do no harm to his soul, for he is still "poor in spirit." To another novice, she expounded her doctrine of empty-handedness:

> There is but one means to compelling God not to judge us: we must take care to appear before Him empty-handed. It is quite simple: lay nothing by, spend your treasures as fast as you gain them. Were I to live to be eighty, I should always be poor, because I cannot economize. All my earnings are immediately spent on the ransom of souls. Were I to await the hour of death to tender my trifling coins, Our Lord would not fail to discover in them some base metal, and they would certainly have to be refined in Purgatory.

According to her, one must be detached from one's religious exercises: "You ought to detach yourself from your own personal labors, conscientiously spending on them the time prescribed, but with perfect freedom of heart. We read that the Israelites, while building the walls of Jerusalem, worked with one hand and held a sword in the other. This is an image of what we should do: avoid being absorbed in our work." Is this not what Lao Tzu meant when he said: "Do your work without setting any store by it?" What the hoary philosopher of China learned from the experience of a long life the green maid of France learned from the School of Love. Love, generous love that knows no measure, set her free and gave wings to her soul. "O my little sister," she said to Céline, "let us be detached from earth, let us hover over the Mount of Love, where dwells the beautiful Lily of our souls. Let us detach ourselves from the consolations of Jesus, that we may be attached to Him alone!" In her hands, detachment has reached a heroic degree. I have an impression that she is detached even from the idea of detachment! The fact is that she is detached even from herself. "That which concerns Thérèse," she said, "is to abandon herself, to surrender herself completely."

And as she has immolated herself, there is nothing to which even the idea of detachment can be attached. She is a vessel, pure and simple, of the Holy Ghost, that's all. God alone has taught his little spouse "to scale the sublime heights of perfection with the agility of a fawn!"

Thérèse has not superseded the other saints, but she has brought sanctity up to date. She is a revolutionary who knows how to effect reforms by way of transformation. The Holy Catholic Church is a living organism, it grows with the centuries, and our twentieth century, which may be called the age of psychological subtlety, has need of a saint like Thérèse, for she is one of the keenest psychologists and the most ruthless analyst that I know of. In her hands, sanctity is no longer merely sublime, it has seeped down like water into the subliminal regions. The Holy Ghost has always raised new saints to forestall and cope with the needs of a new age. It was no accident that in the sixteenth century, the age of dawning individualism, He raised Teresa of Avila, a woman who was a man. Nor is it for nothing that this time He has raised "a baby who is an old man." For our century is an old man who wants very much to be a baby, and the little Thérèse has shown the way. Sensitive, intuitive, paradoxical, humorous, subtle, flexible and ethereal, she did for spiritual life what some of the greatest contemporary minds have done in their own spheres of activity.

9. The Art of Life

When she was in Rome, she made a visit to the famous cemetery "Campo Santo." She has left us a beautiful word-picture of the place:

> The "Campo Santo" filled us with rapture. The whole vast enclosure is covered with marble statues so exquisitely carved as to make one fancy that the chisel of genius has actually imparted life. The apparent negligence with which these wonders of art are everywhere scattered is but an additional charm. Their expression, too, so perfectly portrays a calm and Christian sorrow, that one is almost tempted to console them. Here it is a child throwing flowers on its father's grave, and as the delicate petals seem to fall through its

fingers, the solid nature of the marble is forgotten. Elsewhere a widow's light veil, and the ribbons that bind some young maiden's tresses, appear to float at the bidding of the breeze.

What genius had done to those marble statues, the Divine Sculptor was to do to her character. At first glance, she, too, appears "to float at the bidding of the breeze," but in reality no one could be more solid than this "Little White Flower" of Jesus. It was her hard living that made her so easy to live with. If Thérèse had been a member of the home in Bethany, she would have served Jesus as carefully as Martha did and at the same time cast furtive glances at Him to see whether He was completely happy with Mary sitting at His feet. She would also have loved her sister all the more for having loved Jesus so much. This I infer from what she said herself, "If, by an impossibility, God Himself did not perceive my good acts, I should not be troubled. I love him so much that I would give Him pleasure by my love and my little sacrifices without His perceiving that they come from me. Seeing and knowing, He is, so to speak, obliged to make me a recompense . . . and I would not put Him to that trouble!" The heavier her tasks, the more cheerful she would have appeared. How easy it is to overlook solid virtue hidden beneath an exterior of charming simplicity!

In the art of letters, it is said that hard writing makes easy reading. For true profundity looks limpid. The azure sky is unfathomable, and yet how clear it looks! Justice Oliver Wendell Holmes, for instance, was not only a great jurist but also a great writer. Justice Felix Frankfurter once wrote about his judicial writings: "In their impact and sweep and freshness, his opinions have been a superb vehicle for the views they embody. It all seems so easy—brilliant birds pulled from the magician's sleeve —but it is the delusive ease of great effort as well as great art." Holmes himself wrote to me about style in writing: "When you read Tennyson you feel that he has been carefully searching for the exquisite. When you read Shakespeare you feel as if the splendid speech came without effort, because that was the way he wanted to talk. Stevenson searches for a happy word. Kipling rips an unusual word out of the bowels of the dictionary and on his lips it sounds as natural as slang." Indeed, the greatest art is to conceal art. On the other hand, there is a great deal of truth in what Popocurante in Voltaire's *Candide* remarked à propos a concert: "This noise is amusing for half an hour; but if it lasts longer, it wearies everybody although nobody dares to say so. Music nowadays is merely the art of executing difficulties, and in the end that which is only difficult ceases to please. Perhaps I should like the opera more if they had not made it a monster which revolts me." What is true of music, sculpture and writing is also true of the Art of Life. No one could be more fastidious than little Thérèse in observing the severe Rule of the Carmel. And yet she always appeared light-hearted and contented. As her sisters have testified, "She always appeared gracious and smilingly cheerful, and unless one knew her more intimately, one might imagine that she pursued an easy path full of consolations. This is how it is that many who read her life do not discern the meaning of her smile: they overlook the cross so carefully hidden under the flowers." In a very real sense, to take Holy Orders or to enter a Carmel is already martyrdom. What bigger offerings can one make than to sacrifice all the pleasures of the world and cut off all earthly ties for the sake of God? That Thérèse did not regard her vocation as a sacrifice but a privilege did not make it less a sacrifice in the accepted sense of the word. But how shallow are the hearts of men, and how easily taken in are their minds! Even now, as Father Mateo Crawley-Boevey says, "Some people still imagine that our sweet saint lived her Carmelite life like a nightingale in a grove, singng of Our Lord's tenderness to her and of her own love for Him. She is, indeed, like a nightingale, but let us not forget that, like a nightingale, she sings with her throat against a thorn!" "Should my roses be gathered from amid thorns," she says, "I will sing notwithstanding, and the longer and the sharper the thorns, the sweeter will grow my song."

10. A Self-Revelation

On one occasion a sister remarked to little Thérèse: "They say that you have never suffered much." With a smile she pointed to a glass which contained some medicine of a bright red color.

"Do you see this little glass?" she said. "One would suppose it contained a most delicious draught whereas in reality it is more bitter than anything I take. Well, it is the image of my life. To others it has been all rose color; they imagine that I have drunk of a most delicious wine, but to me it has been full of bitterness. I say bitterness, yet, after all, my life has not been sad, because I have learned to find joy and sweetness in all that is bitter." I think this is the fullest self-revelation Thérèse has given us in a moment of self-forgetfulness. It allows us to have some glimpses into her evasive personality. I seem to see three different layers in her wonderful soul. The layer that lies nearest to the surface is symbolized by her sweet smile. To all appearances she is a care-free sprite! This aspect of hers puts me in mind of a poem by Tu Fu:

> Rows upon rows of flowers
> In the little garden of Madame Huang!
> All the branches are heavy-laden
> With the countless clusters of flowers.
> The carefree buterflies loiter around them,
> And start dancing from time to time.
> The lovely orioles are intoxicated with freedom
> "Cheerio, Cheerio!" they sing.

But probe a little deeper, and you come to the second layer, the layer which is composed of bitterness and sandy desolation. It makes me think of an autumnal song by Hsin Ch'i-chi:

> When I was young and a stranger to Sorrow,
> I loved to gaze from a high terrace:
> I loved to gaze from a high terrace
> To give my new poems a spice of Sorrow.
>
> Now I have drained Sorrow to the bottom,
> I can find no words for it:
> I can find no words for it,
> But merely say: "What a nice cool autumn!"

What pathos, what desolation, what loneliness, what macerations of the heart are revealed by this second stanza, which borders almost on silence! And this is exactly what I find in the second layer of the soul of Thérèse. But, my patient reader, let us probe yet a little deeper, and we shall find in the depths of her soul a fathomless tranquility and serenity, completely unruffled by all the stormy disturbances she experienced a little higher up in her extremely sensitive mind. It is here that we find the hidden Fountain of her joy; a joy that filters patiently through a sandy stratum and issues finally in distilled smiles and sometimes even in spontaneous spurts of congenial humor. Without the sandy stratum, the smile would not be so pure and sweet. Without the hidden Fountain of joy, the smile would have been pathetic, like the silver lining of a black coffin, or like the hysterical laughter of a mad person. But having both the sandy stratum and the Fountain of joy within her, she is at once inebriated and sober! And she is aware of it herself. "Deep down in my soul there is, I own, a joy and transports of delight." With what moderation and mellowness she owns her secret joy! In her little bosom are borne the sorrows of all time and the joy of eternity.

11. The Logic of Love

I confess that at times I am astonished by some of the lightning-like flashes of her insight. But no one could be more astonished than herself. "Since I have taken up my position in the arms of Jesus, I am like a watchman observing the enemy from the hightest tower of a fortress. Nothing escapes me; often I am astonished at seeing so clearly." Hers is a humility that is not only felt by the heart but founded upon the solid knowledge of her own nothingness apart from her Lover. She felt and thought with constant reference to God. Her vision was so clear that she had to resort to parables. Here is one of them that a sister has scribbled down for us:

> She often spoke to me of a well-known toy with which she had amused herself when a child. This was the kaleidoscope, shaped like a small telescope, through which, as it is made to revolve, one perceives an endless variety of pretty, colored figures.
> "This toy," she said, "excited my admiration, and for a long time I wondered what could produce so charming a phenomenon. One day, however, a careful examination showed that it consisted simply of tiny bits of paper and cloth scattered inside. Further scrutiny revealed

three mirrors inside the tube, and the problem was solved. It became for me the illustration of a great truth.

"So long as our actions, even the most trivial, remain within love's kaleidoscope, the Blessed Trinity, figured by the three mirrors, imparts to them a wonderful brightness and beauty. The eye-piece is Jesus Christ, and He, looking from outside through Himself into the kaleidoscope, finds all our work perfect. But, should we leave the ineffable abode of love, He would see nothing but the worthless chaff of worthless deeds."

Love opened the eyes of Little Thérèse to new truths and new reasons for loving Jesus. She was not such a great sinner as Magdalen, and, logically speaking, she did not need as much forgiveness from God as Magdalen. But does it follow that she loved Him the less? No, on the contrary, she loved Him all the more. Love has its own logic that mathematicians have no notion of. "I Love Him," she reasoned, "because He has forgiven me, not much, but all." "He has forgiven me beforehand the sins which I could have committed." She seems to know by intuition what very few theologians have arrived at by their long-winded reasonings. St. Thomas Aquinas had, indeed, pointed out that it is "also a divine benefit that God should keep a man from sins, just as He forgives his past sins." St. Augustine had also confessed: "I put it down to Your grace and mercy that You melted the ice of my sins; I put it down to Your grace also all the sins that I did not, that I could not, commit." But little Thérèse went a step further than these great lights of the Church! She spoke, not in terms of "also," but in terms of "all the more"; and she gave us a very simple illustration of this deep truth:

Let us suppose that the son of a very clever doctor, stumbling over a stone on the road, falls and breaks his leg. His father hastens to his aid, and binds up the fractured limb with all the skill at his command. When cured, the son shows the utmost gratitude—and with good reason.

But, on the other hand, suppose that the father, knowing that a large stone lies on his son's path, anticipates the danger, and, unseen by anyone, hastens to remove it. Unconscious of the accident from which such tender forethought has saved him, the son will not show any mark of gratitude for it, or feel the same love for his father as he would have done had he been cured of some grievous wound. But if

225

he came to learn the whole truth, would he not love his father all the more?

I can imagine Jesus putting His hand gently on her shoulder and saying: "The truth is that you, My dear child, love Me, and want to love Me as I have never been loved before; and you are never at a loss to find reasons in justification of your love. What a subtle logician love has made of My little child!"

12.   Life and Death

With a faith enlivened by such intense love and enlightened by such a transparent vision, it is no wonder that she even conquered death before she died. When a sister asked her permission to weep upon her death, she said in tender reproach: "You will be bewailing my happiness!" When the chaplain asked her: "Are you quite resigned to die?" she answered with a gentle retort: "Ah! my Father, I am even resigned to live! To die, that is the joy I would experience." She actually rose above life and death:

> What matters it then whether life or death?
> My only joy is to love Thee.

This was possible because she had attained a spiritual state where her own will was merged into the Will of God. "I do not like one thing better than another; what the good God likes best and chooses for me, that it is which pleases me most." During the last months of her life she said something, which touches the very core of my heart: "Suppose that the good God should say to me: 'If you die now you shall have a very high degree of glory; if you die at eighty years of age your glory shall be much less, but the pleasure to Me far greater.' Oh, then I would not hesitate to reply: 'My God, I wish to die at eighty, for I do not seek my glory, but only Thy pleasure.'" Her love for God is generous to such a degree that she is even willing to sacrifice Heaven for His sake, if this were indeed possible. She would now be very old, if she had lived. She would be quite happy in remaining a hidden flower in the Carmel of Lisieux, unknown of men. But God wanted her to go back to Him at the age of twenty-four, and make a great saint of her. Is she resting in the arms of her Beloved now? No, for "souls on fire cannot remain inactive." She wished to spend her heaven in doing good upon earth. Her mission is just beginning. "There can be no rest for me," she says, "until the end of the world. But when the angel shall have said: 'Time is no more!' then I shall rest, then I shall be able to rejoice, because the number of the elect will be complete."

In heaven as on earth, the Little Flower of Jesus loves Him with such an abysmal love that she feels her own love is not enough. She wants millions and millions of other souls to love Him as she does. "I invite all the angels and saints to come and sing canticles of love." Even were the whole of creation to participate one day in the living concert of love, she would hardly think of it as more than a tiny drop of water lost in the Infinite Ocean of Divine Love. She would still feel as a little child towards its mother:

> Who says that the heart of an inch-long grass
> Can ever requite the full splendors of a whole Spring?

Date Due

MAY. 22			
MAY. 1 1968			
APR. 13 1972			
NOV 21 1975			
DEC 5 1975			
APR 23 1976			
NOV 10 1978			
APR 23 1979			
MAY 10 1979			
MAY 9 1989			
DEC 05 2007			
JAN 23 2008			
MAR 10 2008			

Demco 293-5